# Literature and Sound Film in Mid-Century Britain

# OXFORD MID-CENTURY STUDIES

The Oxford Mid-Century Studies series publishes monographs in several disciplinary and creative areas in order to create a thick description of culture in the thirty-year period around the Second World War. With a focus on the 1930s through the 1960s, the series concentrates on fiction, poetry, film, photography, theatre, as well as art, architecture, design, and other media. The mid-century is an age of shifting groups and movements, from existentialism through abstract expressionism to confessional, serial, electronic, and pop art styles. The series charts such intellectual movements, even as it aids and abets the very best scholarly thinking about the power of art in a world under new techno-political compulsions, whether nuclear-apocalyptic, Cold War-propagandized, transnational, neo-imperial, super-powered, or postcolonial.

*Series Editors*

Allan Hepburn, McGill University
Adam Piette, University of Sheffield
Lyndsey Stonebridge, University of Birmingham

# Literature and Sound Film in Mid-Century Britain

LARA EHRENFRIED

Great Clarendon Street, Oxford, OX2 6DP,
United Kingdom

Oxford University Press is a department of the University of Oxford.
It furthers the University's objective of excellence in research, scholarship,
and education by publishing worldwide. Oxford is a registered trade mark of
Oxford University Press in the UK and in certain other countries

© Lara Ehrenfried 2025

The moral rights of the author have been asserted

All rights reserved. No part of this publication may be reproduced, stored in a retrieval system, transmitted, used for text and data mining, or used for training artificial intelligence, in any form or by any means, without the prior permission in writing of Oxford University Press, or as expressly permitted by law, by licence or under terms agreed with the appropriate reprographics rights organization. Enquiries concerning reproduction outside the scope of the above should be sent to the Rights Department, Oxford University Press, at the address above.

You must not circulate this work in any other form
and you must impose this same condition on any acquirer

Published in the United States of America by Oxford University Press
198 Madison Avenue, New York, NY 10016, United States of America

British Library Cataloguing in Publication Data
Data available

Library of Congress Control Number: 2024948468

ISBN 9780198950769

DOI: 10.1093/9780198950790.001.0001

Printed and bound by
CPI Group (UK) Ltd, Croydon, CR0 4YY

Links to third party websites are provided by Oxford in good faith and
for information only. Oxford disclaims any responsibility for the materials
contained in any third party website referenced in this work.

The manufacturer's authorised representative in the EU for product safety is Oxford University Press España S.A. of El Parque Empresarial San Fernando de Henares, Avenida de Castilla, 2 – 28830 Madrid (www.oup.es/en or product.safety@oup.com). OUP España S.A. also acts as importer into Spain of products made by the manufacturer.

*To Max and Marga*
*who met at the movies*

# Contents

| | |
|---|---|
| *Acknowledgements* | ix |
| *List of Figures* | xi |
| Introduction | 1 |
| 1. Learning to Talk | 22 |
| 2. Adapting Audio-Vision | 46 |
| 3. Dialogue and Intelligibility | 75 |
| 4. Documenting the Everyday | 106 |
| 5. Networks of Audio-Vision | 137 |
| 6. The Senses at War | 167 |
| Coda | 199 |
| *Films Cited* | 205 |
| *Select Bibliography* | 207 |
| *Index* | 223 |

# Acknowledgements

My sincere thanks go to James Smith, Janet Stewart, and Jo Fox, as well as David Herman, who all supported this project at the University of Durham. Without the guidance, mentorship, and good humour of James Smith, this book would never have seen the light of day. I also gratefully acknowledge the support of the Leverhulme Trust and Durham University's Centre for Visual Arts and Culture, directed by Ludmilla Jordanova, for providing me with the means and intellectual space to complete the original research for this project. I would also like to sincerely thank Elizabeth Archibald, Mark Miller, and the entire community of St Cuthbert's Society.

David Trotter and Patricia Waugh gave valuable feedback when they first examined this work and it was a great pleasure to have them as interlocutors for developing my thoughts further. I am especially grateful to David Trotter for his kindness and advice whenever I required help. Benjamin Kohlmann, Leo Mellor, and Peter Garratt all commented on drafts and presentations at different stages of this project and I would like to thank them for sharing their insights and ideas.

It is thanks to the wonderful Marina MacKay that this book exists and that I first came up with the idea for this project when she suggested I read Patrick Hamilton's *Hangover Square*. I am so grateful to her that she did and that she supported me at Durham and beyond.

The fantastic team at the British Film Institute made studying *The Picturegoer* and *Kine Weekly* an experience that was both enjoyable and exciting. I would like to thank the entire team, and especially Sarah Currant, for their help with my various research requests.

Some parts of Chapter 2 were first published as '"There's a Song there, Really": Evelyn Waugh, the Musical Revue, and Early Sound Film'. Copyright © 2020 Purdue Research Foundation by Johns Hopkins University Press. This article first appeared in *MFS: Modern Fiction Studies*, Volume 66. Number 3 Fall 2020. Published with permission by Johns Hopkins University Press. I am grateful to the Purdue Research Foundation and Johns Hopkins University Press for allowing me to reuse this material.

The mid-century series editors Allan Hepburn, Lyndsey Stonebridge, and Adam Piette were supportive of the idea for this book from the start:

# X ACKNOWLEDGEMENTS

their comments and advice improved this work considerably and I would like to thank them sincerely for their thoughtful feedback.

The wonderful team at Oxford University Press, especially Jack McNichol and Jo Spillane, made the process of publication for a first-time author much less stressful and infinitely more enjoyable than I could have hoped for. I would also like to thank the anonymous peer reviewers, whose reports were a tremendous help when revising the manuscript. I hope they will find the book much improved. The faults that remain are, of course, entirely my own.

I owe particular thanks to Sophie Franklin, who read (too) many drafts with considerable patience and critical acumen. This book is also a product of her friendship, for which I cannot thank her enough.

My family and friends on both sides of the channel sustained me throughout the process of writing and rewriting. Thank you, especially, to my parents Axel and Iris, and to Leander, Moses, Fily, Christine, Arno, Ulla, Julie, Keith, Hannah, Caroline, Claudia, Nadine, Mara, Julia, and Sarah. I could not have completed this work without you.

Harry, this book is yours (the good bits, anyway). Thank you for everything.

# List of Figures

1.1 The landlady's handwritten note; frame grab from the silent version of *Blackmail* (British International Pictures, 1929), directed by Alfred Hitchcock.  23

4.1 Excerpt from the final page of Lewis Grassic Gibbon's *Sunset Song* (1932). Photograph by the author.  124

5.1 Bella's face is reflected in the music box; frame grab from *Gaslight* (British National Films, 1940), directed by Thorold Dickinson.  146

6.1 Jackson attempts to strangle Barbara; frame grab from *The Wicked Lady* (Gainsborough Pictures, 1945), directed by Leslie Arliss.  195

# Introduction

This book is about sound film and literature in twentieth-century Britain. It begins with the first feature-length British sound film, Alfred Hitchcock's *Blackmail* (1929), and traces the paths of film and literary fiction in the two decades following *Blackmail*'s release. I argue that the introduction of sound to film gave rise to two phenomena that transformed how cinema and literature operated at mid-century: audio-vision and synchronicity. 'Audio-vision', a term coined by the film scholar and composer Michel Chion, denotes the linking of sound and image in the cinema and the phenomenological effects of this combination.[1] 'Synchronicity' refers to the experience of sound's temporal alignment with the film image. By placing a new emphasis on the relationship of image and sound, the 'talkies' changed conceptions of cinematic form.

Yet, sound film did not simply marry recorded voices to the moving image. It also fundamentally altered the significance of text in the cinema and introduced the 'cultural specificity' of language to film.[2] By 1915, silent film had established conventions around the use of intertitles and dialogue titles, which also facilitated easy international distribution of productions. The translation of film titles into different languages, for instance, could be accomplished quickly while film's emphasis remained on visual forms of narration. The introduction of sound film, however, meant that written titles on the screen were no longer needed and, instead, the role of *spoken* text—its intelligibility and performance—in conjunction with the moving image became paramount. In this book, I will argue that this development did not solely affect cinema, but that it also stimulated new approaches to writing.

While substantial accounts of the relationship between film and literature have expanded our understanding of twentieth-century film and literary

---

[1] Michel Chion, *Audio-Vision: Sound on Screen*, ed. and trans. Claudia Gorbman (New York: Columbia University Press, 1994), pp. xxv–xxvi.

[2] Michael North, 'International Media, International Modernism, and the Struggle with Sound', in Julian Murphet and Lydia Rainford (eds), *Literature and Visual Technologies: Writing after Cinema* (Basingstoke: Palgrave Macmillan, 2003), 49–66 (p. 51).

## 2 LITERATURE AND SOUND FILM IN MID-CENTURY BRITAIN

culture, most of these analyses focus on the early, the silent, and the avant-garde dimensions of cinema vis-à-vis the literatures of global modernisms.[3] As David Trotter points out, there is a 'historiographical pattern' that tends to give pride of place to canonical modernist writers of the teens and twenties (such as Virginia Woolf, James Joyce, and Dorothy Richardson) on the one hand, and equally canonical filmmakers (such as Charlie Chaplin or Sergei Eisenstein) on the other hand.[4] Avant-garde writing as well as silent cinema form, of course, key contexts for any new study of twentieth-century film and literature. This book thus builds on these existing enquiries and moves the critical focus to the relationship of text and film following the introduction of synchronized sound. In doing so, *Literature and Sound Film in Mid-Century Britain* further develops the territory first surveyed by the coda of Laura Marcus's *The Tenth Muse* and her essay on 'Talking Films', James Purdon's 'Telemediations', and David Trotter's 'Literature between Media'.[5] My aims are methodological as well as literary-critical: I hope to show the productivity of considering media and literary history through the prism of multi-media and multi-sensory dimensions. Second, this book contributes to our understanding of the literature–film relationship *after* the heyday of modernism and approaches the mid-century as the formative age of audio-vision.

The 'mid-century', as Allan Hepburn writes, offers an important sense of 'temporal continuity' from the 1930s through to the 1960s.[6] In this study, I use 'mid-century' as a literary-historical term that opens up ways of reading the literature and culture of this period on its own terms and not merely as a 'foregone conclusion of modernism or bland transition to our contemporary age'.[7] As early as 2007, Marina MacKay and Lyndsey

---

[3] See, for instance, David Trotter, *Cinema and Modernism* (Oxford: Blackwell, 2007); Julian Murphet, *Multimedia Modernism* (Cambridge: Cambridge University Press, 2009); Andrew Shail, *The Cinema and the Origins of Literary Modernism* (Abingdon: Routledge, 2012).

[4] David Trotter, 'Literature between Media', in Vincent Sherry (ed.), *The Cambridge History of Modernism* (Cambridge: Cambridge University Press, 2017), 386–403 (p. 388).

[5] See Laura Marcus's *The Tenth Muse* (Oxford: Oxford University Press, 2007); Marcus, 'Talking Films' and James Purdon's 'Telemediations' both appeared in *A History of 1930s British Literature*, ed. Benjamin Kohlmann and Matthew Taunton (Cambridge: Cambridge University Press, 2019), 177–193 and 194–207, respectively; Lara Feigel's *Literature, Cinema and Politics, 1930–1945* (Edinburgh: Edinburgh University Press, 2016); as well as Laurel Harris's essay on 'Hearing Cinematic Modernism in the 1930s: The Audiovisual in British Documentary Cinema and Virginia Woolf's *Between the Acts*', *Literature & History*, 21.1 (2012), 61–75.

[6] Allan Hepburn, *A Grain of Faith: Religion in Mid-Century British Literature* (Oxford: Oxford University Press, 2018), p. 15.

[7] Claire Seiler, *Mid-Century Suspension: Literature and Feeling in the Wake of World War II* (New York: Columbia University Press, 2020), p. 5.

Stonebridge suggested that 'thinking about mid-century fiction precisely *as* mid-century fiction is…an attempt to get beyond the formalist distinction between experimental and realist fiction that has dominated accounts of this period.'[8] As this study seeks answers to the question of how film and literature constructed themselves around experiences of audio-vision and synchronicity, it widely examines different modes and genres and consciously roams between commercial and non-commercial cinema, between 'highbrow' and 'middlebrow' fiction at mid-century.

Seminal works by Trotter and Marcus offer the conceptual foundations for this book's account of film and literature. Marcus's *The Tenth Muse* (2007) traces the relationship of cinema and literature in the early twentieth century as one of co-construction and development, in which 'issues central to an understanding of cinema…are threaded through [discursive and fictional] writing.'[9] Indeed, Marcus importantly draws attention to the conception of cinema as a 'hybrid form' in the 1920s as it was understood to link 'the representational devices of the verbal and the visual, the word and the image.'[10] *The Tenth Muse* predominantly attends to silent film with its written titles, but the work's coda turns to 'the coming of sound'. Here, I take my cue from Marcus's work and pick up where *The Tenth Muse* concludes.

Focussing on literature and the media ecology between the world wars, Trotter's *Literature in the First Media Age* (2013) argues that 'the combination of new media with new materials gave writers the chance to reimagine both how lives might be lived and how texts might be written.'[11] On this account, it is film and literature ('representational media') that negotiate new strategies of representation in response to 'connective media' (such as the telephone) during the interwar years.[12] Building on Raymond Williams's conception of media as cultural practices, Trotter points out that 'communications technology is an attitude before it is a machine or a set of codes' and that it is precisely this realization which shapes the literary output of the late 1920s and 1930s.[13] More recently, a similar view has been advanced by Kata Gellen's *Kafka and Noise* (2019). Gellen convincingly argues that

---

[8] Lyndsey Stonebridge and Marina MacKay (eds), 'Introduction: British Fiction after Modernism', *British Fiction after Modernism: The Novel at Mid-Century* (Basingstoke: Palgrave Macmillan, 2007), 1–16 (p. 3). See also Hepburn, *Grain of Faith*, p. 15.

[9] Marcus, *The Tenth Muse*, p. 2.  [10] Marcus, *The Tenth Muse*, p. 8.

[11] David Trotter, *Literature in the First Media Age: Britain Between the Wars* (Cambridge, MA: Harvard University Press, 2013), p. 1.

[12] Trotter, *Literature in the First Media Age*, pp. 7–9.

[13] Trotter, *Literature in the First Media Age*, p. 2.

# 4    LITERATURE AND SOUND FILM IN MID-CENTURY BRITAIN

'imaginaries of…media precede their technical realization.'[14] This observation certainly holds for the case of sound film: the idea of synchronized sound–image combination played a role in the cultural imagination long before sound film became a technological reality.[15] As Rick Altman has shown in his study of *Silent Film Sound* (2004), the 1890s and early 1900s saw plenty of experiments geared towards achieving a mechanized connection of moving image and sound: George Demenÿ's Phonoscope of 1892 and Thomas Edinson's Kinetophone of 1895 are only two of many inventions that 'targeted simultaneous presentation of image and sound.'[16] The idea of the seamless combination of sound and image, as Tom Gunning notes, 'is a modern *topoi* [*sic*] that straddled the imaginations of poets and scientists' alike.[17] While my study is not concerned with the prehistory of sound film, the experiments by Edison, Demenÿ, and others gesture towards the concerted drive to facilitate technologically mediated experiences of vision and audition. With the rise of feature-length sound film from the late 1920s, Britain witnessed the large-scale realization of technologically mediated audio-vision. The nation thus experienced a proliferation of audio-visual culture that stimulated different ways of seeing and hearing, and of newly imagining and representing how we see and hear.

*Literature and Sound Film* seeks to extend Trotter's account, in which film and literature are not framed as competitors in the media ecology, but as 'allies' grappling with the challenges posed by technology.[18] As this book will show, there are different ways in which film and literature relate and speak to each other in the 1930s and 1940s and the relationship between these two media forms is one of development and growing synergy. While the late 1920s and early 1930s briefly saw a sense of initial competition between sound film and literary fiction, their shared concerns, as representational media, came to outweigh many of their differences: sound film is

---

[14] Kata Gellen, *Kafka and Noise: The Discovery of Cinematic Sound in Literary Modernism* (Evanston, IL: Northwestern University Press, 2019), p. 201.

[15] Rick Altman and Richard Abel have examined the soundscapes of early cinema in *Silent Film Sound* (New York: Columbia University Press, 2004) and *The Sounds of Early Cinema* (Bloomington: Indiana University Press, 2001) respectively. The prehistory of audio-vision reaches back to the nineteenth century and includes Victorian lantern shows. See Joe Kember, *Marketing Modernity: Victorian Popular Shows and Early Cinema* (Exeter: University of Exeter Press, 2009).

[16] Altman, *Silent Film Sound*, pp. 158–166.

[17] Tom Gunning, 'Doing for the Eye What the Phonograph Does for the Ear', in Richard Abel and Rick Altman (eds), *The Sounds of Early Cinema* (Bloomington: Indiana University Press, 2001), 13–31 (p. 13).

[18] Trotter, *Literature in the First Media Age*, p. 8.

increasingly sustained by literature and especially by the work of the mid-century writer, while literature itself approaches new forms of mediatized textuality. By mediatized textuality, I mean forms of writing that engage with and enact the formal and narrative procedures of other media. Both film and literature test their narrative capacities and limits at mid-century; they follow 'intermedial impulses' as defined by Gellen: 'whenever a work of art tries to reach outside its own medium—when it probes the limits of what can be done within a medium in order to expand its range—it reveals an intermedial impulse.'[19] These ideas have of course been prefigured through, for instance, early twentieth-century (especially avant-garde) literary engagements with photography, radio broadcasting, and sound recording technologies.[20] However, I argue here that audio-vision and synchronicity become essential factors in the developing synergy of literature and film and speed up already operative processes in their engagements with the media ecology.

My analysis of mid-century literature and film is underpinned by a cultural phenomenology of audio-vision. Like Trotter, I conceive of media as cultural practices that, as Lisa Gitelman notes, form 'particular sites for...social as well as historically and culturally specific experiences of meaning.'[21] Gitelman's work opens up a basis for studying media and their histories from the angle of cultural phenomenology. Her approach analyses how culturally and historically specific phenomena appear to us and how we, as cultural actors, make sense of them. On this account, media are 'historical subjects' intricately intertwined with practices of representation: media are themselves 'denizens of the past' and our 'encounters' with media are not simply instances of encountering representations of the past, but, crucially, instances of encountering the representational practices 'produced' by the past.[22] 'Cultural phenomenology', writes Steven Connor, 'attempt[s] to grasp, synthesize, transform and be itself seized by the processes of explanation which are always astir within experiences, processes and objects.'[23]

---

[19] Gellen, *Kafka and Noise*, p. 33.

[20] See, for instance, Michael North, *Camera Works: Photography and the Twentieth-Century Word* (Oxford: Oxford University Press, 2005); Melissa Dinsman, *Modernism at the Microphone: Radio, Propaganda, and Literary Aesthetics During World War II* (London: Bloomsbury, 2017); Angela Frattarola, Modernist Soundscapes: Auditory Technology and the Novel (Gainesville, FL: University Press of Florida, 2018).

[21] Lisa Gitelman, *Always Already New: Media, History, and the Data of Culture* (Cambridge, MA: MIT, 2008), p. 8.

[22] Gitelman, *Always Already New,* p. 5.

[23] Steven Connor, 'Making an Issue of Cultural Phenomenology', *Critical Quarterly*, 42.1 (2000), p. 4.

## 6 LITERATURE AND SOUND FILM IN MID-CENTURY BRITAIN

It is a collective, shared, and intersubjective 'experience becoming explana-tion' that lies at the heart of any project of cultural phenomenology.[24] In the context of this study, my application of cultural phenomenology seeks to mobilize the explanatory potential of audio-vision and synchronicity for understanding a specific period of media history and its evolving strategies of representation.

With a view to developments in media history, William Uricchio further notes that 'moments of tension and instability offer particularly sharp insights into the construction of media form'.[25] He identifies 'transition moments' as particularly pertinent for giving rise to 'forms of instability' that 'threw into question media ontologies (and with them, issues of epistemology, perception, and memory)'.[26] Thus, I contend here that the introduction of synchronized sound technology to film presents such a moment of instability that affected film and literature, as representational media, more pertinently than other, connective media forms (such as the telephone)—and it did so, because the technological possibility of syn-chronized sound–image interaction fundamentally changed the status of text in the cinema.

In the era of silent film, text on screen first appeared in the 1890s and industry conventions for the use of film titles stabilized after 1910. Headers, intertitles, and subtitles could serve concrete narrative functions and ensured the transnational marketability of silent film productions. Intertitles, as Gregory Robinson notes, had the primary function of estab-lishing narrative continuity and could be written with a view to being used in multiple films (titles such as 'the next day' or 'one hour later' could be inserted easily into several different films).[27] Around 1910, silent film also began to use dialogue titles and 'after 1913, dialogue titles typically appeared more frequently, whereas continuity titles appeared less often'.[28] Writing on screen, however, led to debates on the artistic and aesthetic value of text in the cinema. Some critics viewed film titles as a mere 'commercial inevitability'.[29] As Laura Marcus has shown, film titles were 'raising fundamental questions

---

[24] Connor, 'Cultural Phenomenology', p. 4.

[25] William Uricchio, 'Historicizing Media in Transition', in David Thorburn and Henry Jenkins (eds), *Rethinking Media Change: The Aesthetics of Transition* (Cambridge, MA: MIT, 2004), pp. 23–38 (p. 31).

[26] Uricchio, 'Historicizing Media', p. 35.

[27] Gregory Robinson, 'Writing on the Silent Screen', in Deborah Cartmell (ed.), *A Companion to Literature, Film, and Adaptation* (Chichester: Blackwell, 2012), pp. 33–51.

[28] Robinson, 'Writing on the Silent Screen', p. 39.

[29] Robinson, 'Writing on the Silent Screen', p. 39.

INTRODUCTION 7

about the nature of film language.[30] In 1916, Hugo Münsterberg's *Photoplay* stated that written text was not part of the 'original character' of film, whose power ought to remain in the visual image.[31] The film critic Iris Barry equally commended the absence of film titles as 'progress' when reviewing F. W. Murnau's *The Last Laugh* (1924). As Marcus notes, Barry advised writers to become 'visualisers' when working for the screen, thereby underscoring the idea that film was a visual medium upon which text merely intruded.[32]

Despite such debates amongst film critics, writing film titles had become an important industry profession by about 1915. In some cases, title writers attained star-status for establishing a distinctive tone in their work that invited cinema audiences to experience written text as integral to film style and genre. Ralph Spence, whose career is discussed in greater detail by Robinson, achieved critical acclaim and public recognition as 'someone, who could use the right words to take an unsuccessful movie and make it profitable'. It was Spence's specialty to turn unsuccessful drama into popular comedy, simply by writing and revising film titles.[33] Although not many writers achieved the same fame as Spence, the profession was key to film production between 1910 and 1930. Like Spence, Anita Loos worked as a successful title writer from 1912 onwards. She had begun her career writing for films starring Douglas Fairbanks (*His Picture in the Paper* of 1916 and *American Aristocracy* of 1917). Fairbanks had witnessed the positive audience response to Loos's titles on their first joint project and subsequently asked her to write titles for all his films—a major coup for Loos given Fairbanks's popularity and power in the industry at the time.[34] Loos's particular appeal, according to Laura Frost, was her ability to 'challeng[e] the separation of literature and cinema' by 'develop[ing] a mode of writing in which literature and cinema together unmoor the conventional relationship of the image to the word. In both media, words exceed their contexts and signify not only through their meaning, but also through their literal status as objects.'[35] Although not many writers found the same public recognition that Loos and Spence experienced, their cases show that title writers, for at least two decades, conducted integral work in the film industry that was

---

[30] Marcus, *The Tenth Muse*, p. 290.
[31] Hugo Münsterberg, *The Photoplay: A Psychological Study and Other Writings*, ed. Allan Langdale (London: Routledge, 2002), p. 82.
[32] Marcus, *The Tenth Muse*, p. 291.     [33] Robinson, 'Writing on the Silent Screen', p. 47.
[34] Robinson, 'Writing on the Silent Screen', p. 44.
[35] Laura Frost, *The Problem with Pleasure: Modernism and its Discontents* (New York: Columbia University Press, 2013), p. 211.

8   LITERATURE AND SOUND FILM IN MID-CENTURY BRITAIN

especially well-received by audiences. Written text on screen shaped the reception of film in the decades preceding the introduction of sound.

With the advent of feature-length sound film, the status of the written word in relation to cinema changed. Synchronized sound film no longer required intertitles or dialogue titles and written text was largely displaced from the visual realm of the screen. While Iris Barry had advised writers to become visualizers in silent cinema, sound film reconfigured such a view. In the talking film, the script would offer the basis for the actors' performance and their recitation of the written word. Spoken performance, as Gellen rightly points out, 'upends and transforms the status of authorship by reconfiguring the relationship between writer, work, performer, and audience'.[36] In the sound film, text does not signify as a literal object projected onto the screen, but as spoken performance whose 'authorship' is co-constructed by several parties. In the early years of sound film especially, this change appeared to bring film closer to the theatre and the scriptwriter somewhat closer to the profession of dramatist; it also meant that professional writers, as authors of physical text printed on a page, regained some of their sovereignty over the realm of letters. On the one hand, sound film thus allowed authors to reclaim text for literature; on the other hand, it simultaneously challenged them to reimagine writing in an audio-visual media ecology. In order to explore these ideas further, the following section discusses the mid-century emergence and later development of audio-vision and synchronicity as key concepts in film history, before moving to a consideration of how these phenomena might also bear on the literary text.

## Audio-Vision and Synchronicity

The history of cinema is a history of audio-vision: Victorian lantern shows, an important precursor to cinema, were often accompanied by music and a lecturer or narrator.[37] With the advent of film from the 1890s, silent film screenings usually took place with some element of sonic accompaniment, ranging from live narration, to sound effects and music (either live or pre-recorded). Sometimes, exhibitors would employ actors to voice characters from behind the screen. The first few decades of film, then, were already geared towards establishing links between seeing and hearing. As James

---

[36] Gellen, *Kafka and Noise*, p. 92.
[37] Kember, *Marketing Modernity,* pp. 40–41 and pp. 60–68.

Buhler has shown, the conceptualization of film sound then gained traction from about 1926, when the relationship of sound to the image was debated by Gilbert Seldes, Rudolf Arnheim, Béla Balázs, and Sergei Eisenstein.[38]

In his work *The Spirit of Film* (1930), the Hungarian film theorist Balázs was one of the first to offer comprehensive reflections on the sound film as a fundamentally audio-visual medium: the 'challenge' faced by sound film, Balázs argues, 'is not merely that of complementing the silent film and making it resemble nature more closely, but of approaching nature from a completely different perspective. The challenge is to open up a new sphere of experience.'[39] This 'new sphere of experience' consists of the nuanced interplay of sound and image. Balàzs proceeds to set out his thoughts on sound effects, music, and dialogue and their respective relationships to the visual image. The sound film's capacity to present synchronous as well as asynchronous image–sound combinations would reconfigure audience perception.[40] The task of the filmmaker, according to Balázs, is to 'lead our ears as he led our eyes'—the sound film requires careful direction and curation of material in recognition of its new, audio-visual nature.[41] By asserting that the interaction of moving image and sound will create, first, an entirely new film form and, second, establish a wholly new experience of cinema, Balázs also anticipates core elements of Michel Chion's theory of audio-vision.

In the late 1930s, while filming *Alexander Nevsky* (1938), the Soviet director Sergei Eisenstein began to theorize what he termed 'vertical montage' in film. Eisenstein's writing on the topic (c. 1940–1941) first appeared in English in Jay Leda's translation of Eisenstein's *The Film Sense* (1957). Here, Eisenstein notes the fundamental synaesthetic properties of film that may emerge from the 'inner synchronization' of music and moving images.[42] The shared common denominator of sound and image, according to Eisenstein, is movement, which allows both elements to be combined to produce an 'audio-visual score'.[43] Indeed, 'combinations should...proceed from the trace of *movement* in a given musical or visual piece, where that work's line and shape can become the foundation for a corresponding visual or musical

---

[38] James Buhler, *Theories of the Soundtrack* (Oxford: Oxford University Press, 2018), pp. 23–56.

[39] Béla Balázs, *Bela Balázs: Early Film Theory: 'Visible Man' and 'The Spirit of Film'*, ed. Erica Carter, trans. Rodney Livingstone (New York: Berghahn, 2011), p. 184.

[40] Balázs, *Early Film Theory*, pp. 183–210.  [41] Balázs, *Early Film Theory*, p. 185.

[42] Sergei Eisenstein, *The Film Sense*, trans. Jay Leda (New York: Meridian, 1957), p. 81.

[43] Eisenstein, *The Film Sense*, p. 74.

10   LITERATURE AND SOUND FILM IN MID-CENTURY BRITAIN

composition...to the final convergence of the two in vertical montage.[44] Eisenstein thus conceptualizes film as a multi-sensory and multi-dimensional medium. As Kia Afra convincingly argues, Eisenstein's theory of vertical montage outlines his 'audio-visual practice' as a filmmaker.[45]

Eisenstein also provides his own account of the prehistory of image–sound interaction: 'to remove the barriers between sight and sound...To bring about a unity and a harmonious relationship between these two opposite spheres. What an absorbing task! The Greeks and Diderot, Wagner and Scriabin—who has not dreamt of this ideal?'[46] He provides excerpts from Karl von Eckartshausen's 'Theory of Ocular Music' (1784) and Arthur Rimbaud's 'Voyelles' (1883) amongst other sources to evidence historical (and artistic) interest in the construction of audio-visual combination (here, colour and music).[47] Crucially, Eisenstein uses this excursus into what he views as the prehistory of audio-vision to illustrate his ideas about different possible types of image–sound synchronization in film. He distinguishes, for instance, between 'inner' and 'physical' synchronization. While 'physical' synchronization denotes the technological process of aligning image and sound, 'inner synchronization' denotes the expressive *effect* produced by a careful curation of image–sound interaction. This endeavour aims at a 'complete fusion' that pushes beyond the boundaries of physical image–sound alignment into the realm of interpretation and phenomenological effect.[48]

Both Eisenstein and Balázs discuss synchronization in different forms— and they do so, importantly, by distinguishing the physical process from its psychological impact. In his *Spirit of Film*, Balázs also uses the term 'synchronicity': 'a sound may continue to reverberate in our ears, even though we can no longer hear it in the following image. Here we can speak of a psychic effect of synchronicity, which enables the creation of the subtlest of moods and the deepest associations.'[49] From both Eisenstein's account of 'inner synchronization' and Balázs's discussion of synchronicity's 'psychic effect' on the audience, a distinction between synchronization and synchronicity emerges: synchronization denotes the technological process of achieving the concurrence in time of image and sound; synchronicity points instead to the *experience* produced by synchronization.

---

[44] Kia Afra, '"Vertical Montage" and Synaesthesia: Movement, Inner Synchronicity, and Music–Image Correlation in *Alexander Nevsky* (1938)', *Music, Sound, and the Moving Image* 9.1 (2015), 33–61 (p. 38).

[45] Afra, 'Vertical Montage', p. 36, n. 4.   [46] Eisenstein, *The Film Sense*, p. 87.

[47] Eisenstein, *The Film Sense*, pp. 88–109.   [48] Eisenstein, *The Film Sense*, pp. 81–84.

[49] Balázs, *Early Film Theory*, p. 201.

INTRODUCTION 11

This distinction is underpinned further from another mid-century angle: Carl Gustav Jung applied the term 'synchronicity' (*Synchronizität*) in the 1930s to his work in psychiatry and psychoanalysis. For Jung, the concept denoted the psychological experience of 'circumstances that appear meaningfully related yet lack a causal connection'.[50] He therefore called synchronicity an 'acausal connecting principle' that could be used to psychologically construct meaning out of two or more unrelated occurrences or events.[51] Jung's idea can be mapped easily onto cinema: the technological process of aligning image track and soundtrack, so that (for example) the sound of a gunshot firing would concur in time with the image of a character pulling the trigger, is synchronization. As the audience watches such a scene in the cinema, they will see a shot being fired and also hear the shot being fired simultaneously. Sound and image are thereby also experienced as causally and meaningfully related. Connecting the image and the sound only takes a fraction of a second: the gun, with its trigger being pulled, immediately appears to our minds and our senses as the source of the sound. The effect of synchronization is the experience of synchronicity. However, it is important to remember that the image is not the source of the sound that audiences hear. These two are distinct, concrete events that have been spliced together to appear meaningfully related to us. To experience synchronicity in the cinema means to build causal connections between vision and audition; but we do so, because these connections are artificially curated for us.

While conceptions of audio-vision and the distinction between synchronization and synchronicity thus emerge historically from their mid-century context, these terms have been developed further by scholars of film sound: seminal works in the field by Michel Chion, Elisabeth Weis and John Belton, Rick Altman, K. J. Donnelly, Lea Jacobs, and James Lastra have been invaluable for this study.[52] Building on Chion, I contend that sound–image interaction is key to understanding the experience offered by

---

[50] Laura K. Kerr, 'Synchronicity', *Encyclopedia of Critical Psychology*, ed. Thomas Teo (New York: Springer, 2014), 1905–1908 (pp. 1905–1906).

[51] C. G. Jung, *Synchronicity: An Acausal Connecting Principle*, trans. R. F. C. Hull (Princeton, NJ: Princeton University Press, 1973).

[52] John Belton and Elisabeth Weis (eds), *Film Sound: Theory and Practice* (New York: Columbia University Press, 1985); Rick Altman (ed.), *Sound Theory, Sound Practice* (New York: Routledge, 1992); K. J. Donnelly, *Occult Aesthetics: Synchronization in Sound Film* (Oxford: Oxford University Press, 2014); Lea Jacobs, *Film Rhythm after Sound: Technology, Music, and Performance* (Oakland, CA: University of California Press, 2015); James Lastra, *Sound Technology and the American Cinema* (New York: Columbia University Press, 2000).

12 LITERATURE AND SOUND FILM IN MID-CENTURY BRITAIN

film: 'films, television, and other audiovisual media do not just address the eye. They place their spectators—their audiospectators—in a specific perceptual mode of reception.'[53] The 'audiovisual combination', Chion writes, signifies the mutual influence of seeing and hearing on each other.[54]

Chion's ideas echo some earlier themes articulated in the classical phenomenological tradition of Edmund Husserl, Martin Heidegger, and Maurice Merleau-Ponty. Like Chion, the phenomenologists had emphasized the holistic and unified character of our perceptual, sensory experience of the world. In the *Phenomenology of Perception* (1945), Merleau-Ponty criticized empiricist conceptions of our experience that tended to treat perception as composed of isolated sensations—patches of colours, tones, or noises—which somehow combine into our perception of definite objects. Such a picture, Merleau-Ponty argued, introduces artificial, theoretical constructs that do not correspond with our experience.[55] Instead, what we perceive is defined by its relation to the background or perceptual field against which the object of our perception not only stands out but which in turn shapes how that object is perceived. Second, the empiricist overlooks the centrality of our being embodied subjects, where how we perceive is shaped by our interests and habits, the potential actions open to us, the emotional as well as other aspects of our experience. That is to say, we find the world already saturated with meaning and our embodied perception of the world 'expresses a nexus of living meanings'.[56] Indeed, Merleau-Ponty goes on to offer a visceral description of the 'synaesthetic' (meaning here the fundamentally multi-sensory) quality of our experience:

> one sees the hardness and brittleness of glass, and when, with a tinkling sound, it breaks, this sound is conveyed by the visible glass.... One sees the weight of a block of cast iron which sinks in the sand, the fluidity of water and the viscosity of syrup. In the same way, I hear the hardness and unevenness of cobbles in the rattle of a carriage, and we speak appropriately of a 'soft', 'dull' or 'sharp' sound.[57]

---

[53] Chion, *Audio-Vision*, p. xxv.    [54] Chion, *Audio-Vision*, p. xxvi.

[55] For further discussion of 'holistic perception' in the phenomenological tradition and its critique of empiricism, see Shaun Gallagher and Dan Zahavi, *The Phenomenological Mind* (New York: Routledge, 2012), pp. 105–112.

[56] Maurice Merleau-Ponty, *The Phenomenology of Perception*, trans. Colin Smith (London: Routledge, 2010), p. 175.

[57] Merleau-Ponty, *Phenomenology of Perception*, pp. 266–267. I wish to thank Harry Lewendon-Evans, who shared his knowledge of phenomenology and pointed me to this particular section in Merleau-Ponty's work.

From the perspective of film studies, and aligning with Merleau-Ponty's writing, K. J. Donnelly notes that the idea of 'audiovisual combination' captures what neuropsychological accounts of sound–image experience refer to as a 'cross-modal effect'—meaning that our perception of what we see is transformed by what we hear (and vice versa).[58]

The combination of image and sound leads to a surplus, or in Chion's words, an 'added value', of film. It is something that can be achieved when hearing and vision appear to act *together*.[59] As such, cinematic audio-vision is defined by its multi-dimensionality: the temporal dimension of sound and the spatial dimension of vision come together in the sound and image tracks of the film, thus producing a unique experience that engages the audience's sense of time and space—and of story and character unfolding within this matrix.[60]

Donnelly builds on Chion's work to examine cinema as an 'audiovisual enterprise' whose 'highly particular aesthetic' consists of the 'synergetic effect' of sound and image.[61] This sound–image interaction can be achieved in a number of ways: location sound and image can be filmed together at the same time. This, as Donnelly notes, is still frequently done for live television and was also 'the norm on classical Hollywood soundstages'.[62] A second option is the use of pre-recorded sound during filming whereby the soundtrack forms the guiding principle for the filming of the visual track (for example, in a musical film or a music video where a pre-recorded track is played while a dance routine is filmed). Finally, adding post-production sound is also possible; for example, when music or sound effects are added or enhanced after filming has concluded.[63] The interaction of sound and image is key to achieving the viewer's mind and senses, but this interaction does not have to be built on perfect synchronization at all times. Sound film can easily 'move between moments of synchrony between sound and image and points where there is no synchronization'.[64]

Rick Altman famously declared synchronized sound–image interaction to be 'the sound film's fundamental lie: the implication that sound is

---

[58] Donnelly, *Occult Aesthetics*, p. 24.     [59] Chion, *Audio-Vision*, p. 5.

[60] See Chion's chapter on 'Projections of Sound on Image', *Audio-Vision*, pp. 3–24.

[61] Donnelly, *Occult Aesthetics*, p. 13 and p. 27.     [62] Donnelly, *Occult Aesthetics*, p. 30.

[63] Donnelly, *Occult Aesthetics*, p. 30.

[64] Donnelly, *Occult Aesthetics*, p. 8. Asynchrony in film has been more comprehensively theorized than synchrony. See chapter 8 of Donnelly's *Occult Aesthetics* (pp. 181–199). Asynchrony and the idea of using sound as counterpoint to the film image is central to early writing on film sound, including Sergei Eisenstein, W. I. Pudovkin, and G. V. Alexandrov's 'Statement on Sound'. See *The Eisenstein Reader*, ed. Richard Taylor (London: BFI, 1998), pp. 80–81.

## 14   LITERATURE AND SOUND FILM IN MID-CENTURY BRITAIN

produced by the image when in fact it remains independent of it'.[65] Sound film, then, creates a multi-sensory illusion that derives its value from perceptual trickery by technological means. This illusion is achieved by the use of synch points: a synch point is a particular moment at which sound and image give the impression of concurrence in time and of causal relation. Dialogue is one of the most frequent synch points in sound film as it offers ample opportunity for visible lip movement to be matched to the sounds of words being articulated by the actors. Sound effects can equally form synch points, for instance when visible events on the image track are combined with a 'sonic counterpart'.[66] These synch points are key to producing the impression of sound emanating from the image.

To sustain this illusion, a sound film needs to include a number of synch points throughout its duration. A phenomenological account of 'time-consciousness' supplies a possible explanation for the importance of synch points in sound film: Husserl and Merleau-Ponty outline how our perception of every moment in time is not an isolated event.[67] Rather, our perception of every moment in time is shaped by what has immediately preceded it and an anticipation of what will follow it:

> when I experience a melody, I don't simply experience a knife-edge presentation of one note, which is then completely washed away and replaced with the next knife-edge presentation of the next note. Rather, consciousness retains the sense of the first note as I hear the second note, a hearing that is also enriched by an anticipation of the next note.[68]

'Retention' and 'protention' (anticipation) inform each present moment and can 'constitut[e] a coherency that stretches over an experienced temporal duration'.[69] If applied to sound cinema, this suggests that throughout the duration of a film, the experience of each new synch point, together with the retention of previous synch points and anticipation of future synch points, can constitute the experience of coherence and meaningful temporal duration. If, for any reason, the soundtrack breaks down or suddenly

---

[65] Rick Altman, 'Introduction', *Yale French Studies* 60 (1980), 3–15 (p. 6).

[66] Donnelly, *Occult Aesthetics*, p. 4.

[67] For a comprehensive discussion of 'temporality' that expands Husserl's account of time consciousness, see Merleau-Ponty, *Phenomenology of Perception*, pp. 476–503. A clear introduction to this topic is supplied by Gallagher and Zahavi, *The Phenomenological Mind*, pp. 77–97.

[68] Gallagher and Zahavi, *The Phenomenological Mind*, p. 84.

[69] Gallagher and Zahavi, *The Phenomenological Mind*, p. 84.

INTRODUCTION 15

ceases to align with the image track, the audience's reaction might be surprise, shock, or annoyance because the experience no longer aligns with the anticipation (protention) of what is to come. Synch points, then, are an important technological feature by which the sound film creates the experience of coherence and meaning.

In the early years of the film industry's move to sound, industry professionals quickly developed new understandings of how sound should be applied in conjunction with the image. Rather than a faithful reproduction of the original recording event, the effect produced by sound–image interaction took centre stage.[70] These effects carry perceptual and interpretive consequences for audiences: the combination of sound and image can, for instance, 'temporalize' the visuals: sound, especially through synch points, can create the impression of temporal succession or a temporal structure.[71] Similarly, sound also lends spatial depth to a two-dimensional image and embeds the visuals into a diegetic space that appears much larger than the part one sees projected onto a cinema screen. 'Sound cinema', as Lea Jacobs explains, 'is about the sync, about harnessing diverse components of sound and picture to form a rhythmically compelling whole.'[72]

I want to conclude this section by reflecting on the question of how audio-vision and synchronicity might operate in relation to literature. With the rise of sound studies since the 1980s, and following R. Murray Schafer's coinage of the term 'soundscape' in 1977, the idea of the 'literary soundscape' has gained traction.[73] Yet, the critical interest in 'listening to literature' or 'literary sound' may, at times, produce analytic slippages by applying direct comparisons. An analysis of literary soundscapes in *The Waste Land* (1922), for instance, might lead to the conclusion that Eliot's poem is like a gramophone record. However, such an analysis might conflate the individual representational capacities of different media forms: a printed text cannot mediate sound in the same way that a gramophone record can.[74] There are, however, other ways in which a more nuanced account may be reached. Building on Caroline Levine's *Forms: Whole, Rhythm, Hierarchy, Network*

---

[70] Lastra, *Sound Technology*, p. 195. On production practices for sound film and the increasing professionalization of sound staff in the commercial film industry, see Helen Hanson, *Hollywood Soundscapes: Film Sound Style, Craft and Production in the Classical Era* (London: BFI, 2017).

[71] Chion, *Audio-Vision*, pp. 13–16.    [72] Jacobs, *Film Rhythm after Sound*, p. 218.

[73] R. Murray Schafer, *The Soundscape: Our Sonic Environment and the Tuning of the World* (Rochester, VT: Destiny, 1994), p. 4 and p. 7.

[74] This problem is addressed in relation to cinema and literature by Maria Di Battista in 'This is not a movie: *Ulysses* and Cinema', *Modernism/Modernity*, 13.2 (2006), 219–235.

# 16    LITERATURE AND SOUND FILM IN MID-CENTURY BRITAIN

(2015), Helen Groth suggests that studying literary sound means to ask how literary texts 'capture, import, or converge with extra-textual forms or structures for hearing, voicing, sounding.'[75] In other words, textual engagements with audition and vision intersect directly with the history of the senses and the historically specific practices of their representation.

Furthermore, as Kata Gellen suggests, the vocabulary of both sound studies and narrative theory are perhaps not quite enough for an in-depth examination of literary sound and vision. In *Kafka and Noise*, Gellen convincingly demonstrates the benefits of mobilizing the critical repertoire of film studies (and especially of studying film sound) for discussing prose narrative in particular.[76] One way of applying such tools provided by film studies for an analysis of prose narrative is shown by Laurel Harris, who argues that Virginia Woolf's *Between the Acts* (1941) is built on a multi-dimensional and multi-sensory repertoire: the sonic dimension of the gramophone record is synthesized with the visual pageant performance and 'Woolf's characteristic narrator...focalizes the narrative of *Between the Acts* through overheard dialogue, environmental noise, and visual impressions that can best be integrated through the model of the audiovisual.'[77] Harris convincingly identifies 'the audiovisual' as a key component of Woolf's novel that pushes beyond a metaphorical understanding of literary sound and vision. Building on this suggestion, I argue that mid-century literature is fundamentally concerned with finding ways of textually mediating multi-sensory experience: these narratives do not simply offer literary soundscapes (or literary imagery), but textually adapt and enact experiences of audio-vision and synchronicity. This is done, for instance, by Evelyn Waugh in *Vile Bodies* (1930). Here, different characters in different places are suddenly connected by hearing the same song:

> Father Rothschild heard it and turned his face to the wall.
> Kitty Blackwater heard it....
> The Captain heard it....'[78]

What readers see on the page is how the novel visually arranges these one-line paragraphs one below the other, narrating a number of scenes that

---

[75] Helen Groth, 'Literary Soundscapes', in Anna Snaith (ed.), *Sound and Literature* (Cambridge: Cambridge University Press, 2020), 135–153 (p. 143).

[76] Gellen, *Kafka and Noise*, pp. 7–8.

[77] Harris, 'Hearing Cinematic Modernism in the 1930s', p. 67.

[78] Evelyn Waugh, *Vile Bodies* (London: Penguin, 2000), p. 17.

suggest temporal concurrence as they are linked diegetically by song and formally by parallel syntax and verbal repetition. In proposing such a reading, I concur with Jonathan Foltz's account that cinema 'reawaken[ed] the sense that not all forms of storytelling have been exhausted by the novel, nor all forms of experience been defined by its terms'.[79] Waugh's novel does not simply evoke or allude to sound, but forms an incisive textual response to forms of cinematic audio-vision at the very time of their emergence. Literary engagements with image–sound combination and its perceived synchronism might also take various other forms, such as onomatopoetic inserts (the *click!* and *crack!* of Patrick Hamilton's *Hangover Square* discussed in Chapter 5) or the narration of synaesthetic perception (as is frequently the case in the writing of Henry Green). These may form ways of showing a textual drive to capture cross-modal experience in a given moment of narrated time. Yet others might integrate actual images of musical notation into the text itself (this happens, for instance, in Lewis Grassic Gibbon's *Sunset Song* discussed in Chapter 4). As I show throughout this book, mid-century writing configures many different ways of narrating multi-sensory experience. The novel moves towards a mediatized textuality that articulates the historically specific experience of audio-vision.

While form and narration are key in considering literary engagements with sound–image interaction, mid-century writers also deal in other thematic and conceptual ways with this issue: Elizabeth Bowen and Henry Green, for instance, extensively theorize dialogue alongside similar contemporary discourses in the film industry. They reflect a wider concern with the power of voice and ask how speech might construct scenes and characters that create, as Green writes, 'life, of a kind, in the reader'.[80] In pursuing fictional literary as well as non-fictional discursive engagements with audio-vision alongside British film history, this book attempts to broaden the archive of sources that may conceivably be used to study the resonant and pervasive presence of audio-vision in twentieth-century culture.

The ways in which this book deals with the specific problem of 'literary' audio-vision draws further inspiration from recent methodological reflections in the study of radio and literature As Debra Rae Cohen writes for the case of '"literary" radio studies', a rigorous approach ought to be

[79] Jonathan Foltz, *The Novel after Film: Modernism and the Decline of Autonomy* (New York: Oxford University Press, 2018), p. 2.

[80] Henry Green, 'A Novelist to his Readers', *Surviving: The Uncollected Writings of Henry Green* (London: Harvill, 1993), 136–142 (p. 137).

# 18 LITERATURE AND SOUND FILM IN MID-CENTURY BRITAIN

'necessarily intermedial, and necessarily political: attentive to industry specificities, cultural dynamics, the protocols of broadcast and reception and the resonant metaphorics of wireless derived from the phenomenological particularities of listening practice'.[81] As the following outline of the book's structure will show, each chapter examines a set of distinct film industry practices and their cultural contexts, the specificities of film as a medium grounded in the technological mediation of performance, and the 'phenomenological particularity' of cinema as multi-sensory, audio-visual experience. Each chapter traces how this set of film-specific issues relates to forms of mid-century literary practice.

## Looking Ahead

This book follows a chronological and thematic structure, moving from the late 1920s to the late 1940s. Each chapter addresses a different film genre and a different set of texts to show the range of material that gains new legibility through my approach. The writers featured in this study (with the exception of Ivy Compton-Burnett) were born in the 1890s and 1900s and reached adulthood in an age of silent film, before witnessing first-hand the transition to sound film. Many of them forged, at least temporarily, careers as scriptwriters and film reviewers in addition to their literary writing. In addition to such biographical considerations, each of my case studies also responds individually to existing lines of enquiry in the study of mid-century writers and media culture: there are, for instance, excellent discussions of George Orwell and Elizabeth Bowen vis-à-vis radio; of the role played by the gramophone and telephone in the works of Jean Rhys and Evelyn Waugh; and illuminating accounts of Christopher Isherwood, Graham Greene, and Henry Green with a view to the camera work of photography and (silent) film.[82] Here, I re-examine these writers, alongside some lesser-known authors of their generation, to complement such existing accounts and to demonstrate the centrality of audio-vision to their engagements with the media ecology at mid-century.

---

[81] Debra Rae Cohen, 'Wireless Imaginations', in Anna Snaith (ed.), *Sound and Literature* (Cambridge: Cambridge University Press, 2020), 334–350 (p. 344).

[82] See, for example, Emily C. Bloom, *The Wireless Past: Anglo-Irish Writers and the BBC, 1931–1968* (Oxford: Oxford University Press, 2016) on Bowen and radio; Frattarola, *Modernist Soundscapes* (2018) on Rhys and the gramophone; Foltz, *The Novel after Film* (2018) on Green in relation to photography and film.

The discussion presented here is by no means exhaustive. As a study of the specifically British context, this book predominantly considers the British (and, at times, Hollywood) film industry as well as the British response to sound film at the expense of more detailed accounts of, for instance, French, Soviet, and German developments that have been addressed elsewhere.[83] I cover the two decades following the release of the first British sound film because this period is most immediately affected by the introduction of sound cinema. However, my readings could conceivably be expanded well into the 1950s and beyond (one might think, for instance, of Muriel Spark and Christine Brooke-Rose alongside New Wave cinema). Readers will find that this book, at times, also speaks to some of the key issues in the study of the 1930s and 1940s, including discussions of middlebrow and gender, the culture of celebrity, and the relationship between media and Empire. However, these topics do not form the primary focus of this study and will only feature in relation to my analyses of audio-vision in selected chapters.

Chapter 1, 'Learning to Talk', addresses the shift from silent to sound film and its wide-ranging consequences for mid-century cinema and literature. I discuss Alfred Hitchcock's *Blackmail*, which was released as a silent version and as a sound version in 1929. Comparing these two versions, I make two foundational arguments for the following chapters: first, I argue that Hitchcock's film develops an audio-visual aesthetic that comprehensively answered, for the first time, critical questions regarding the nature and form of sound film. Second, I argue that the film illustrates the changing status of image, sound, and text in the 'talkie', which, in turn, had significant implications for literature. The chapter briefly introduces the group of mid-century writers discussed in this volume and reflects on their varied engagements with sound film throughout their careers.

Chapter 2, 'Adapting Audio-Vision', considers the early years of sound cinema vis-à-vis the affordances of theatre, film, and literature. Early sound film was viewed as particularly suited to adapting material from the theatre. Thus, revue and cabaret came to act as templates for the production of successful revue and musical films in the 1930s. Sound film's appropriation of

---

[83] Buhler's *Theories of the Soundtrack* discusses Soviet, French, and German film sound theory. Charles O'Brien notes important differences in national film cultures: 'whereas the emphasis in 1930s Hollywood was on sound's intelligibility within a film's story-world, French filmmaking implies an alternative model, whereby sound serves to reproduce a performance staged for recording'. My focus is therefore limited to British sound film and some selected interactions of the British film industry with Hollywood. See O'Brien, *Cinema's Conversion to Sound*, pp. 1–16 and pp. 156–164.

20 LITERATURE AND SOUND FILM IN MID-CENTURY BRITAIN

stage forms, however, also drew writers to the issue of cross-media adaptation and raised wider questions regarding the possibilities and limits of the literary text: how might writers adapt stage forms for a prose text? How could literature translate modes and effects of audio-vision into its own narrative procedures? I argue that Evelyn Waugh's *Vile Bodies* (1930) as well as Christopher Isherwood's *Mr Norris Changes Trains* (1935), *Goodbye to Berlin* (1939), and *Prater Violet* (1945) address such questions sparked by the rise of sound film. They highlight literature's adaptability in an evolving media ecology and underscore the literary text's own capacity to become mediatized in the age of audio-vision.

Chapter 3, 'Dialogue and Intelligibility', turns to one of the most significant changes synchronized sound brought to the film industry: spoken dialogue and its synchronization with the film image. The chapter argues for the mid-century emergence of a new, audio-visual poetics of dialogue, meaning a way of conceiving of dialogue and its effects as a matter of vision and audition. By analysing film dialogue in Alexander Korda's British take on screwball comedy, *The Divorce of Lady X* (1938), and by correlating this work with selected literary texts, essays, and broadcasts by Elizabeth Bowen, Henry Green, and Ivy Compton-Burnett, the chapter evidences film and text's rapidly growing proximity in their efforts to conceptualize dialogue audio-visually.

Chapter 4, 'Documenting the Everyday', addresses film and literature's pervasive questioning of representational conventions in response to the 'documentary impulse' of the 1930s. This very act of questioning matters, because audio-vision, like the documentary itself, is never apolitical. I discuss General Post Office (GPO) documentary films *The Song of Ceylon* (1934) and *Night Mail* (1936) alongside novels by Lewis Grassic Gibbon (*Sunset Song*, 1932) and George Orwell (*A Clergyman's Daughter*, 1935 and *Keep the Aspidistra Flying*, 1936) to argue that these works share a preoccupation with demonstrating the artificial, curated nature of their form in order to undermine any possible claim to documentary realism at a time when audio-vision might easily seduce the viewer into believing that one can gain 'unmediated' or 'direct' access to documentary's subjects.

Chapter 5, 'Networks of Audio-Vision', pursues two related lines of thought: first, I argue that audio-vision is a networked phenomenon, meaning that it builds on the entire media ecology. Audio-vision is so powerful and expressive, because it links different technological and sensory channels and grounds its effect in a network of media forms. I show how this development becomes particularly clear in the thriller, one of the most popular cinematic and literary genres of the Thirties and Forties. I correlate Thorold Dickinson's psychological thriller *Gaslight* (1940) with texts by Eric Ambler and Graham Greene to show how networks of audio-vision are mobilized for the thriller's characteristic presentation of violence, suspense, and threat. In a second step, the chapter zooms out to show that these audio-visual networks are circulating more broadly in the mid-century mediascape. Patrick Hamilton's *Hangover Square* (1941) and Jean Rhys's *Good Morning Midnight* (1939), for instance, also rely on audio-visual networks to construct their narrative strategies, creating new literary idioms for the representation of violence, crisis, and distress. In their works, characters become media and the human sensorium becomes part of the network.

Chapter 6, 'The Senses at War', establishes unlikely connections between the Gainsborough melodrama cycle, produced in Britain between 1943 and 1947, and Home Front fiction by Elizabeth Bowen, Henry Green, and James Hanley. I argue that these works jointly pursue what I call an 'aesthetics of excess'. They engage in the production of textual, visual, and sonic excesses as well as complicated temporalities, thereby calling into question the possibility of any kind of linear understanding of time, space, and lived experience in wartime. In a world menaced by totality, excess might also become resistance. The Coda examines Evelyn Waugh's novella *The Loved One* (1948) as a sly Wavian comment on the film industry and the mid-century writer's alleged complicity in it.

Taken together, these chapters invite readers to think anew about the relationship between sound film and literature. This matters, not simply because it produces new readings of canonical and less canonical twentieth-century writers and films, but because it advocates for a multi-sensory and intermedial approach to studying mid-century culture. As I will show throughout this book, the mid-century witnessed an unprecedented synthesis of technologically mediated vision and audition alongside a growing synergy of film and literature—and it is no accident that these events coincided.

*Literature and Sound Film in Mid-Century Britain.* Lara Ehrenfried, Oxford University Press.
© Lara Ehrenfried 2025. DOI: 10.1093/9780198950790.003.0001

# 1
# Learning to Talk

When Alfred Hitchcock's first sound film *Blackmail* was released in 1929, *The Daily Mail* called it a British 'triumph' and the 'best talk-film yet'.[1] The paper praised the film as 'far in advance of all other talking films which have hitherto been shown', stating that 'for the first time intelligent use is made of sound'.[2] Initially planned as a silent film for British International Pictures (BIP), *Blackmail* was moved to sound when production was already under way. Filming at Elstree Studios, which had been fitted with sound equipment by April 1929, Hitchcock had to reshoot scenes to accommodate the film's shift to synchronized sound.[3] *Blackmail* thus remains of critical relevance as the film's extant silent and sound versions invite audiences to consider the challenges posed to film by the industry's move to sound. *Blackmail* widely earned critical acclaim, not least because it addressed key issues of cinematic form that would continue to preoccupy filmmakers, artists, and audiences throughout the following decade: the impact of synchronization, the shifting status of written text and spoken language within the image-world of film, and the changing significance of silence.

*Blackmail* tells the story of Alice White, a young woman who stabs the painter Crewe in self-defence when he assaults her in his artist's studio. Too scared to go to the police, Alice conceals the murder. Her fiancé Frank is a detective at Scotland Yard and gets assigned to the case. Frank quickly finds out that Alice killed Crewe, but decides to keep quiet until the couple are blackmailed by a witness. The silent version of *Blackmail* contains many of Hitchcock's trademark features, showing the influence of expressionist cinema: the marked play of light and shadow, the use of slightly distorted camera angles and framing devices. Mirrors, doors, telephone booths, and window panes enclose characters as they move or converse with others. The silent film also relies on a high volume of diegetic, written text alongside

---

[1] 'Best Talk-Film Yet', *The Daily Mail*, 24 June 1929, p. 11.

[2] 'Best Talk-Film Yet', p. 11.

[3] *Blackmail*, dir. by Alfred Hitchcock, starring Anny Ondra and John Longden (British International Pictures, 1929). See also Murphy, 'Coming of Sound to the Cinema in Britain', p. 155.

intertitles and dialogue titles. Characters are often shown writing or reading notes, perusing newspapers, and glancing at posters to convey action and character psychology: a note carried by Alice in her handbag suggests an eagerly awaited rendezvous with Crewe and a newspaper poster announces the police hunt for the murderer. This reliance on diegetic text is toned down in the sound version of *Blackmail*, where, in some instances, sound effects and synchronized dialogue entirely replace the textual inserts of the silent version. When, for instance, Crewe's landlady is interviewed by the police following the murder, the silent version shows a close-up of her last handwritten note to Crewe about a mysterious visitor who had been calling three times before his death (see Figure 1.1).

In *Blackmail*'s silent version, audiences are permitted to read the handwritten note in full as the camera lingers on the piece of paper in the landlady's hands. In the sound version, the film shows a medium-long shot of Mrs Humphries and the police sitting together in an office at Scotland Yard. Mrs Humphries holds the handwritten note and briefly looks at it while its content is discussed by the characters, but the film does not show a close-up

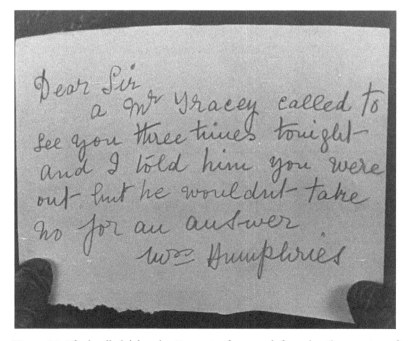

**Figure 1.1** The landlady's handwritten note; frame grab from the silent version of *Blackmail* (British International Pictures, 1929), directed by Alfred Hitchcock.

24 LITERATURE AND SOUND FILM IN MID-CENTURY BRITAIN

of the paper or the actual text. Here, information is solely conveyed through verbal exchange: speech replaces written text in the sound film.

This difference between the silent and sound versions of *Blackmail* exemplifies a crucial shift taking place in the late 1920s: the reconfiguration of the roles played by text, sound, and image in cinema. As Michel Chion notes, 'the writing of words and the sound of speech, which seem to be similar, are in fact quite different; [...] the presence of language redivides what we perceive in a film'.[4] In the silent film the visualization of written text on the screen had performed vital utilitarian and aesthetic functions, whereas the sound film places much greater attention on text that is spoken, but unseen. In both cases, language interacts with the moving image. However, intertitles, dialogue titles, and other forms of text in the silent film could be easily integrated as written material into the visual composition of film. As film titling work became professionalized and more sophisticated, the visualization of the written word evolved into an integral part of the silent film as a coherent entity. The sound film, however, upended this relation between moving image and written text while the speaking voice turned central to filmic communication: 'as soon as speech appears in a film, voices cease to belong completely to the world of concrete sound, for they have become the vehicles of language'.[5] In sound film, the voice conveys spoken language, which has to be married as seamlessly as possible to the visual composition of film.

The positive reception of Hitchcock's *Blackmail*, then, had much to do with the way it handled this reconfiguration of sound, image, and text. Indeed, the production's self-conscious engagement with the possibilities and limits of synchronized sound cemented its status as a milestone in the history of British cinema. John Belton notes that *Blackmail* cleverly uses sound 'to foreground its central character's inability to speak', while Matthew McDonald suggests that the film showcases Hitchcock's anxiety surrounding the precise control of film sound and, especially, of the speaking voice.[6] As the story of the eponymous blackmail relies on the protagonists' efforts to keep quiet, there is a marked tension between the film's capacity for technologically

---

[4] Michel Chion, *Words on Screen*, ed. and trans. Claudia Gorbman (New York: Columbia University Press, 2017), p. 1.

[5] Chion, *Words on Screen*, p. 200.

[6] John Belton, 'Awkward Transitions: Hitchcock's 'Blackmail' and the Dynamics of Early Film Sound', *Musical Quarterly*, 83.2 (1999), 227–246 (p. 243); Matthew MacDonald, 'Hitchcock's *Blackmail* and the Threat of Recorded Sound', *Music and the Moving Image*, 8.3 (2015), 40–51.

mediated, synchronized sound and the plot's motivation to remain silent. The sound version thus, paradoxically, constructs a sustained emphasis on silence by disembodying the speaking voice, by contrasting Alice's speech-lessness with other characters' incessant chatter, by deliberately excluding the audience from sonic information, and by distorting dialogue and sound effects to underline the unspeakability of Alice's crime.

Camera perspective and editing are used to avoid visible lip-synchronization in many of the dialogue scenes, which tend to be composed of reaction shots, whereby the camera focuses in close-up or medium upper-body shots on the listener of a dialogue sequence while the voice of the speaker is heard. Hitchcock often applied such reaction shots and recognized their function in retaining the speed and agility of camerawork in the sound film: 'this over-running of one person's image with another person's voice is a method peculiar to the talkies; it is one of the devices which help the talkies to tell a story faster than a silent film could tell it, and faster than it could be told on the stage.'[7] While this strategy simplified the process of adding sound to film, the lack of visible lip-synchronization also visually separates the speaking voice from its on-screen body. This impression of the disembodied voice is especially striking in Alice's case, because it reflects the actual record-ing process for *Blackmail*'s soundtrack: Anny Ondra, who plays Alice, spoke English with a Czech accent. BIP deemed her accent and speaking voice unsuitable for *Blackmail*'s sound version and hired the English actress Joan Barry to deliver Ondra's lines by standing just off-stage while Ondra mimed her lines in front of the camera.[8] *The Daily Mail*'s review of the film makes a special point of telling its readers that Ondra does not actually speak in the film: 'the finest talk in the film comes from the lips of the girl. But those tones are not the authentic voice of Miss Ondra. Miss Joan Barry "doubled" for her in the dialogue. That fact, unhappily, is not mentioned anywhere in the programme or in the...list of characters.'[9] Silence is thus central to both plot and production: the part of the speechless woman is performed by a woman whose voice was muted and substituted in the filming process.

---

[7] Alfred Hitchcock, 'Direction', in Charles Davy (ed.), *Footnotes to the Film*, Reader's Union Edition (New York: Arno Press & *The New York Times*, 1970), 3–15 (p. 9). This edition is a reprint of the 1938 edition.

[8] Laura Marcus, 'Talking Films', in Benjamin Kohlmann and Matthew Taunton (eds), *A History of 1930s British Literature* (Cambridge: Cambridge University Press, 2019), 177–193 (pp. 179–180).

[9] See 'Best Talk-Film Yet', *The Daily Mail*, 24 June 1929, p. 11.

## 26 LITERATURE AND SOUND FILM IN MID-CENTURY BRITAIN

The sound version of *Blackmail* further plays with the contrast between sound and silence by excluding the audience from sonic information. The film underscores the idea that, even in a sound film, access to sonic information is a privilege and not a certainty. Film scenes exploiting this technique are grouped around a phone booth in the shop of Alice's father. When, for instance, Alice's fiancé Frank receives a call in the phone booth, the door of the booth is initially left open and audiences can hear Frank's response to the caller. When a presumably significant piece of information is communicated to the policeman, he suddenly closes the door of the booth and audiences can no longer hear his replies, thus effectively excluding the audience from the rest of his phone conversation. At other times, Alice and Frank retreat to the phone booth for private conversations. When they close the door, they are visible through the glass walls of the booth, but their conversations remain unheard. Laura Marcus points out that this use of the phone booth alludes to early sound cameras which had to be installed in heavy cases ('blimped') in order to soundproof them.[10] These cameras could capture visual information but were prevented from picking up unwanted ambient noise on the film set. Similarly, the phone booth in the film excludes the audience from sonic information while still maintaining access to the visual image.

The manipulation and distortion of sound continues throughout the film, foregrounding Alice's state of shock and her silence. The iconic breakfast scene, for instance, contains one of Hitchcock's most interesting experiments with sound: as Alice is at breakfast with her parents on the morning after the murder, a visiting neighbour gossips about the murder with Alice's mother. The camera focuses on Alice as she sits at the table while the dialogue in the background between her mother and the neighbour becomes increasingly unintelligible. The camera shows close-ups of Alice's tormented face while only the word 'knife' remains intelligible. The word is repeated several times, becoming louder and shriller with each repetition. Marcus argues that Hitchcock produces the equivalent of a close-up with sound rather than image by rendering all other words unintelligible and by drawing the auditory focus to the word 'knife'.[11] One might add here that this particular effect is based on image–sound combination: the camera's persistent focus on Alice's face coupled with the manipulated background noise expresses Alice's silent anxiety and distorted perception in the aftermath of

---

[10] Marcus, *The Tenth Muse*, p. 424.    [11] Marcus, *The Tenth Muse*, p. 422.

LEARNING TO TALK 27

the crime. The shrill repetition of 'knife' is so effective and meaningful, because it is synthesized with close-ups of Alice's face. Like the *Daily Mail*, *The Times* praised Hitchcock for succeeding in controlling sound without sacrificing image, acting, or sound quality. *The Times* review continues that the film

> frees us from the idea that the camera must be transfixed and the pictorial flow of the film arrested merely for the pleasure of recording a variety of strange noises.…Indeed, the dialogue throughout is admirably written and enters with a frank and pleasing cadence into its graphic background.[12]

The reviewer commends Hitchcock's film for retaining the fluid camera movements and visual agility that were known to audiences from silent film. To Hitchcock's credit, *Blackmail* was able to combine such features with recorded dialogue, music, and sound effects to create a new audio-visual aesthetic. The reviewer also emphasizes the director's achievement in well-written dialogue that matches the 'graphic background', thereby gesturing to the implicit assumption that sound and image tracks should achieve a new audio-visual synthesis. In 1938, Hitchcock himself stated that his aim in filmmaking was to 'put my film together on the screen, not simply to photograph something that has been put together already in the form of a long piece of stage acting.… The screen ought to speak its own language, freshly coined.'[13] Hitchcock understood very early that sound film required new means of expression to link visual flow and verbal utterance. As synchronized sound had introduced the cultural specificity of spoken language to the image world of film, both image and sound had to be developed and spliced together to form a coherent unity. Reflecting on his process as a filmmaker, Hitchcock underlines the importance of precise scripting, of conceiving of film 'directly in visual terms', and of using actors who are 'cinema-minded', meaning those who understand that acting in a film functions entirely differently from acting in the theatre.[14] The audio-visual 'language' of the screen must be wholly its own, wholly suited to its medium. These remarks directly address two wider issues pertaining to sound film in the transition years of the late 1920s and early 1930s. First, the need to establish 'the talkies' as a *sui generis* media form distinct from both silent film and theatre; and second, the need to conceptualize anew the interplay of

---

[12] 'Regal Theatre: "Blackmail". A British International Picture', *The Times*, 24 June 1929, p. 12.
[13] Hitchcock, 'Direction', p. 7.     [14] Hitchcock, 'Direction', pp. 6–7.

text, sound, and image in sound film. As I will show in the remainder of this chapter, both of these issues, which had already clearly emerged from the production of *Blackmail*, had significant consequences for cinema and mid-century literature.

## Beyond *Blackmail*

Hitchcock's *Blackmail* certainly stood out against a number of early synchronized sound films that were released relatively quickly in and around 1929 to capitalize on the new sound technology with varying degrees of success. This trend received mixed responses from the British trade press. In January 1930, *Kinematograph Weekly* critically reviewed the events of the past year, stating that

> there were those who rushed in talkie equipment at such speed that the apparatus could not possibly be expected to work properly, and there were those who, when good talkies were scarce, put on anything that talked with no thought of whether it entertained or not. This remarkable combination of atrocious reproduction and bad entertainment made thousands of enemies for the talkies...[15]

Spurred on by the successful American sound film *The Singing Fool*, released in the UK in November 1928, the British film industry intensified its efforts to move to sound.[16] At the time, numerous different sound systems were available on American and British markets, including RCA's Photophone, Western Electric's Vitaphone, American Powers-Cinephone, German Tobis-Klangfilm, British Phototone, British Acoustic, and Marconi-Visatone.[17] These different systems could be divided into two categories: sound-on-disc and sound-on-film systems. Sound-on-disc, such as Vitaphone, was a system for which the soundtrack was recorded on a separate disc and, during a film

---

[15] '1929–1930', *Kinematograph Weekly*, 2 January 1930, p. 113.

[16] Detailed accounts of the transition to sound in Britain can be found in Robert Murphy, 'Coming of Sound to the Cinema in Britain', *Historical Journal of Film, Radio and Television*, 4.2 (1984), 143–160 (p. 146); Laraine Porter, 'The Talkies Come to Britain', pp. 87–98; Geoff Brown, 'When Britannia Ruled the Sound Waves: Britain's Transition to Sound in its European Context', *Music, Sound, and the Moving Image*, 12.2 (2018), 93–119; and Rachael Low, *The History of the British Film, 1929–1939: Film Making in 1930s Britain* (London: Allen & Unwin, 1985).

[17] Murphy, 'Coming of Sound', p. 147.

screening, the soundtrack on the disc had to be played separately from the image track on the film reel. While sound reproduction with this system offered relatively good intelligibility, accurate synchronization was quite difficult to achieve as the system required manual adjustment. Sound-on-film, for instance the German Tobis-Klangfilm or RCA's photophone, contained image and sound tracks on the film strip. This allowed for better synchronization, but the sound quality was generally worse than the standards offered by sound-on-disc systems. Both systems, however, changed the practicalities of filmmaking considerably: cameras had to be soundproofed prior to sound recording and microphone placement had to be devised carefully, often adversely affecting lighting and set design. Microphones and heavy soundproofed cameras restricted the possibilities of movement for actors while the sensitivity of early recording equipment also made on-location filming virtually impossible.[18] The film industry thus had to grapple with changed conditions of production and, as suggested by the *Kine Weekly* review of events in 1929, the results were often rather unsatisfactory.

As a result, as Laura Marcus shows in *The Tenth Muse*, many intellectuals, film critics, and avant-garde writers remained rather critical of the talking film, not least because of the initial practice to 'put on anything that talked' with no regard for its quality.[19] Moreover, the intrusion of the speaking voice into film's visual realm was viewed, by some, as fatal to cinema's form. The British writer and film critic Ernest Betts, for instance, was convinced that cinema's appeal came from its poetic play of 'light and shadow'.[20] Betts saw film as a strictly silent domain in which spoken dialogue had no place. Similarly, in *The Film till Now* (1930), the British documentary filmmaker Paul Rotha stated his early concerns over sound as a potential distraction for the viewer. He argued that having to follow dialogue on screen would take the viewer's attention away from the image, thus likely interfering with audiences' attentive reception of film.[21] Some popular entertainers agreed, among them notably Charlie Chaplin, who wrote in

---

[18] The problems raised by early sound equipment for the film production process are discussed by Barry Salt, 'Film Style and Technology in the Thirties: Sound', in Elisabeth Weis and John Belton (eds), *Film Sound: Theory and Practice* (New York: Columbia University Press, 1985), pp. 37–43.

[19] Marcus, *The Tenth Muse*, pp. 404–437.

[20] Betts summarizes his attitude in the short journal article 'Why Talkies are Unsound', reprinted in James Donald, Anne Friedberg, and Laura Marcus (eds), *Close Up 1927–1933: Cinema and Modernism* (London: Cassell, 1998), pp. 89–90. See also Ernest Betts, *Heraclitus or The Future of Films* (London: Kegan Paul, 1928).

[21] Paul Rotha, *The Film Till Now: A Survey of World Cinema*, revd edn (London: Vision, 1949), pp. 405–409.

30  LITERATURE AND SOUND FILM IN MID-CENTURY BRITAIN

*The Daily Mail* in February 1931 that his 'screen character' would remain 'speechless from choice'.[22] A more mixed reaction to synchronized sound came from the Soviet directors Sergei Eisenstein, Vsvolod Pudovkin, and Gregori Alexandrov. They published their 'Statement on Sound' in 1928 in Leningrad and a translation for the avant-garde film journal *Close Up* made the 'Statement' available to an English-speaking audience.[23] Eisenstein already enjoyed a reputation as a brilliant director due to the international success of his silent film *Battleship Potemkin* (1925). He welcomed sound as a cinematic innovation and advocated for treating sound as an additional element in the practice of montage which featured centrally in his own aesthetic programme for film.[24] Colliding shots and creating conflicting impressions by means of image and sound montage would, according to Eisenstein, produce a layering of visual and acoustic effects.[25] This 'contrapuntal use' of sound and image was the Soviet director's ideal for cinematic production under the conditions of the new technology. However, Eisenstein and his colleagues also feared that synchronized sound could be used to solely increase industry profits and as a contributing factor to the proliferation of mass entertainment, rather than film art.[26] The use of sound for a 'photographed presentation of theatrical order' would merely return film to its 'repressed other', the theatre.[27] To Eisenstein, Pudovkin, and Alexandrov, this issue pertained especially to the practice of synchronization for, as James Buhler notes, synchronized dialogue would make the filmic 'segments less pliable' and thus potentially less flexible for the purpose of montage.[28]

Building on the 'Statement on Sound', but more open and pragmatic, are some of Pudovkin's individually authored pieces on *Film Technique* and *Film Acting*, which establish sound as a key element whose purpose is to 'augment the potential expressiveness of the film's content'.[29] Regarding the question of synchronization, Pudovkin observed that the precise overlap of

---

[22] Charlie Chaplin, 'Why I Prefer Silent Films', *Daily Mail*, 7 February 1931, p. 10.

[23] James Donald, 'Introduction', in James Donald, Anne Friedberg, and Laura Marcus (eds), *Close Up 1927–1933: Cinema and Modernism* (London: Cassell, 1998), 79–82.

[24] Sergei Eisenstein, W. I. Pudovkin, and G. V. Alexandrov, 'Statement on Sound', in Richard Taylor (ed.), *The Eisenstein Reader* (London: BFI, 1998), pp. 80–81.

[25] Sergei Eisenstein, 'The Dialectical Approach to Film Form', in Richard Taylor (ed.), *The Eisenstein Reader* (London: BFI, 1998), pp. 93–110.

[26] Eisenstein et al., 'Statement on Sound', pp. 80–81.

[27] Eisenstein et al., 'Statement on Sound', pp. 80–81. See also Altman, 'The Evolution of Sound Technology', p. 51.

[28] James Buhler, *Theories of the Soundtrack* (Oxford: Oxford University Press, 2018), pp. 26–27.

[29] Vsevolod Pudovkin, *Film Technique*, in Ivor Montagu (trans.), *Film Technique and Film Acting: The Cinema Writings of V. I. Pudovkin* (New York: Bonanza, 1949), p. 156.

visual image and audio track is merely one possibility amongst many. As Buhler writes, Pudovkin

> finds the related approach of editing the scene to follow the dialogue with each change of speaker bringing a cut to the image of the new speaker to be something of an improvement, because it at least recognizes that film receives its power from selecting pertinent elements from the whole and giving them emphasis.[30]

Pudovkin's view focuses on sound as an element that can be shaped during the editing process. Synchronization does not preclude the possibility of using sound as counterpoint per se.[31] Like Pudovkin, the Hungarian-born writer and film critic Bela Balázs initially welcomed sound technology as an opportunity to innovate film production and to create new cinematic experiences. In his monograph *The Spirit of Film* (1930), Balázs cautioned his readers not to view sound as a mere complement to silent film. In his opinion, hearing was a more powerful sense than sight and thus synchronized sound film would open up a completely new dimension for reaching audiences.[32] While Balázs acknowledged that technological limitations would put an initial strain on filmmakers' and actors' creative freedom when working with sound, a far greater problem was 'the untutored state of our hearing'.[33] Hence, the filmmaker's main task had to be the 'creation of linguistic and acoustic landscapes' to educate audiences' hearing in relation to the image.[34] Balázs's writing makes clear the degree to which he understood that sound film must establish itself as its own independent medium with an evolving form based on the interaction of spoken language, sound effects, and image.

These views exemplify how synchronized sound film was a contested issue for intellectuals and film critics. On the other hand, exhibitors and cinema audiences seemed more favourably disposed towards the talkies. Between 1929 and 1933, the majority of British cinemas were equipped with sound, which was widely seen as a viable financial investment by exhibitors since 'sound equipment would generally mean increased attendance'.[35]

---

[30] Buhler, *Theories of the Soundtrack*, p. 29.
[31] Buhler, *Theories of the Soundtrack*, pp. 29–30.
[32] Bela Balázs, *Bela Balázs: Early Film Theory: 'Visible Man' and 'The Spirit of Film'*, ed. Erica Carter, trans. Rodney Livingstone (New York: Berghahn, 2010), p. 184.
[33] Balázs, *Early Film Theory*, pp. 185–187.    [34] Balázs, *Early Film Theory*, p. 195.
[35] Murphy, 'Coming of Sound', p. 151.

32    LITERATURE AND SOUND FILM IN MID-CENTURY BRITAIN

The British fan magazine *The Picturegoer* published a series of letters debating the pros and cons of sound film in the late 1920s and early 1930s. In January 1931, for instance, the magazine printed the following letter containing an extensive defence of sound film by an exhibitor:

> Highbrows are constantly denouncing the American accent, which they erroneously suggest is to be heard in all talking films. May I suggest, and I feel sure that most readers of *The Picturegoer* will agree, that a talking film made in America and dealing with American life would not have any pretensions to reality if it were not spoken in the tongue normally used by the characters the film portrays?...As regards the music the new entertainment provides, 'canned' is an expression which is often used, in such a tone of voice that one is left with little doubt as to the speaker's opinion of it. In reality, exhibitors find that talkie music is vastly more satisfactory than the music of silent days. It should be remembered that during the latter period, orchestras did not play during the whole of the continuous performance....[W]ith talkies installed, a kinema provides an equally good show at every portion of the performance. When music is heard, it is now often the result of the efforts of the highest paid musicians in the world.... Talkies are held responsible for the displacement of large numbers of musicians. This is true, but we must remember that scores of new posts have to be filled from sources not originally connected with the kinema industry. The installation and service of equipment alone is responsible for a great increase in employment on behalf of talkie houses.[36]

This defence of the talking film responds, from an industry and trade perspective, to some of the most pertinent points of criticism levelled against the sound film in Britain: the presence of American accents, the provision of music, job opportunities, and the overall quality and intelligibility of sound reproduction were frequently debated by fan magazines and the trade press. By January 1930, *Kinematograph Weekly*, which usually commented on a number of elements for each reviewed film ('story', 'acting', 'production', 'setting', and 'photography'), had added a new category to its reviews section: 'sound technique'. Reviewer comments in this section included information on whether a film's recordings were of good quality, whether accents spoken were (too) strong, and whether the voices heard in

---

[36] 'Truth about the Talkies', Letter by F. Williams, *The Picturegoer*, 21.121 (January 1931), p. 52.

the film were generally 'pleasant', clear, and intelligible.[37] Between 1930 and 1931, many readers of *The Picturegoer* wrote to the magazine to express their opinion that an unfair comparison with silent cinema was held against the sound film: 'talkies…are still in their infancy, though making rapid headway day by day, and it is unfair to compare the silent film of some fourteen years' experience with the very immature talking picture'.[38] Responses such as these indicate audiences' readiness to forgive some of the perceived shortfalls of early sound film. More importantly, there was a clear awareness of sound film's new audio-visual form, still in its 'infancy' and in the process of becoming, that had to be recognized as entirely separate from the silent film.

## Sound Film and the Mid-Century Writer

1929, the year of *Blackmail*'s release, also saw the publication of Elizabeth Bowen's *Joining Charles and Other Stories*, her third short story collection. 'Dead Mabelle', one of the stories in this collection, forms an unlikely companion piece to Hitchcock's film. Bowen's short story reflects on the move from silent to sound film and equally considers the reconfiguration of the roles played by text and moving image as part of this development. Karen Schaller reads 'Dead Mabelle' as Bowen's response to modernist debates about cinema, especially due to its 'language of motion' and its 'acute awareness of anxieties about the consuming powers of the cinema and its fleetingness'.[39] One of the key contexts for 'Dead Mabelle', however, is the emergence of cinematic audio-vision and image–sound synchronization. The story traces a bank clerk's obsession with the deceased silent film star Mabelle Pacey. William Stickford, the story's protagonist, is an isolated man, socially awkward and sexually inexperienced. The story begins by introducing him as an avid reader: 'he was intelligent, solitary, self-educated, self-suspicious; he had read, without system, enough to trouble him endlessly; text-books…popular translations, fortnightly publications (scientific and so on) complete in so many parts, potted history and

---

[37] 'Reviews of the Week', *Kinematograph Weekly*, 2 January 1930, p. 83.
[38] 'What do you think?', Letter by M. L. Sheffield, *The Picturegoer*, 21.122 (February 1931), p. 54.
[39] Karen Schaller, ' "I know it to be synthetic but it affects me strongly": "Dead Mabelle" and Bowen's Emotion Pictures', *Textual Practice* 27.1 (2013), 163–185 (p. 165 and p. 169).

34    LITERATURE AND SOUND FILM IN MID-CENTURY BRITAIN

philosophy.[40] William reads and observes his environment; his social awkwardness initially conveyed in the visual language of a camera: 'he couldn't quite get Jim into focus but he supposed he liked him all right'; William is 'cinema-shy' until, one day, his colleague Jim drags him to watch a film featuring Mabelle Pacey.[41] William quickly becomes enamoured with Mabelle's film image, the projected close-up of her face, and his obsession with Mabelle then grows day by day. He begins to tour around various cinemas to catch screenings of Mabelle's films. His steady consumption of Mabelle's image also transforms his capacity to think, feel, and read: 'Thought, as he understood thought, became pale and meaningless, reading scarcely more than a titillation of the eye-balls.'[42] William's intense encounter with the silent films of Mabelle draw him into her 'black-and-white world of abstractions', and reading text becomes just one superficial visual stimulus amongst many as text itself is anchored in the world of film in William's new, cinema-minded consciousness.[43]

While the story thus mirrors, perhaps even slyly comments on, the connections woven between text and silent film image in the early to mid-1920s, the story's timeline also takes up the issue of cinema's changing form in the late 1920s: 'Dead Mabelle' begins in 1927, the year of the successful American sound film *The Jazz Singer*, followed by a prolonged flashback to 1924, the moment when William first encounters the silent films of Mabelle. Now, in 1927, however, the violent death of the silent film star also expresses the decline of her medium: 'her films would be recalled—boiled down, they said. He had heard old films were used for patent leather; that which was Mabelle would be a shoe, a bag, a belt round some woman's middle.'[44] Bowen here likely alludes to the fact that cellulose nitrate, the base layer of most film stocks well into the 1950s, could be repurposed in different ways. Recycling of film stocks for their various chemical components, especially silver and cellulose, occurred regularly. The glossy finish on patent leather shoes could be achieved relatively affordably by applying a celluloid treatment. William's anxiety over the re-commodification of the chemical components of Mabelle's films thus highlights the likelihood of their destruction as both cultural and economic necessity in line with standard practices for recycling film stock. His anxiety also reflects the conflation of reel and real,

---

[40] Elizabeth Bowen, 'Dead Mabelle', *The Collected Stories of Elizabeth Bowen* (London: Vintage, 1999), 302–312 (p. 303).
[41] Bowen, 'Dead Mabelle', p. 303.     [42] Bowen, 'Dead Mabelle', p. 305.
[43] Bowen, 'Dead Mabelle', pp. 304–306.     [44] Bowen, 'Dead Mabelle', p. 311.

as 'that which *was* Mabelle would be a shoe, a bag, a belt'. The film image does not represent, but *is* Mabelle; William's obsession with the film star turns image into reality. This, of course, makes the idea of Mabelle, recycled as fashionable commodities for other women, even more disturbing.

The juxtaposition of the story's present (1927) and past (1924) highlights that the 'boiling down' of Mabelle's silent image is driven by the coming of sound. When William reads of Mabelle's death in the local paper, he decides to buy all other magazines and newspapers reporting on her death, as if to permit himself to read the story from all possible angles. As he carries the papers home, 'he met the wind tearing down the street. He stood on the kerbstone, not knowing which way to go; the wind got into the papers and rattled and sang in them; they gave out an inconceivable volume of sound to which he believed the whole town must turn round and listen.'[45] The news of the death of the silent film (star) is accompanied by a new sensitivity to sound, a new audio-visual world in which William now comes to move and which, once back at home, leads him to 'walk[ ] about in a state of suspension, looking, without connection of thought, at his books and pictures.'[46] Mabelle's death heralds a state of suspension, followed by a new order (or reconfiguration), of the status inhabited by text, image, and sound.

'Dead Mabelle' is one of the earliest pieces by Bowen to reflect explicitly on the implications of media change and, especially, on cinematic developments. It is a foundational text in Bowen's writing on cinema, which strongly supports a reading of Bowen as one of the most perceptive, 'cinema-conscious' writers of her generation. Having come of age in the era of silent film, followed by her witnessing first-hand the transition to sound cinema, Bowen, like her contemporaries, was uniquely positioned to reflect on filmic audio-vision and its implications for writing. In her essay 'Why I Go to the Cinema' (1938), she presents herself as an avid cinemagoer, as 'a fan, not a critic'.[47] She reports that she visits the cinema 'to be distracted (or "taken out of myself"); I go when I don't want to think; I go when I do want to think and need stimulus.'[48] The screen offers both escapist fantasy and a vital source of inspiration to the writer. Her fictional characters, Bowen asserts, are often 'composite copies' assembled from 'the novelist's memory,'

---

[45] Bowen, 'Dead Mabelle', p. 307.     [46] Bowen, 'Dead Mabelle', p. 312.

[47] Elizabeth Bowen, 'Why I Go to the Cinema', in Charles Davy (ed.), *Footnotes to the Film*, Reader's Union Edition (New York: Arno Press & *The New York Times*, 1970), 205–220 (p. 207).

[48] Bowen, 'Why I Go to the Cinema', p. 205.

36  LITERATURE AND SOUND FILM IN MID-CENTURY BRITAIN

as well as from 'pictures, photographs, the screen'.[49] As the novelist's representation of character must be directed towards the creation of 'palpable physical reality', characters 'must be not only see-able (visualizable); they must be to be felt.... Physical personality belongs to action: cannot be separated from it. Pictures must be in movement. Eyes, hands, stature, etc., must appear, and only appear, *in play*.'[50] Similarly, 'scene' is composed from memory as well as 'pictures, photographs, the screen'.[51] Both scene and character of a novel must be written to 'direct the reader's visual imagination'.[52]

As I will show in Chapter 3, Bowen's attention to movement and vision is coupled with a particular emphasis on dialogue, which must be 'illustrative' as well as 'functional'.[53] Her theoretical reflections on the novel and the craft of the fiction writer are shaped by the experience of 1930s film as, ultimately, 'the novelist's relation to the novel is that of the director's relation to film. The cinema, cinema-going, has no doubt built up in novelists a great authoritarianism. This seems to me good.'[54] Sound cinema is useful because it supplies the novelist with the experience of a combination of movement, visual image, and spoken dialogue—all in the service of 'the fullest possible realization of the director's idea'. Cinema as a model for the writer holds clues to the 'completest possible surrounding of the subject'. This idea of 'completion' or 'full realization', in Bowen's poetics, is built on the combination of vision, movement, and audition. 'In effect', she asserted in her later essay 'A Matter of Inspiration' (1951), 'the page is like a cinema screen'.[55]

Perhaps surprisingly, such a comparison between the cinema screen and the pages of a literary text is echoed by Evelyn Waugh after the Second World War Although he lamented in 1947 that the 'talking apparatus set [cinema] back to its infancy',[56] elsewhere, he also noted that

---

[49] Elizabeth Bowen, 'Notes on Writing a Novel', in Hermione Lee (ed.), *The Mulberry Tree: Writings of Elizabeth Bowen* (London: Vintage, 1999), 35–48 (p. 39).

[50] Bowen, 'Notes on Writing a Novel', p. 38. Italics in the original.

[51] Bowen, 'Notes on Writing a Novel', p. 40.

[52] Bowen, 'Notes on Writing a Novel', p. 40.

[53] Bowen, 'Notes on Writing a Novel', p. 42.

[54] Bowen, 'Notes on Writing a Novel', p. 43.

[55] Elizabeth Bowen, 'A Matter of Inspiration', in Allan Hepburn (ed.), *People, Places, Things: Essays by Elizabeth Bowen* (Edinburgh: Edinburgh University Press, 2008), 263–268 (p. 266).

[56] Evelyn Waugh, 'Why Hollywood is a Term of Disparagement', in Donat Gallagher (ed.), *The Essays, Articles and Reviews of Evelyn Waugh* (London: Methuen, 1983), 325–331 (p. 326). The article was first published in the *Daily Telegraph* on 30 April 1947.

it is the cinema which has taught a new habit of narrative.... It is as though, out of the indefinite length of film, sequences have been cut which, assembled, comprise an experience which is the reader's alone.... The writer has become director and producer.[57]

Waugh's comments suggest that sound film of the 1930s and 1940s brought a key question to the mind of the writer, namely the question of whether, and to what extent, literature might learn from or adapt to the experience offered by sound film. The writer as 'director and producer' treats their material, and the matter of textual representation, differently. Waugh suggests here that literature adapts to media change and becomes itself more mediatized in the process.

Similar to Bowen and Waugh, the Scottish writer Lewis Grassic Gibbon (James Leslie Mitchell) noted that 'the Big Picture' might act as 'a Muse in tar and feathers' to the novelist.[58] Film admittedly had its shortfalls, but it could still be a significant source of inspiration for the writer. Indeed, there is evidence to suggest that Grassic Gibbon himself considered the ways in which sound film might be mobilized for his fictional and non-fictional writing. For his unfinished autobiography *Memoirs of a Materialist*, he had planned to structure the text as a film. Notes and a synopsis show that Grassic Gibbon was planning to adapt a layout and narrative structure made up of 'camera eye' sequences, 'stills', 'reels', and individual 'scenario scripts' addressing scenes and events of his life.[59] In one of his last published essays, 'A Novelist Looks at the Cinema' (1935), he vehemently advocates for cinema as an art form that ought to stand on its own.

If only she [the cinema] would practice the courtezan [*sic*] to the full, not drape her lovely figure in the drab domestic reach-me-downs of stage drama. Too often—in fifteen out of twenty of the Big Pictures that reach our bug house—she is clad not even in reach-me-downs. Instead, she is tarred and feathered or sprayed with saccharine in the likeness of a Christmas cake; and

---

[57] Waugh, '*Felix Culpa?* Review of the *Heart of the Matter* by Graham Greene', in Donat Gallagher (ed.), *The Essays, Articles and Reviews of Evelyn Waugh* (London: Methuen, 1983), 360–365 (p. 362).

[58] Lewis Grassic Gibbon, 'A Novelist Looks at the Cinema', *Cinema Quarterly*, 3.2 (1935), 81–85 (p. 85).

[59] Valentina Bold (ed.), *Smeddum: A Lewis Grassic Gibbon Anthology* (Edinburgh: Canongate, 2001), pp. 781–786.

38  LITERATURE AND SOUND FILM IN MID-CENTURY BRITAIN

unendingly, instead of walking fearless and free, she sidles along with her hands disposed in a disgustingly Rubens-like gesture.[60]

He criticizes film's apparent dependency on materials and stories taken from the theatre and stresses the importance of achieving sound film's complete independence from the stage.

Sound film, Grassic Gibbon asserts, does not 'suffer' the same 'limitations' as theatre. The willing suspension of disbelief can be facilitated much more easily by cinema; it can provide 'the free and undefiled illusion' sought by an audience.[61]

Henry Green (Henry Vincent Yorke) appeared equally concerned with sound film's means of communication, its sensory world, and its relation to the novel: 'media change', he insisted retrospectively in a 1958 interview for *The Paris Review* with Terry Southern, would always occupy the novelist.[62] When Green was asked directly by Southern whether he thought that 'films and television will radically alter the format of the novel', he responded that it was 'impossible for a novelist not to look out for other media.... The novelist is a communicator and must therefore be interested in any form of communication.'[63] Although Green remained largely unwilling to theorize extensively on his approach to writing (as an undergraduate, he claimed to have 'discovered that literature is not a subject to write essays about'),[64] his pervasive interest in media change and media forms as means of communication characterizes his work as a novelist. As I discuss in Chapters 3 and 6, Green's literary fiction of the 1930s and 1940s responds quite clearly to the changes brought about by audio-vision and synchronicity.

His second novel *Living*, yet another work appearing in 1929, presents cinema-going as an audio-visual and communal experience. Of *Living*, he wrote to his friend Nevill Coghill that it was conceived rather in the form of a 'disconnected cinema film'.[65] In the novel, the young working-class woman Lily Gates enjoys her visits to the local cinema. Above all, it is the phenomenological, affective response to film, in which Lily is swept up and which is

---

[60] Grassic Gibbon, 'A Novelist Looks at the Cinema', p. 85.

[61] Grassic Gibbon, 'A Novelist Looks at the Cinema', p. 85.

[62] Henry Green, 'The Art of Fiction', Interview by Terry Southern, first published in *The Paris Review* 19 (1958), pp. 60–77. Reprinted in Matthew Yorke (ed.), *Surviving: The Uncollected Writings of Henry Green* (London: Harvill, 1993), 234–250 (p. 248).

[63] Henry Green, 'The Art of Fiction', pp. 247–248.

[64] Henry Green, *Pack My Bag: A Self-Portrait* (London: Hogarth, 1979), p. 213.

[65] D. J. Taylor, *Bright Young People: The Rise and Fall of a Generation, 1918–1940* (London: Vintage, 2008), p. 253.

LEARNING TO TALK 39

mapped by the text with great sensitivity. The pictures, sounds, movement, and the community of the auditorium merge and create a joyful, sensory abandon:

> They were in cinema. Band played tune tum tum did dee dee. She hugged Dale's arm. She jumped her knees to the time. Couple on screen danced in ballroom there. She did not see them. Dee dee did da. Tum tum tum tum tum. Dale did not budge. Dee dee de did dee. She hummed now. She rolled his arm between her palms. Da da did dee—did dee dee tum, ta.... Tune was over. She clapped hands and clapped. Applause was general. But film did not stop oh no heroine's knickers slipped down slinky legs in full floor. Eeeee Lily Gates screamed. OOEEE the audience.[66]

Through extensive use of onomatopoeia and elliptic syntax, Green's early novel explores the immediacy of vision and audition in the auditorium and presents film-going as communal experience, in which the individual viewer echoes and becomes herself part of the crowd.

As if in dialogue with Green's Lily Gates, Jean Rhys reports her own visits to the cinema in her unfinished autobiography *Smile Please* (1979). Like Green's Lily Gates, Rhys records her experience of cinema as both communal and deeply sensuous:

> Yesterday at the cinema in the one and threes, watching the usual thing. Biff. Bang. Why, you dirty-double-crossing. Bang. Biff. I am so sick of fights. It is a funny sort of...I cannot remember the word. Anodyne. Lovely lovely word. Anodyne. Sitting in the darkness in the one and three. Bang, Biff. Revolver shots. Surrounded by small boys, infants in arms who wail, fat mothers, old age pensioners. After a long speech from the screen, small boy, 'I wanna know what the lady was saying.' Mother, 'Don' know, ducks.' Small boy, 'What was the gentleman saying, Mum?' Mother, 'You keep quiet or you'll get smacked.' You can't do this to me, You dirty double-crossing.[67]

While Rhys does not reflect on film's direct relation to literature, her textual representation of this visit noticeably draws on the interaction of spoken

---

[66] Henry Green, *Living, Loving, Party Going* (London: Vintage, 2005), p. 224.
[67] Jean Rhys, *Smile Please: An Unfinished Autobiography* (Harmondsworth: Penguin, 1984), p. 160.

40  LITERATURE AND SOUND FILM IN MID-CENTURY BRITAIN

dialogue, sound effects, and vision. It shows how her response to film is shaped by watching the image and listening both to the screen and to the soundscape created by the audience. By coupling her descriptions of the sound of the revolver, the speech emanating from the screen, the babies wailing, and the apparent problems of understanding the soundtrack in the noisy auditorium, her autobiographical narration indicates the extent to which her memory of cinema is grounded in audio-visual experience.[68]

Graham Greene's engagement with cinema was more overt than Waugh's or Rhys's. It is well known that Greene was one of the most prolific film critics of his time, writing for *The Spectator* and the magazine *Night and Day*. In addition, he made a number of radio broadcasts on film criticism and supplemented his income with work on film scripts, including John Boulting's adaptation of *Brighton Rock* (1948) and Carol Reed's *The Third Man* (1949). As David Parker notes, Greene's early film criticism was notably shaped by his reading of the avant-garde magazine *Close Up* in the 1920s and the magazine's early resistance to the coming of sound.[69] In light of Greene's interest in *Close Up*, it is hardly surprising that he wrote some critical assessments of early sound film. In 'A Film Principle', first published in *The Times* on 10 July 1928, he warned that 'film has reached a point where it must choose finally between developing as a cheap imitation of the stage or as a separate art. Silence is not its vice but its virtue.'[70] Greene's initial rejection of synchronized sound gradually gave way to a more nuanced view. He began to see sound film as an important commercial opportunity and as a source of income for professional writers. He indicated that sound film could also empower writers. They were 'no longer merely a spectator or

---

[68] For an in-depth discussion of Jean Rhys's literary engagements with film, see Chapter 4 of Lisa Stead, *Off to the Pictures: Cinema-going, Women's Writing and Movie Culture in Interwar Britain* (Edinburgh: Edinburgh University Press, 2016), pp. 93–126. Elizabeth Bowen also presents film as a sensory and bodily experience: 'the success of a film with its house communicates a tingling physical pleasure—joining and heightening one's private exhilaration.... There is no mistaking that tension all round in the dark, that almost agonised tension of a pleased house—the electric hush, the rapt immobility.' Like Rhys, Bowen also uses the word 'anodyne'. Bowen, 'Why I Go to the Cinema', p. 208 and p. 210.

[69] David Parker (ed.), 'Introduction', *Mornings in the Dark: The Graham Greene Film Reader* (Manchester: Carcanet, 2007), xi–xxxvii (p. xiii and p. xvii). On *Close Up*, see Michael North, 'International Media, International Modernism, and the Struggle with Sound', *Literature and Visual Technologies: Writing after Cinema*, ed. Julian Murphet and Lydia Rainford (Basingstoke: Palgrave Macmillan, 2003), pp. 49–66; James Donald, Anne Friedberg, and Laura Marcus (eds), *Close Up 1927–1933: Cinema and Modernism* (Princeton: Princeton University Press, 1998).

[70] Graham Greene, 'A Film Principle', *Mornings in the Dark: The Graham Greene Film Reader*, ed. David Parkinson (Manchester: Carcanet, 2007), 392–394 (p. 393).

the critic of the screen. Suddenly the cinema needed him [the writer]; pictures required words as well as images.[71] Greene followed his own advice: he became *The Spectator*'s film reviewer in 1935 and likely began writing scenarios for film as early as 1936.[72] As a reviewer, Greene often had unfavourable responses to commercial films produced in Hollywood and Britain (not even successful British directors like Alfred Hitchcock or Alexander Korda could attain his approval). Instead, documentary films by John Grierson and Basil Wright were praised by Greene, as well as a number of Soviet and Dutch films. On the relatively unknown Dutch production *Dood Wasser* (1934), Greene wrote that 'neither the stage nor prose can present' the montage of images, voices, and music. He especially commended the film's 'lyrical use of a human voice'—a rarity to be found in his reviews.[73] The successful combination of sound and image track also drew him to Grigori Alexandrov's Soviet musical film *Jazz Comedy* (1934). Greene ecstatically claimed that the film was

> the best thing that has happened to the cinema since René Clair made *The Italian Straw Hat*....The opening sequence...is the most lovely a moving camera has yet achieved, as it follows [the protagonist] with the quickness of his long stride over hills and rocks, streams and veranda, while he sings, knocking the tune out on the slats of a bridge or the bars of a paling.[74]

The film's visual language, progression of action, coupled with music and a minimum of synchronized dialogue, led Greene to pronounce *Jazz Comedy* a work of 'genuine cinema'.[75] In 1938, Greene reiterated this view in his essay on 'Subjects and Stories'.[76] In this piece, written for Charles Davy's collection *Footnotes to the Film*, Greene praises Basil Wright's documentary

---

[71] Graham Greene, 'The Novelist and the Cinema—A Personal Experience', in David Parkinson (ed.), *Mornings in the Dark: The Graham Greene Film Reader* (Manchester: Carcanet, 2007), pp. 441–445 (p. 444).

[72] See David Parker's notes on an unknown film which Greene may have been working on as early as 1936 and preceding his work on *The Green Cockatoo* in 1937. David Parker (ed.), *Mornings in the Dark: The Graham Greene Film Reader* (Manchester: Carcanet, 2007), p. 700.

[73] Graham Greene, Review of 'Dood Wasser, Me and Marlborough, The Barretts of Wimpole Street', in David Parkinson (ed.), *Mornings in the Dark: The Graham Greene Film Reader* (Manchester: Carcanet, 2007), pp. 24–25.

[74] Graham Greene, Review of 'Jazz Comedy, Two for Tonight', in David Parkinson (ed.), *Mornings in the Dark: The Graham Greene Film Reader* (Manchester: Carcanet, 2007), pp. 30–32.

[75] Greene, 'Jazz Comedy', p. 32.

[76] Graham Greene, 'Subjects and Stories', in Charles Davy (ed.), *Footnotes to the Film*, Reader's Union Edition (New York: Arno Press & *The New York Times*, 1970), 57–70.

## 42   LITERATURE AND SOUND FILM IN MID-CENTURY BRITAIN

*Song of Ceylon* (1934) because it shows the promise of 'poetic cinema' that could not be achieved by the image alone.[77] On *Song of Ceylon*, Greene noted that it

> contained more of what we are looking for, criticism implicit in the images, life as it is containing the indications of life as it should be, the personal lyric utterance. It was divided, it may be remembered, into four parts, and opened with a forest sequence...and here, as a priest struck a bell, Mr Wright used one of the loveliest visual metaphors I have seen on the screen. The sounding of the bell startled a small bird from its branch, and the camera followed the bird's flight and the bell notes across the island, down from the mountain side, over forest and plain and sea, the vibration of the tiny wings, the fading sound.[78]

While Greene calls this scene a 'visual metaphor', one may add here that the sequence he describes is in fact a key example for image–sound combination: the sounding of the bell and the motion of the bird are presented as synchronous events linked by two important synch points: as the bell strikes for the first time, the bird takes flight and, a little later, the sound fades in parallel with the vibration of the bird's wings. Audio-vision and synchronicity play key parts in achieving what Greene views as 'poetic' cinema. To Greene, this meant a successful interplay of visual track, music, and sound effects, coupled with a more restrained and carefully crafted approach to spoken dialogue.

Like Greene, Eric Ambler and Christopher Isherwood worked as novelists and scriptwriters. Ambler's film credits are extensive, beginning with work in the early 1940s on Carol Reed's *The Way Ahead* (1944) for which he co-wrote the script with his friend Peter Ustinov. After the Second World War, Ambler also received an Academy Award nomination for his screenplay of *The Cruel Sea* (1953), a war film produced by Michael Balcon for Ealing. As a young man of sixteen who had just begun reading for an engineering degree, Ambler first tried his hand at writing plays and song lyrics before turning to novels.[79] His interest in theatre, music, and cinema undoubtedly

---

[77] On this point, see Greene's comments on Flaherty's *Man of Aran* whose camera work he describes as 'arty' but the film does not achieve a 'poetic' meaning or form for Greene. Greene, 'Subjects and Stories', p. 61.

[78] Greene, 'Subjects and Stories', p. 63.

[79] Joel Hopkins, 'An Interview with Eric Ambler', *Journal of Popular Culture* 9.2 (1975), 285–93 (p. 286).

LEARNING TO TALK 43

fed into his writing, although he never theorized his relationship to sound film specifically. In an interview with Joel Hopkins, Ambler called the film industry an 'occupational hazard' for the novelist of his time:

> It's an occupational hazard because very little screenwriting is writing. It's drawing blueprints for someone else to make a movie. The hazard is it earns large sums of money which tend to raise the living standard, therefore, the writer gets to a point where he is reluctant to reduce. He wants to go on making movies, not because he enjoys it, which is the only proper criteria, but because he wants to make the same kind of money.... During the war I learned a great deal about film making at the Army's expense. So for the next ten years that's what I did. Coming back to writing novels was an extraordinary effort. But there was nothing more exciting to do, and that's when I decided to come back to writing novels.[80]

By his own account, the lure of financial security (alongside his service in the Army Film and Photographic Unit until the end of the Second World War) impacted Ambler's decision to abandon novel-writing for a while and to focus on film in the 1940s, before returning to writing thrillers in the 1950s.

Christopher Isherwood, like Ambler, clearly suffered from the same 'occupational hazard' and became involved in the film industry early in his writing career. In an interview with Charles Higham in 1968, he spoke highly of film's influence on his work as a novelist and his experiences in film production. Isherwood began his career in writing for film in 1933, when he became the scriptwriter for Berthold Viertel's *Little Friend* (1934). This was followed by contributions to *A Woman's Face* (1941), *Crossroads* (1942), *The Great Sinner* (1949), and *Diane* (1956).[81] On Isherwood's own account, his practice of writing novels was deeply influenced by his work in sound film: 'you must remember that all my novels, or almost all, have been written post-screenwriting'.[82] Accordingly, Isherwood argues that it is 'very good in the first place for most writers to be forced to visualize: you have to learn to stop relying on the word and thinking in terms of possible silent sequences or sequences *where dialogue plays against the image*'.[83] Isherwood

---

[80] Hopkins, 'An Interview with Eric Ambler', p. 291.
[81] Christopher Isherwood, 'Isherwood on Hollywood' (1968), Interview with Charles Higham, in James J. Berg and Chris Freeman (eds), *Conversations with Christopher Isherwood* (Jackson: University Press of Mississippi, 2001), 45–51 (pp. 47–48).
[82] Isherwood, 'Isherwood on Hollywood' pp. 47–48.
[83] Isherwood, 'Isherwood on Hollywood', p. 47, my emphasis.

knew that the relation between spoken words and moving image in sound film was key to the success of the production. Dialogue, when it occurs, would have to add another dimension to the visuals, instead of merely providing redundant information that is already supplied by image and movement.[84] Of course, he is often cited for the beginning of *Goodbye to Berlin*: 'I am a camera with its shutter open, quite passive, recording, not thinking.'[85] As Glyn Salton-Cox notes, while this phrase has become something of an iconic reference to Isherwood's style, the statement is neither apolitical nor quite as 'unthinking' and 'passive' as it makes itself out to be.[86] As I note in Chapter 2, Isherwood repeatedly reflects on the different affordances of text and film in the age of audio-vision and his professional experience in sound film considerably shaped his approach to his literary writing.

In contrast to Greene, Isherwood, and Ambler's extensive work in the film industry, their contemporary Patrick Hamilton only took some short excursions into screen writing and primarily remained a novelist and dramatist for radio and the stage. Hamilton had been an avid cinemagoer since his early childhood days and became a star overnight with his play *Rope* (1929).[87] Following *Rope*'s success in the West End and at Broadway, Hamilton tried his hand at a screenplay for Hitchcock's film adaptation. However, Hamilton's script was later rejected and Hitchcock made the film based on a new screenplay created by Arthur Laurents instead.[88] Despite this more limited experience as a scriptwriter for film, Hamilton went on to publish one of the most 'cinematic' novels of the 1940s: *Hangover Square* (1941). As I discuss in Chapter 5, the novel's protagonist George conceives of his life as a 'talkie' in which, occasionally, the 'sound-track' fails. The interplay between film sound and its intermittent failure is an instrumental part of the novel's narrative strategy. *Hangover Square*, like all literary works discussed in this volume, evinces a new preoccupation with audio-vision and synchronicity.

[84] Christopher Isherwood, 'A Writer and the Films', in James J. Berg (ed.), *Isherwood on Writing* (Minneapolis: University of Minnesota Press, 2007), 99–113 (pp. 106–107).

[85] Christopher Isherwood, *Goodbye to Berlin*, in *The Berlin Novels* (London: Vintage, 1999), p. 243.

[86] Glyn Salton-Cox, *Queer Communism and the Ministry of Love: Sexual Revolution in British Writing of the 1930s* (Edinburgh: Edinburgh University Press, 2021), pp. 44–45.

[87] Nigel Jones, *Through a Glass Darkly: The Life of Patrick Hamilton* (London: Scribners, 1991), p. 33 and p. 97; Nathalie Blondel, 'Patrick Hamilton', *Oxford Dictionary of National Biography* (2004). https://doi.org/10.1093/ref:odnb/38308, accessed 3 June 2024.

[88] Bruce Hamilton, *The Light Went Out: The Life of Patrick Hamilton by His Brother Bruce Hamilton* (London: Constable, 1972), pp. 97–98.

LEARNING TO TALK    45

Of course, not all mid-century writers were as cinema-minded as Ambler, Bowen, Greene, Isherwood, and Hamilton: Ivy Compton-Burnett, for instance, famously said of herself that she did not have 'any real or organic knowledge of life later than about 1910' and that she had a 'dislike…of dealing with modern machinery and inventions'.[89] Similarly, George Orwell, as Jeffrey Meyers writes, had 'no interest in film as art'. And yet, Orwell's letters of the 1930s to his close friend Brenda Salkeld occasionally reference his visits to the cinema: 'I went to the pictures last week and saw Jack Hulbert in *Jack Ahoy* which I thought very amusing, & a week or two before that there was quite a good crook film, which, however, my father ruined for me by insisting on telling me the plot beforehand.'[90] In the autumn of 1940, Orwell even accepted work as a film reviewer for *Time and Tide* and continued writing in this capacity for the magazine until the summer of 1941.

While one might view Orwell's and especially Compton-Burnett's engagements with cinema as considerably more limited than that of many of their contemporaries, they still remain part of a group of authors who were born, grew up, and came of age in the era of silent film, which was then followed by their witnessing first-hand the transition to sound cinema. This book is an invitation to reconsider how this particular experience of media change may have mattered to all of them and to their literary practices. As sound film reconfigured the relationships between text, sound, and image, these mid-century writers could reclaim the written word from the cinema screen and create new forms of textuality for the age of audio-vision.

*Literature and Sound Film in Mid-Century Britain*. Lara Ehrenfried, Oxford University Press.
© Lara Ehrenfried 2025. DOI: 10.1093/9780198950790.003.0002

---

[89] Charles Burkhart (ed.), 'I. Compton-Burnett and M. Jourdain: A Conversation', in *The Art of I. Compton-Burnett: A Collection of Critical Essays* (London: Gollancz, 1972), 21–31 (p. 27).
[90] Jeffrey Meyers, *Orwell: Life and Art* (Urbana, IL: University of Illinois Press, 2010), p. 94; George Orwell, Letter to Brenda Salkeld, Tuesday Night [late August 1934], in *George Orwell: A Life in Letters*, selected by Peter Davison (New York: Liveright, 2013), 33–35 (p. 33).

# 2
# Adapting Audio-Vision

The transition to sound, as discussed in Chapter 1, reconfigured the roles of text, sound, and image. It raised the question of how film and literature might adapt to a changing media ecology, in which audio-vision and synchronicity came to play ever greater parts. As I will show, this development also brought about new reflections on the affordances of media form. This chapter argues that adaptation is key to understanding the paths taken by cinema and literature in response to audio-vision in the 1930s. I draw on recent work in adaptation theory as outlined by Lars Elleström, who suggests that adaptation can be broadly conceived as 'media transformation'. This transformation, in turn, can take several (sometimes overlapping) forms: while 'transmediation' refers to the 'representation of media characteristics in another medium', 'media representation' denotes the representation or description of one medium in another.[1] Both transmediation and media representation enhance our understanding of film and literature in the early sound years and beyond, as sound film first heavily relied on and then gradually extricated itself from a close association with the theatre. Stage entertainment seemed to provide a model for testing sound cinema's new capacities and limits, and thus sound film itself came to deal with the question of adaptation in a double sense: adapting, formally and materially, to the requirements of audio-vision, and doing so by adapting stories and forms taken from the theatre.

Mid-century writers such as Evelyn Waugh and Christopher Isherwood did not remain unaffected bystanders to these events; transmediation and media representation equally became staple features of their works, not least as a means of testing the affordances of the literary text in the age of audio-vision. The complex relation between theatre and early sound film substantially informed mid-century literature. In what follows, I examine sound film's adaptation of theatrical forms with a focus on musical revue and cabaret, followed by an analysis of how Waugh and Isherwood respond

---

[1] Lars Elleström, 'Adaptation and Intermediality', in Thomas Leitch (ed.), *The Oxford Handbook of Adaptation Studies* (Oxford: Oxford University Press, 2017), 509–526 (p. 511).

to sound film's appropriation of theatre. What emerges in the cases of Waugh and Isherwood is a consistent engagement with the question of adaptation vis-à-vis textual form. Both authors write novels of transmediation and media representation, thereby readily engaging in a new mediatized textuality that is grounded in the mid-century encounter with audio-vision and synchronicity.

## Stage Entertainment and Early Sound Film

In the late 1920s and early 1930s, it was mainly musical theatre and its associated forms (revue, operetta, cabaret, and music-hall) which seemed to offer film studios and producers the plots, scripts, sheet music, lyrics, and performers that could be easily appropriated to capitalize on the newness of synchronized sound in the cinema. The connection between film and the theatre had been firmly established long before sound even entered the film industry: during the silent era, studios frequently turned to the stage for inspiration, adapting successful plays, operetta, and canonical dramatic works for the screen.[2] That is not to say that the proximity between film and stage was always viewed favourably. For many film critics and industry professionals, the evolution of cinema as an art form was taken to depend on the medium's ability to distinguish itself from the theatre.[3] Rick Altman notes that theories of montage in the early twentieth century by Sergei Eisenstein and other filmmakers chiefly emerged from a desire to differentiate silent film from the theatre: 'to such a world, devoted to minimalization of the language which recalls…the theater, the coming of sound could hardly have represented a welcome innovation. For the coming of sound represents the return of the silent cinema's repressed.'[4] Synchronized sound sparked renewed interest in dramatic forms, stage performers, and stories either directly stemming from or, at the very least, set in the world of

---

[2] For instance, a 1915 silent film production of *Carmen* by Cecil B. DeMille starring Geraldine Farrar and Erich von Stroheim's *The Merry Widow* (1925), which was based on the operetta of the same name by Franz Lehár. The production company Vitagraph released a successful cycle of silent Shakespeare adaptations between 1908 and 1912. On the latter see, for instance, the discussion in Judith Buchanan, *Shakespeare on Silent Film* (Cambridge: Cambridge University Press, 2009), pp. 105–145.

[3] On this point, see the chapter on 'Thirty Differences between the Photoplays and the Stage' in Vachel Lindsay, *The Art of the Moving Picture* (New York: Modern Library Paperback, 2000), pp. 105–115.

[4] Rick Altman, 'Introduction', *Yale French Studies*, 60 (1980), 3–15 (p. 13).

## 48  LITERATURE AND SOUND FILM IN MID-CENTURY BRITAIN

theatre. As early as 1923, it was reported that Lee De Forest's 'Phono-Film' would be mainly used 'for the reproduction of musical, vaudeville numbers, and solos'.[5] Indeed, sound film was originally conceived of as a 'virtual broadway' that would create a space in which audiences could experience the most popular shows, musical performances, and comedy acts regardless of their physical location and financial means.[6] The idea that sound film could, in effect, mainly function as a virtual stage also derived from synchronized sound's original, intended purpose: the technology had been developed for recording live music and songs to accompany silent film screenings. Accordingly, a substantial part of the source material for early sound film productions came from revue, music-hall, and operetta.

For studios and producers, musical theatre was also deemed a suitable model for film in the early sound era: audio-visual combination lies at the heart of musical theatre, thereby offering early sound film a template to emulate. Plots derived from musical theatre were already tailored towards a narrative integration of spectacular visuals, music, and song-and-dance routines. Adaptations of successful stage entertainments allowed film studios to copy existing scripts, music, lyrics, and choreographies, and gave film producers leverage for drafting popular stage performers with appropriate voice training from the theatre. In the early sound years, these conditions led to a fairly direct transfer of stage material onto the cinema screen. Warner Bros.' *The Desert Song* (1929), for instance, was one of these early 'literal transcriptions', as discussed by Richard Barrios.[7] Based on a successful operetta of the same name which had had its Broadway premiere in 1926, the film offered audiences a replica of the stage version with minimal alteration.[8] By the mid-1930s, the ways in which sound film drew on stage shows had become more sophisticated and complex, but musical films remained a staple feature of the entertainment industry throughout the decade. Indeed, musical films are still estimated to have been one of the biggest outputs of the British film industry in the 1930s overall, not least since

---

[5] 'Phono-Films Weekly', *The Film Daily*, 7 April 1923, p. 1.

[6] Donald Crafton, *The Talkies: American Cinema's Transition to Sound, 1926–1931* (New York: Scribner, 1997), p. 70.

[7] Richard Barrios, *A Song in the Dark: The Birth of the Musical Film* (New York: Oxford University Press, 2010), p. 59.

[8] Barrios comments that 'the two-act stage structure was rigidly adhered to, with a few songs cut…and most of the purplest stage dialogue retained'. Barrios, *Song in the Dark*, pp. 76–77.

viewers were 'still predisposed towards musical and variety theatre, [and] could relate to the musical film as an offshoot of it'.[9]

The years 1929 and 1930 introduced and marketed a particular type of film musical to British audiences: the revue film. British International Picture's *Elstree Calling* (1930) was advertised as a 'A Cine-Radio Revue'.[10] The film's loose linking narrative concerns an elderly couple who attempt to tune into a television broadcast. Their home TV set is broken and the pair spend the duration of the broadcast trying to fix the equipment with little success. *Elstree Calling*'s frame narrative self-referentially presents the film as a televised item and shows how live acts are filmed for broadcast through switching between three different settings: the backstage setting in the film studio, the proscenium arch stage on which performers are filmed, and the elderly couple trying to view the show on their TV at home. Co-directed by Adrian Brunel and Alfred Hitchcock, *Elstree Calling* brings together some of Britain's most popular actors, musicians, dancers, and comedians of the late 1920s.[11] Hosted by comedian Tommy Handley, who appears between performances (usually in the backstage setting), the film combines popular songs ('I've fallen in love' performed by Cicely Courtneidge), music-hall entertainment (by comedians Will Fyffe and Lily Morris), and dance performances by the 'Adelphi Girls' and the 'Charlot Girls'. Recurring scenarios provide a sense of structure and add to the comedy element: there are several scenes in which an unemployed Shakespeare actor is denied stage time, suggesting slyly that audiences no longer want highbrow theatre, but light-hearted comedy and musical revue. *The Times* reviewed the production favourably, calling it a 'monumental affair' and praised its 'smoothness and continuity'.[12]

*Elstree Calling* was the British response to a film revue craze following MGM's considerable success with *The Hollywood Revue of 1929*. MGM's

---

[9] Stephen Guy, 'Calling All Stars: Musical Films in a Musical Decade', in Jeffrey Richards (ed.), *The Unknown 1930s: An Alternative History of the British Cinema, 1929–1939* (London: Tauris, 2000), 99–118 (pp. 100, 118).

[10] *Elstree Calling*, dir. by Adrian Brunel and Alfred Hitchcock, starring Will Fyffe, Cicely Courtneidge, and Tommy Handley (British International Pictures, 1930).

[11] Hitchcock was under contract with British International Pictures in 1929. After his work on *Blackmail*, he was asked to complete *Elstree Calling* and reshot some scenes after BIP's management encountered difficulties with the revue's original writer and director, Adrian Brunel. It remains unclear to what extent Hitchcock's direction actually shaped the final version of the film. In the opening credits, 'sketches and other interpolated items' are attributed to him. Hitchcock's potential contribution to *Elstree Calling* is addressed in greater detail by Alain Kerzoncuf and Charles Barr in *Hitchcock Lost and Found: The Forgotten Films* (Lexington, KY: University Press of Kentucky, 2015), pp. 88–97.

[12] 'Elstree Calling', *The Times*, 10 February 1930, p. 10.

50  LITERATURE AND SOUND FILM IN MID-CENTURY BRITAIN

revue was so popular that it sparked a number of similar productions, not-ably *The Show of Shows* (Warner Brothers, 1929) and *Paramount on Parade* (Paramount Pictures, 1930). Revue seemed to present a convenient template for filming with sound and for marketing a large number of performers contracted to each production's studio. The revue films offered entertainment that consisted of songs, dance, and comedy sketches, relying heavily on existing acts and productions, thereby minimizing the amount of new material that was needed to put the film together. Affirming the industry belief in revue as a viable model for the sound film, *The Spectator*'s film critic Celia Simpson wrote in 1929 that revue presented 'the sort of entertainment which is most suitable and capable of success in the talking film medium'.[13]

The revue had its roots in both variety theatre and musical comedy. It contained different short 'turns' which were loosely based on a common theme or topic.[14] Revues had a basic storyline, narrated through intermit-tent scenes and usually featuring a compère or emcee leading through the programme. In contrast to traditional musical comedy, the development of a sustained plot was of little importance. Gaining momentum in the Edwardian period, the revue slowly replaced musical comedy as the most popular form of stage entertainment in Britain.[15] One of the revue's most important features was its eclectic style, which allowed for easy incorpor-ation of other popular forms: revue could contain elements of music-hall, burlesque, variety, and slapstick comedy. It also sometimes featured short film clips as part of its programme, leading scholars such as Len Platt to suggest that revue was 'a multi-media practice' with 'parody and pastiche bec[oming] hallmarks' of the form.[16]

Originally devised as an end-of-year review show, the revue used a com-bination of popular songs, dialogue scenes, comedy, dance numbers, and even acrobatics to present and mock 'events and personalities which had preoccupied the public to a greater or lesser extent during the course of the year'.[17] Slapstick, parody, timing, and pace were key elements of successful

---

[13] Celia Simpson, 'The Cinema: Star-Gazing', *The Spectator*, 2 November 1929, p. 623.

[14] Allardyce Nicoll, *English Drama, 1900–1930: The Beginnings of the Modern Period*, Part 1 (Cambridge: Cambridge University Press, 2009), p. 169.

[15] David Linton, 'English West End Revue: The First World War and After', in Robert Gordon and Olaf Jubin (eds), *The Oxford Handbook of the British Musical* (Oxford: Oxford University Press, 2016), 143–169 (p. 144).

[16] Len Platt, *Musical Comedy on the West End Stage, 1890–1939* (Basingstoke: Palgrave Macmillan, 2004), p. 134.

[17] Raymond Mander and Joe Mitchenson, *Revue: A Story in Pictures* (London: Peter Davies, 1971), p. 1.

revue shows.[18] In the interwar years, revue arguably became more self-critical. Not only did it parody events and people, but it also mocked its own form and its obsession with musical trends and fashions.[19] The British West End revue of the interwar period was largely influenced by American and French productions and performance styles. On the one hand, it took inspiration from the Broadway producer Florenz Ziegfeld, whose revues were lavish affairs. Known as the 'Ziegfeld Follies', these shows featured a large chorus of beautiful female performers, elaborate set designs, and extravagant costumes.[20] On the other hand, the West End revue also drew on a more intimate French style which was popularized in Britain by André Charlot, who worked as a producer in London from 1912 to 1937.[21] After the First World War, C. B. Cochran and Charlot began to produce British revues, notably *On with the Dance* (1925) and *This Year of Grace* (1928), both written by Noël Coward. *On with the Dance* was a review of different dance styles, containing four different ballet sequences and a sketch titled *Fête Galante* (about a vicarage garden party).[22] Evelyn Waugh watched the revue with his friend Alistair Graham and noted in his diary that Ernest Thesiger's performance during the show 'was quite marvellous'.[23] In the same year as *On with the Dance*, one of Cochran's competitor's, Norman Lee, released the *London Revue* at the Lyceum Theatre. 'Riotously funny', the production featured scenes set in Kew Gardens and Piccadilly Circus, and contained 'impersonations of music-hall stars' and parodies of stereotypical members of the capital's population.[24]

With the introduction of synchronized sound to the film industry in the late 1920s, the revue began to be adapted by the screen. This development also coincided with the large-scale displacement of British music halls and theatres by cinemas. According to Robert Murphy, London's West End, for instance, rapidly gained purpose-built cinemas as these venues could

---

[18] Jenkins focusses on the interaction between vaudeville, anarchistic or raucous humour, and early sound film in the United States. Henry Jenkins, *What Made Pistachio Nuts? Early Sound Comedy and the Vaudeville Aesthetic* (New York: Columbia University Press, 1992).

[19] Linton, 'English West End Revue', p. 159.

[20] Ziegfeld is credited with having 'invented' the concept of the showgirl in the early twentieth century. See, for instance, Michael Lasser, 'The Glorifier: Florenz Ziegfeld and the Creation of the American Showgirl', *The American Scholar*, 63.3 (1994), 441–448.

[21] Linton, 'English West End Revue', pp. 147–149.

[22] 'On with the Dance', *The Times*, 1 May 1925, p. 12.

[23] Evelyn Waugh, *The Diaries of Evelyn Waugh*, ed. Michael Davie (Harmondsworth: Penguin, 1979), p. 217.

[24] 'The London Revue', *The Times*, 3 September 1925, p. 8.

# 52    LITERATURE AND SOUND FILM IN MID-CENTURY BRITAIN

'assimilate more of [music halls' and theatres'] functions'.[25] In addition, exhibitors and studios came to see synchronized sound as a viable financial investment during the economic downturn of the late 1920s and early 1930s. The consolidation of synchronized sound film, alongside more protectionist legislation (such as the British Cinematograph Films Act of 1927), is now credited with stabilizing American and British film industries during the Great Depression. Sound film's economic success was partly due to its pure novelty and to its audience appeal, but, in economic terms, sound film also proved highly effective in creating multiple revenue streams in exchange for a one-off investment in production.[26]

## Evelyn Waugh's Musical Revue

Just two weeks ahead of the 1930 release of *Elstree Calling*, Evelyn Waugh beat the sound film at its own game: his second novel *Vile Bodies* was published to great acclaim. From the outset, early reviews compared *Vile Bodies* to a stage revue, drawing attention to the novel's amalgamation of entertaining yet unrelated scenes. Edward Shanks wrote for the *New Statesman* that Waugh had written 'what must be called rather a revue, between covers. He does not lack even a female chorus, which we meet on the second page.... [The scenes] succeed one another with a snap and variety that many a revue-producer might envy.'[27] Rose Macaulay similarly called *Vile Bodies* a revue:

> *Vile Bodies*, a novel more crowded, less classic and clear-cut in plot, more dispersed in interest, more of a revue show...[T]he giddy whirl of *Vile Bodies* snatches up in its dance at least a dozen separate groups of people, each with their own story, as in a ballet where groups perform in different corners of the stage....The mass effect of unsteady, extravagant fantasy and sick and squalid reaction is breath-taking.[28]

---

[25] Robert Murphy, 'Coming of Sound to the Cinema in Britain', *Historical Journal of Film, Radio and Television*, 4.2 (1984), 143–160 (p. 145).

[26] See Dennis Kennedy, 'British Theatre 1895–1946: Art, Entertainment, Audiences', in Baz Kershaw (ed.), *The Cambridge History of British Theatre*, Vol. 3 (Cambridge: Cambridge University Press, 2004), pp. 1–33; Murphy, 'The Coming of Sound', pp. 143–160.

[27] Edward Shanks, Review of *Vile Bodies*, in Martin Stannard (ed.), *Evelyn Waugh: The Critical Heritage* (London: Routledge & Kegan Paul, 1984), pp. 100–101. The review was first published in the *New Statesman* on 8 February 1930.

[28] Rose Macaulay, 'Evelyn Waugh', in Martin Stannard (ed.), *Evelyn Waugh: The Critical Heritage* (London: Routledge & Kegan Paul, 1984), pp. 109–112. The review was first published in *Horizon* in December 1946.

Ronald Knox, commenting more widely on Waugh's fiction, claimed that Waugh's early novels 'were…a show being put on for your benefit; it was revue, not drama.'[29] These reviews leave little doubt about the fact that some of the novel's early readers saw a connection between the style, structure, and themes of Waugh's novel and the stage revue. Echoing such sentiments, Ralph Straus, writing for the *Bystander*, commented that 'I assure you that "Vile Bodies" is one of the drollest and most entertaining affairs that ever strayed into print. It is a masterpiece of inconsequence. It has irony and the right amount of malice.'[30] Straus's phrasing suggests that *Vile Bodies* was felt to be quite a different form of entertainment that had only by chance found its way between the covers of a book. The sensation of novelty stirred by the text could only be explained by its otherness from the novel and its kinship with the revue. Perhaps unsurprisingly, the text's show qualities, as outlined by Shanks and Macaulay, led to two rather hasty efforts to produce stage adaptations of the novel. The first, written by Arthur Boscastle, was presented at the Arts Theatre on 8 October 1931. Reviews were mixed: on the one hand, Richard Jennings, writing for *The Spectator*, commented favourably on the cast's performances. Jennings praised 'the two totally unsentimental lovers, Nina and Adam (Mr. Robert Douglas and Miss Eileen Peel), whose scenes are in the best Restoration comedy manner' and noted that 'the dialogue, inspired or borrowed from a book that managed to be at once delightful and depressing, show that Mr. Waugh could write a complete play in that convention.'[31] On the other hand, the *Daily Telegraph* described the play as suffering from 'ineffectiveness' because it was unable to match the 'delicately fashioned caricature' crafted by the novel.[32] The play did not receive a licence for public performance. Just a few months later in April 1932, a second version written by Dennis Bradley premiered at the Vaudeville Theatre. This adaptation was a rewritten version of Boscastle's earlier attempt and consisted of twelve episodes. Bradley had added a compère who appeared between scenes and led through the action. The play fared much better and was praised as 'something rather in the nature of a revue.'[33]

---

[29] Ronald Knox, 'The Reader Suspended', *Month*, 8.4 (October 1952), 236–238 (p. 237).

[30] Ralph Straus, 'Vile Bodies', in Martin Stannard (ed.), *Evelyn Waugh: The Critical Heritage* (London: Routledge & Kegan Paul, 1984), pp. 95–96. The review was first published in *Bystander* on 15 January 1930.

[31] Richard Jennings, 'The Theatre', *The Spectator*, 17 October 1931, p. 12.

[32] '*Vile Bodies*: Difficulties of Stage Presentation', *Daily Telegraph*, 9 October 1931, p. 8.

[33] 'The Censor Relents', *Daily Telegraph*, 26 March 1932, p. 6.

## 54 LITERATURE AND SOUND FILM IN MID-CENTURY BRITAIN

A keen observer, as well as participant, of popular culture in his youth, Waugh was no stranger to stage revue and cinema. His early years were shaped by frequent visits to the movies, plays, and live revue shows. Prior to the publication of *Vile Bodies*, he was involved in the making of an amateur film during his years at Oxford and maintained a close friendship with actors Elsa Lanchester and Tony Bushell. Waugh frequently visited the *Cave of Harmony* nightclub in Soho, which was co-owned by Lanchester and renowned for its late-night cabaret and revue shows.[34] In his diary, Waugh reported one of the convivial nights spent with Lanchester and his brother Alec on 12 July 1924:

> In the evening Keith Chesterton was giving a party.... There were a comic collection of all the early Cave of Harmony set.... Elsa sang some few Cockney songs including *Yiddisher Boy* which I love. The man who wrote that delightful parody of *Our Betters* in the Little Revue was there.... I got home in broad daylight at 5 and this morning feel more than a little weary.[35]

In addition to his outings with Lanchester and the Cave of Harmony crowd, Waugh visited different revue shows: in August 1925, he went to *On with the Dance*, which he 'had long wanted to see'.[36] In August 1927, he saw C. B. Cochran's *One Damn Thing after Another*, wryly commenting that this revue was not 'particularly good but the whole quite brisk and jolly and well organized'.[37] These visits to revue shows are instructive because they clearly indicate the wider context in which Waugh's thoughts on writing literary fiction were evolving. The 1920s marked a time at which he was grappling with developing his own theory of writing. In a review essay on the works of Ronald Firbank, Waugh summarized the elements of Firbank's style which he admired most: a dialogic, conversational, 'unobtrusive' style of

---

[34] Martin Stannard, *Evelyn Waugh: The Early Years 1903–1939* (London: Dent & Sons, 1986), p. 93 and pp. 101–102. On the Cave of Harmony and Elsa Lanchester, see Rohan McWilliam, 'Elsa Lanchester and Bohemian London in the Early Twentieth Century', *Women's History Review*, 23.2 (2014), 171–187. McWilliam notes that 'an evening at the Cave usually began at nine with dancing followed by a cabaret or revue commencing at twelve and then dancing till two.... The evenings embodied a spirit of experimentation; the succession of dancing and performance could be likened to the use of montage by figures in the avant-garde' (p. 179).

[35] Waugh, *Diaries*, p. 169. The 'Little Revue' Waugh mentions here was most likely a revue show put on by the Little Theatre, John Street, London.

[36] Waugh, *Diaries*, p. 217.      [37] Waugh, *Diaries*, p. 288.

narration and narrative that was 'directed for entertainment'.[38] Such features seemed somehow related to film. According to Waugh:

> [Firbank's] later novels are almost wholly devoid of any attributions of cause to effect; there is the barest minimum of direct description; his compositions are built up intricately and with a balanced alternation of the wildest extravagance and the most austere economy, with conversational nuances. They may be compared to cinema films in which the relation of caption and photograph is directly reversed; occasionally a brief, visual image flashes out to illumine and explain the flickering succession of spoken words.[39]

Not only does this appraisal of Firbank suggest that Waugh was keen to develop his own writing style based on authors he greatly admired, but it also demonstrates that Waugh was contemplating cinema's role for thinking about the affordances of text.[40] It is in his reflections on Firbank that Waugh is already conceiving of an audio-visual understanding of 'good' literary fiction: 'the flickering succession of spoken words' and the 'visual image' combine to form an impression in the reader: the function of the image is to support and explain the dialogue. Waugh's careful phrasing ('they may be compared to cinema films') indicates that he may have tried to avoid a direct comparison between Firbank's fiction and film. Rather, Waugh expresses here how his understanding of 'good' literary writing was influenced by his understanding of cinema as a matter of audio-visual combination and effect. Waugh uses the comparison to describe his experience of Firbank's writing, because film seems to have offered him a way of thinking figuratively about specific features of literary writing that he thought worth emulating.

The formative relationship between film and literature that Waugh expresses in his thoughts on fiction has led some scholars to propose that he approaches his fiction as a 'director'.[41] This does not limit itself to film,

---

[38] Evelyn Waugh, 'Ronald Firbank', in Donat Gallagher (ed.), *The Essays, Articles and Reviews of Evelyn Waugh* (London: Methuen, 1983), pp. 56–59. The review essay was first published in *Life and Letters* in March 1929.

[39] Waugh, 'Ronald Firbank', pp. 57–58.

[40] A more extensive discussion of the young Waugh's thoughts on fiction writing can be found in Robert Murray Davis's *Evelyn Waugh and the Forms of his Time* (Washington: Catholic University of America Press, 1989), 68–89. Davis observes that the young Waugh had 'a surprising tolerance for commodity fiction' (p. 74).

[41] George McCartney, *Evelyn Waugh and the Modernist Tradition* (New Brunswick, NJ: Transaction, 2004), p. 121.

## 56   LITERATURE AND SOUND FILM IN MID-CENTURY BRITAIN

but extends to the theatre. Robert Frick, for instance, notes the presence of repetitive 'speaker identifiers', such as 'he said' and 'she said', in *Vile Bodies* and their similarity to 'theatrical prompts'.[42] Waugh's short story *The Balance* (1925) is another early testament to his preoccupation with both stage forms and the screen and demonstrates his quest for ways to productively mobilize the entertainment forms of his time for writing prose fiction.[43] *The Balance* 'is a strange mixture of narrative and dramatic modes', which may have been an early rehearsal for some of the stylistic and structural features of *Vile Bodies*.[44] Using revue as a model for *Vile Bodies*, Waugh gave himself a head start: his strategy allowed him to write a commercially successful book while simultaneously experimenting with different forms of writing. Transferring the structures and themes of revue onto the page of his novel also gave Waugh an ideal opportunity to slyly demonstrate the novel's own capacity for adaptation as media transformation: in adapting features of stage revue for the novel, the text directly speaks to the sound film's own practices of adaptation.

*Vile Bodies* commences with a ship crossing the channel from Calais to Dover. As most passengers become seasick, the text adapts and parodies the principles of stage revue's song-and-dance numbers. The evangelist Mrs Ape tries to keep up morale aboard by instructing her choir girls, her 'Angels', and all other passengers to sing:

> The ship creaked in every plate, doors slammed, trunks fell about, the wind howled; the screw, now out of the water, now in, raced and churned, shaking down hatboxes like ripe apples; but above all the roar and clatter there rose from the second-class ladies' saloon the despairing voices of Mrs Ape's angels, in frequently broken unison, singing, singing, wildly, desperately, as though their hearts would break in the effort and their minds lose their reason, Mrs Ape's famous hymn, *There ain't no flies on the Lamb of God*.[45]

The ship, tossed about by the rough waters, 'creaks', the wind 'howls', luggage topples over and doors 'slam'. Yet, amidst all this 'roar and clatter',

---

[42] Robert Frick, 'Style and Structure in the Early Novels of Evelyn Waugh', *Papers on Language and Literature*, 28.4 (1992), 417–441 (p. 436).

[43] Evelyn Waugh, 'The Balance', in Ann Pasternak Slater (ed.), *The Complete Short Stories and Selected Drawings* (London: Everyman's Library, 1998), pp. 3–38.

[44] Frederick L. Beaty, *The Ironic World of Evelyn Waugh: A Study in Eight Novels* (DeKalb, IL: Northern Illinois University Press, 1992), p. 12.

[45] Evelyn Waugh, *Vile Bodies* (London: Penguin, 2000), pp. 12–13.

ADAPTING AUDIO-VISION  57

Mrs Ape's choir sings 'wildly' with 'despairing voices'. The title of Mrs Ape's 'famous hymn', 'There ain't no flies on the Lamb of God', acerbically juxtaposes the serious connotations of a religious hymn with its wholly inappropriate title. The girls do not have proper names (and if they do, they are not used by anyone). Rather, Mrs Ape calls them by their stage names: 'Faith', 'Charity', 'Fortitude', and so on. The girls are all young and attractive, wearing angel's wings for a costume. Despite Mrs Ape's efforts to sell her choir as a charitable Christian endeavour to audiences, the girls are sexualized, either directly or through innuendo, at every turn: 'Creative Endeavour lost her wings....She got talking to a gentleman in the train.'[46] Another girl, 'Chastity', has become a sex worker in all but name by the end of the novel. The angels mimic the fashionable type of the chorus girl or revue girl that was popularized in the interwar era by Ziegfeld's spectacular revue productions on Broadway. The 'Ziegfeld Girls' were selected primarily for their looks and danced in perfect synchrony, lending each of Ziegfeld's shows spectacle, glamour, and sex appeal through a deliberate objectification of the female performer. An equivalent dance troupe had formed in Britain as early as 1889, the Tiller Girls. They performed in Manchester, London, Berlin, and Paris, and were particularly renowned for their perfectly coordinated movements, attractiveness, and athletic bodies. Initial recruitment of the girls did not actually involve any dancing, but 'a thorough inspection of each candidate's teeth and legs'.[47] They were also one of the first dance troupes to use the 'precision kick line' in 1910.[48] Having witnessed the Tiller Girls perform in 1927, Siegfried Kracauer subsequently wrote in 'The Mass Ornament' that the dancers were 'no longer individual girls, but indissoluble girl clusters whose movements are demonstrations of mathematics. As they condense into figures in the revues, performances of the same geometric precision are taking place.'[49] Likening the precision dancing and perfectly synchronized bodies to Fordist ideals of capitalist production that can be endlessly and internationally replicated, Kracauer observes how women, as part of the dance troupe, become objects of desire and an expression of modern consumer culture. The Tiller Girls, like the Charlot Girls and the

[46] Waugh, *Vile Bodies*, p. 8.
[47] Kara Reilly, 'The Tiller Girls: Mass Ornament and Modern Girl', in Kara Reilly (ed.), *Theatre, Performance and Analogue Technology: Historical Interfaces and Intermedialities* (Basingstoke: Palgrave Macmillan, 2013), pp. 117–132 (p. 119).
[48] Reilly, 'Tiller Girls', p. 117.
[49] Siegfried Kracauer, 'The Mass Ornament', in Thomas Y. Levin (trans. and ed.), *The Mass Ornament: Weimar Essays* (Cambridge, MA: Harvard University Press, 1995), 75–86 (pp. 75–76).

## 58   LITERATURE AND SOUND FILM IN MID-CENTURY BRITAIN

Ziegfeld Girls, embodied the new twentieth-century type of the 'girl': a sexually liberated (and yet also highly sexualized) woman who appeared independent, perpetually unattainable, and beautiful.[50]

In Waugh's novel, the performances of Mrs Ape and her angels are interspersed with scenes featuring the main characters Adam, Nina, and Agatha Runcible.[51] There are several references to song and dance, such as Chastity's comment that Lady Metroland's party offers 'nothing to make a song and dance about'.[52] Interlinking the singing 'female chorus' with the rest of the novel appears to imitate stage revue's characteristic interpolation of sketches and song-and-dance routines for the novel. This happens, for instance, during the ship's crossing, when Mrs Ape forces her fellow passengers to join in the singing:

> 'We're going to sing a song together, you and me.' ('Oh, God', said Adam). 'You may not know it, but you are. You'll feel better for it body *and* soul.... There's the song on the back. Now all together... sing. Five bob for you, steward, if you can shout me down. Splendid, all together, boys.' In a rich, very audible voice Mrs Ape led the singing. Her arms rose, fell and fluttered with the rhythm of the song. The bar steward was hers already—inaccurate sometimes in his reading of the words, but with a sustained power in the low notes that defied competition. The journalist joined in next and Arthur set up a little hum. Soon they were all at it, singing like blazes, and it is undoubtedly true that they felt the better for it.[53]

In a process of transmediation, the novel here emulates the stage revue's musical sequences, in which a song takes centre stage and disrupts the continuity of the action.

At the same time, Waugh's novel here also begins to show its capacity for adapting to the requirements of cinematic audio-vision and synchronicity: Mrs Ape's command to sing takes hold of the passengers ('the bar steward was hers already') and her speech is accompanied by Adam's comment in brackets, suggesting that the two characters' speeches are happening

---

[50] This new type of 'girl' was popularized in literature and film of the 1920s and 1930s by works like Anita Loos' *Gentlemen Prefer Blondes* (1925) and Irmgard Keun's *Das kunstseidene Mädchen* (1932). See Katharina von Ankum, 'Material Girls: Consumer Culture and the "New Woman" in Anita Loos' *Gentlemen Prefer Blondes* and Irmgard Keun's *Das kunstseidene Mädchen*', *Colloquia Germanica*, 27.2 (1994), 159–172.

[51] Waugh, *Vile Bodies*, pp. 16–17, 84–85.    [52] Waugh, *Vile Bodies*, p. 77.

[53] Waugh, *Vile Bodies*, p. 16.

simultaneously. Visual description and action are led by song, and sound itself is described visually: 'Soon they were all at it, singing like blazes.' The song then becomes the narrative's anchoring point for the subsequent paragraphs of text, each starting with somebody 'hearing it':

> Father Rothschild heard it and turned his face to the wall.
> Kitty Blackwater heard it....
> The Captain heard it....
> The Bright Young People heard it. 'So like one's first parties,' said Miss Runcible, 'being sick with other people singing.'[54]

The white lines between paragraphs move the reader's focus from character to character, and, rather than establishing chronological order, the song disrupts such ordering and conveys the impression of simultaneity and synchronicity by focussing on various passengers at the precise moment of hearing the song. The song thus takes on a function that appears similar to a filmic 'synch point' within the narrative. As Donnelly writes, 'music...provides a number of synch points with the action on-screen, marking an activity most obviously with an emphasized "hit," a stinger or sonic punch', as well as possibly 'indicating the conclusion of a sequence or...entering at a significant point to provide and enhance dramatic aspects of the narrative'.[55] While the arrangement of sentences in Waugh's novel gives the impression of temporal concurrence as they are linked by parallel syntax and verbal repetition, the song also gives the impetus for each new line (each new scene), thereby functioning as textual equivalent to a synch point.

The episodic plot of the novel, which moves quickly back and forth between different characters and strings together only loosely related incidents, further adopts revue's rather cavalier treatment of narrative continuity and coherence:

> The whole show, although written as a unified text with designed songs, dance routines and sketches, had far less interest in narrative coherency than musical comedy. It was not that revue was too unsophisticated to sustain traditional story, as is sometimes thought, but rather that it eschewed what it saw as the narrative simplicity and romanticism of the earlier form.[56]

---

[54] Waugh, *Vile Bodies*, p. 17.    [55] Donnelly, *Occult Aesthetics*, p. 4.
[56] Platt, *Musical Comedy*, p. 134.

60   LITERATURE AND SOUND FILM IN MID-CENTURY BRITAIN

Waugh could have given his novel a more traditional plot, but, as becomes clear from his reflections on Firbank, he did not want to pursue the 'simplicity' of cause-and-effect narrative. Instead, *Vile Bodies* contains variations on a number of themes: Adam and Nina's on-off relationship, Adam's quest for money, and the conflict between generations. Grouped around these themes is a cluster of scenes (the motor-car races, the ship, the nursing home, the film at Doubting Hall), which all contribute to an acerbic picture of the society in which Adam and Nina move.

Although Waugh's text gives the superficial impression of chaos, it is carefully structured: fourteen chapters essentially form two blocks of six chapters with a concluding chapter each.[57] In theatrical terms, we might understand the novel as having two acts of six scenes each, with an intermission (chapter 7) and a finale ('Happy Ending'). The action notably moves back and forth between different party settings and pseudo-domestic settings: following chapter 2 (the customs scene), chapters 3, 5, and 9 take place in pseudo-domestic settings such as Shepheard's Hotel and Doubting Hall. Chapter 7 forms a break or intermission in the flow of events as the chapter foregrounds Adam's quest for domestic bliss by becoming Mr Chatterbox to raise the money needed to marry Nina. In contrast, chapters 4, 6, 8, and 10 focus on the different parties: Archie Schwert's party, Lady Metroland's party, the party in the airship, and the fatal raucous gathering of the Bright Young People at the motor car races. These movements between locations indicate that Waugh structured the novel spatially with a view to setting. George McCartney remarks on the novel's careful structuring, but attributes this to Waugh's use of cinematic techniques:

> Even at his most knockabout, his fiction always exhibits the craftsman's attention to design. He learned a good deal of his craftsmanship from cinema, which supplied him with the mechanics to build underlying patterns into his narratives, no matter how helter-skelter their surfaces might seem to the casual reader.[58]

While McCartney's assessment is plausible, one should note the origins of such a structural concept in revue: '"running order" was crucial in revue;

---

[57] Further comments on the structure of *Vile Bodies* can be found in Davis, *Evelyn Waugh*, pp. 128–145 and in Richard Jacobs, 'Introduction', Evelyn Waugh, *Vile Bodies* (London: Penguin, 2000) pp. ix–xxxiv.

[58] McCartney, *Evelyn Waugh*, p. 100.

not only did the sequence of song and sketch…need careful attention, costume-changing had to be figured in and a fully staged segment had to be followed by a front-cloth act'.[59] The point here, then, is that Waugh's text structurally adapts features of stage revue: there is a similar use of different scenarios, a reliance on common themes rather than sustained, coherent plot, and a surface impression of disorder which masks a carefully curated, underlying structure. The novel's thinly veiled, parodic treatment of political and socialite figures of the late 1920s also calls to mind the revue's capacity to mock and parody personalities in the public sphere. *Vile Bodies* is notably concerned with characters taking on different roles and inventing new personalities: Nina pretends to be a maid when answering the phone; Adam becomes the gossip columnist Mr Chatterbox and invents famous socialites such as Imogen Quest; and Colonel Blount signs the cheque for Adam as 'Charlie Chaplin'.[60]

Reading the novel as chiefly inspired by revue also supports readers' understanding of narration in *Vile Bodies*. It has been noted that the novel appears to contain at least two different narratorial voices: 'the intrusive, knowing voice of the Society pages' on the one hand, and the 'detached, impersonal orchestrator of modernist aesthetics' on the other.[61] Naomi Milthorpe, for instance, argues that one voice can be attributed to the main body of the text, and that the other voice is linked to the novel's 'paratextual devices', such as footnotes, parentheses, and white lines.[62] In contrast, Damon Marcel DeCoste insists that 'the division between modernist detachment and gossip-columnist obtrusiveness does not always observe those paratextual boundaries'.[63] However, I would argue that to understand narrative voice in *Vile Bodies*, we must, again, turn to its adaptation of revue. From this perspective, the narration only *seems* to be split between these two voices, because the narrator performs a role modelled on the compère in stage revue. A compère would normally lead through the programme of a performance, making announcements, commenting on acts, and interacting with the live

---

[59] James Ross Moore, 'Girl Crazy: Musicals and Revue between the Wars', in Clive Barker and Maggie B. Gale (eds), *British Theatre between the Wars, 1918–1939* (Cambridge: Cambridge University Press, 2000), 88–112 (p. 94).

[60] Waugh, *Vile Bodies*, p. 28 and p. 69, and p. 91.

[61] DeCoste, Damon Marcel, ' "(AND YOU GET FAR TOO MUCH PUBLICITY ALREADY WHOEVER YOU ARE)": Gossip, Celebrity, and Modernist Authorship in Evelyn Waugh's *Vile Bodies*', *Papers on Language and Literature*, 49.1 (Winter 2013), 3–36 (pp. 6 and 17–18).

[62] Naomi Milthorpe, *Evelyn Waugh's Satire: Texts and Contexts* (Madison, NJ: Fairleigh Dickinson University Press, 2016), p. 48.

[63] DeCoste, 'Gossip, Celebrity, and Modernist Authorship', p. 18.

## 62  LITERATURE AND SOUND FILM IN MID-CENTURY BRITAIN

audience. The compère would also be responsible for maintaining order and for providing some short, improvised entertainments between acts. In *Vile Bodies*, the narrator performs these multiple functions that are closely related to those of the compère. First, the narrator addresses the audience directly, establishing a sense of community by drawing them into the circle of shared secrecy and gossip: 'You see, that was the kind of party Archie Schwert's party was.'[64] Second, the narrator's voice announces some of the 'acts' before they actually happen in the novel ('He did this with a man called Ginger').[65] And, finally, the narrator repeatedly comments on the events as they unfold: '(all that succession and repetition of massed humanity...Those vile bodies...).'[66] Performing these different functions, the narrator of *Vile Bodies* appears both as a detached commentator and as an insider, who acts simultaneously in the midst and on the fringes of the novel. This double function may lead to the impression of split narratorial voices, but this impression is created by the novel's adaptation of the role of the compère in revue.

In addition to these forms of transmediation, of adapting features of stage revue for the textual form of the novel, *Vile Bodies* also engages in more direct media representation, this time of sound film itself. The novel contains an intricate critique of early sound film which goes far beyond the suggestion that Waugh was simply influenced by sound film. Rather, the novel engages in different forms of adaptation, transmediation, and media representation, to demonstrate how the literary text might successfully supersede the sound film in its ability to adapt stage entertainment. There is evidence in the novel that Waugh was concerned with a critique of both cinematic sound reproduction more broadly as well as musical and revue film specifically. Waugh builds up to his direct attack on sound film by first planting various clues to attune his readers to the challenges of modern sound reproduction. Waugh's soundscapes are often constructed to demonstrate a total lack of intelligibility:

The engine was running and the whole machine shook with fruitless exertion. Clouds of dark smoke came from it, and a shattering roar which reverberated from concrete floor and corrugated iron roof into every corner of the building so that speech and thought became insupportable and all the senses were numbed.[67]

---

[64] Waugh, *Vile Bodies*, p. 43.  [65] Waugh, *Vile Bodies*, p. 98.
[66] Waugh, *Vile Bodies*, p. 104.  [67] Waugh, *Vile Bodies*, p. 135.

The narrator draws attention to how modern noise prevents intelligible human interaction as well as conscious sensory experience. Attending the motor car races, Adam, Nina, and Agatha Runcible witness 'scraps of highly technical conversation'. The novel here uses ellipses and fragments of speech to show disrupted communication, eschewing intelligible dialogue and using the evocation of noise to undermine and impede characters' interaction and the progression of action:

> '...Burst his gasket and blew out his cylinder heads...'
> '...Broke both arms and cracked his skull in two places...'
> '...Tailwag...'
> '...Speed-wobble...'
> '...Merc...'
> '...Mag...'
> '...crash...'[68]

Recording disintegrated speech as fragments of noise, the narrator does not care whether these sound bites may or may not be meaningful to the reader. In its recording of sound fragments, Waugh's text alludes to the shortfalls of early cinematic sound reproduction. Early microphones, for instance, were omnidirectional and not selective enough (hence the need for comprehensive sound-proofing on an early sound film set). The slightest sound was picked up by the recording device which could lead to a cacophony of noises that made it extremely difficult for the listener to distinguish between 'meaningful' sound and mere noise.[69] As noted in Chapter 1, debates on the poor intelligibility of film sound were conducted in the daily newspapers, film magazines, and in the trade press throughout the late 1920s and early 1930s.[70] The fragmentation of speech and the novel's references to noise cleverly alludes to the shortfalls of synchronized sound in the cinema: non-selectivity and unintelligibility of spoken interaction convey a cacophony

---

[68] Waugh, *Vile Bodies*, p. 134.

[69] More detailed discussions of the challenges faced by film industries in the US, France, and Britain can be found in Charles O'Brien, *Cinema's Conversion to Sound: Technology and Film Style in France and the U.S.* (Bloomington, IN: Indiana University Press, 2005); James Lastra, *Sound Technology and the American Cinema* (New York: Columbia University Press, 2000); Barry Salt, *Film Style and Technology: History and Analysis* (London: Starword, 2009); Donald Crafton, *The Talkies: American Cinema's Transition to Sound, 1926–1931* (New York: Scribner, 1997); and Lea Jacobs, *Film Rhythm after Sound: Technology, Music, and Performance* (Oakland, CA: University of California Press, 2015).

[70] See *Kinematograph Weekly*'s critique of 'atrocious reproduction and bad entertainment' in '1929–1930', *Kinematograph Weekly*, 2 January 1930, p. 113.

64 LITERATURE AND SOUND FILM IN MID-CENTURY BRITAIN

without depth, direction, and purpose. Although everything is recorded, it lacks cohesive narrative integration and meaning.

These more covert hints at the failure of sound reproduction culminate in Waugh's direct attack on the sound film: the novel represents the making of a musical film that, ironically, cannot be played with its soundtrack due to a lack of equipment. The film is co-financed by Nina's father, Colonel Blount, and shot on his estate Doubting Hall. It tells a sensational and non-sensical account of the life of John Wesley, produced by 'The Wonderfilm Company of Great Britain' and overseen by a Mr Isaacs, who explains to Adam that the film 'marks a stepping stone in the development of the British Film Industry. It is the most important All-Talkie super-religious film to be produced solely in this country by British artists and management and by British capital'[71] Suggesting the making of a musical film, Isaacs boasts to Adam that the film team are 'recording extracts from Wesley's sermons and we're singing all his own hymns'[72] Singing and music are repeatedly shown to be prominent elements of the film as Adam, upon his arrival at Doubting Hall, first hears 'distant shouting and what seemed to be a string band'[73] As he wanders onto the film set, he encounters 'a dozen or so men and women in eighteenth-century costume...singing strongly'[74] They are guided by a conductor and, yet again, accompanied by 'a string band'[75] Even the Colonel is part of the ensemble, financially and vocally supporting the film venture. However, when Colonel Blount shows the finished film to Nina and Adam, the screening does not go as planned:

> There came in breathless succession four bewigged men in fancy costume, sitting round a card table. There were glasses, heaps of money and candles on the table. They were clearly gambling feverishly and drinking a lot. ('There's a song there, really', said the Colonel, 'only I'm afraid I haven't got a talkie apparatus yet.')[76]

While the live performance of Mrs Ape and her angels, earlier in the novel, has the capacity to take hold of the novel's characters, the sound film, as represented by the text, lets down its audiences on and off the page. The 'most important All-Talkie super-religious film' is not a talking film at all. The ambitious project fails and the screening of the film without

---

[71] Waugh, *Vile Bodies*, p. 122.    [72] Waugh, *Vile Bodies*, p. 123.
[73] Waugh, *Vile Bodies*, p. 119.    [74] Waugh, *Vile Bodies*, p. 120.
[75] Waugh, *Vile Bodies*, p. 120.    [76] Waugh, *Vile Bodies*, p. 177.

appropriate equipment makes the Colonel revert back to an explanatory live commentary: 'there's a song there really'. The film, which is meant to mark a 'stepping stone in the development of the British Film Industry', does not mark anything significant at all but points to the failure of the new audio-visual medium and invalidates the grand claims made by Isaacs and Colonel Blount. Indeed, the failure of sound film in the novel may call to mind the real warnings issued by the trade paper *Kinematograph Weekly* that 'atrocious reproduction' would lead to 'thousands of enemies for the talkies'.[77] While sound film is thus framed as wholly unreliable in its reproduction of sound, Mrs Ape's choir, the numerous telephone conversations, and the scenes at the motor car races demonstrate that the literary text does not fail its readers when it comes to adapting the principles of stage revue for the novel and 'reproducing', albeit textually, its sound and sound–image relationships.

The failure of sound film in *Vile Bodies* draws attention to Waugh's ambivalent attitude towards cinematic innovation. Critical of new technologies such as sound and colour, Waugh felt that synchronized sound degraded cinema as an art form. In an article for the *Daily Mail* published in May 1930, he made it clear to his readers that he held early sound film in rather low esteem and criticized the displacement of music-halls, of staged live entertainment, that was increasingly replaced by the movie palaces:

> I feel that nowadays, since the introduction of what are charitably known as 'Talking Pictures', writing about the cinema is like writing about the music-hall; it tends to become a mere lament of a disappearing art.... [O]ur appreciation is dimmed by the intrusion of uncouth voices, which we strive to dissociate from the actors and actresses who have so often delighted us....I know that I am in the minority in this feeling, and I hope fervently that this disturbing new invention will soon be tamed so that we can once more look upon the cinema—silent or 'talky'—not as an imitation stage play but as genuine and self-sufficient art.[78]

Waugh's critique focusses on sound film's creation of 'imitation stage play[s]' whose mere function is to capitalize on synchronized sound. Waugh is

---

[77] '1929–1930', *Kinematograph Weekly*, 2 January 1930, p. 113.
[78] Waugh, 'My Favourite Film Star', in Donat Gallagher (ed.), *The Essays, Articles and Reviews of Evelyn Waugh* (London: Methuen, 1983), pp. 68–70 (p. 68). The essay was first published in *The Daily Mail* on 24 May 1930.

66 LITERATURE AND SOUND FILM IN MID-CENTURY BRITAIN

clearly targeting musical and revue films like *The Hollywood Revue of 1929* and *Elstree Calling* and their typical manner of adapting and appropriating stage entertainment to showcase film's new, audio-visual form. Waugh criticizes the sound film's lack of originality, intelligibility, and sophistication. Such a critique also becomes clear in *Vile Bodies'* media representation of the sound film as a pointless, plotless, and speculative endeavour that culminates in a considerable loss of financial assets for all parties involved. The 'Wonderfilm' episode of *Vile Bodies* exemplifies the dissociation of voice and image through the lack of technological equipment. There is no synchronized sound film, no audio-visual aesthetic and no experience of synchronicity, because the technological means are lacking. *Vile Bodies* is Waugh's claim that the novel, as carefully curated written text, does not fail its readers when it comes to audio-vision and synchronicity whereas the sound film itself is represented as an unreliable venture.

Despite Waugh's criticism of sound film, he did not seem to mind that *Vile Bodies* was eventually turned into a television revue in 1939. Waugh is credited with having contributed to parts of the script. The revue called *Table d'Hôte* was in part based on Waugh's novel and featured a sketch called 'Doubting Hall' which starred the characters of Adam and Nina. According to the *BBC Radio Times*, the programme was first broadcast on 26 June 1939 at 9.20 pm.[79] No recording of the show survives as these TV broadcasts took place live. In the absence of surviving records, readers are left to wonder whether this was a worthy outlet for Waugh's 'revue between covers'.

*Vile Bodies* presents one answer to the question of how the novel, of how the mid-century writer, might adapt to the conditions of audio-vision and synchronicity. Waugh's focus here firmly lies on processes of adaptation: *Vile Bodies* takes up elements of stage revue and transmediates them. At the same time, the novel also engages in the direct, unflattering media representation of sound film. In its textual and literary capacities for adaptation, *Vile Bodies* thus beats early sound film at its own game, thereby also forming a core text for understanding mid-century literature's move towards a more mediatized textuality.

---

[79] 'Table D'Hôte', *BBC Radio Times*, 23 June 1939, p. 16. Enquiries with the British Film Institute and the BBC Written Archives Centre have confirmed that there appears to be no surviving recording of the TV revue. The BBC Archives do not hold a script of the revue either. Waugh and Dennis H. Bradley, who adapted *Vile Bodies* for the stage, are listed as contributors to the TV revue in the *BBC Radio Times* entry for 23 June 1939.

## Isherwood's Weimar Cabaret and the Musical Film

Like Waugh's *Vile Bodies*, Christopher Isherwood's *Mr Norris Changes Trains* (1935) and *Goodbye to Berlin* (1939) often behave more like stage shows than as novels. *Goodbye to Berlin* consists of six short stories, all of which, according to their author, 'are the only existing fragments of what was originally planned as a huge episodic novel of pre-Hitler Berlin.'[80] Chronicling Isherwood's life in Berlin between 1929 and 1933, these episodes present a politically tumultuous, decadent city on the brink of collapse. While *Goodbye to Berlin* is now widely known as the source material for John Van Druten's play *I am a Camera* (1951) and for the stage and film versions of the musical *Cabaret* (1966 and 1972), these later adaptations of Isherwood's text capitalize on a key feature that already underscores *Goodbye to Berlin* as well as Isherwood's related works in their entirety; namely, the structural, formal, and thematic borrowings from the cabaret stages of the Weimar Republic. As I will show in the remainder of this chapter, Isherwood, like Waugh, rehearses different strategies of adaptation in his literary works, thereby also devising his own response to the affordances of media form in the age of audio-vision and synchronicity.

Cabaret offered Isherwood a model for constructing *Mr Norris Changes Trains* and *Goodbye to Berlin*: a form of small stage performance (*Kleinkunst*) mixing art, political satire, and popular entertainment, cabaret originated from the bohemian bars and clubs of Paris, especially Montmartre's *Chat Noir* (1881). It spread across Europe from the late nineteenth century onwards with Vienna, Zurich, Munich, and Berlin becoming important artistic centres. Like stage revue, cabaret consisted of a quick succession of different acts or scenes, usually an elastic mixture of songs, poetry recitals, dance numbers, erotic performance art, political satire, and parody. Cabaret distinguishes itself from revue by its performance venue, which is usually a bar, nightclub, or restaurant with a small stage. The setting creates intimacy and interaction between audiences and performers. One might think of revue as cabaret's more moderate, pretty cousin: especially in a German-speaking context, *Kabarett* is often characterized by its acerbic, sarcastic, and dissenting tone, its socio-political criticism, and its attempts to shock and provoke audiences. At the time of Isherwood's life in Berlin, cabaret was a mainstay of the local entertainment culture and performance

---

[80] Christopher Isherwood, untitled preface, *Goodbye to Berlin*, in *The Berlin Novels* (London: Vintage, 1999), p. 240.

68   LITERATURE AND SOUND FILM IN MID-CENTURY BRITAIN

venues like *Die Katakombe* (1929–1935) provided important outlets for political protest and parody as Fascism's grip on Germany tightened. Some of the best-known, German-speaking writers of the period, such as Bertolt Brecht, Kurt Tucholsky, Joachim Ringelnatz, and Erich Kästner produced lyrics, poems, and performance pieces for the cabaret stages and published their work in the cabaret scene's associated magazines, *Simplicissimus* and *Die Weltbühne*.[81] Although Stephen Spender later insisted that Berlin life 'wasn't a Cabaret', he and Isherwood were frequent readers of *Simplicissimus* and *Die Weltbühne*, watched stage productions by Brecht and Max Reinhardt, and immersed themselves in the cinema and theatre culture of Berlin.[82] Like revue, the cabaret setting emphasizes performance as performance: it does not aim for the audience's suspension of disbelief, but actively deconstructs the fourth wall. Cabaret performance directly addresses (and often comments on, shocks, or offends) the audience and, as such, it may have had a crucial influence on the development of Bertolt Brecht's understanding of drama.[83]

Cabaret's emphasis on self-referential performance also inherently underscores the narrative style of *Goodbye to Berlin* and other works based on Isherwood's Berlin life (*Mr Norris Changes Trains, Down There on a Visit, Christopher and His Kind, Prater Violet*). *Goodbye to Berlin*'s characters act performatively. Like the cabaret dancers in a local nightclub, who are 'showing in their every movement a consciousness of the part they were playing', the narrator's encounters with Sally, Otto, and the Nowak family are a constant reminder of life as lived performance.[84] Arguments between Otto and his mother are conducted more loudly and aggressively whenever

---

[81] Lisa Appignanesi, *Cabaret: The First Hundred Years* (London: Methuen, 1984), pp. 31–44 and 99–105.

[82] Stephen Spender, 'Life wasn't a Cabaret', *New York Times*, 30 October 1977, p. 198.

[83] See Lisa Appignanesi, *Cabaret: The First Hundred Years* (London: Methuen, 1984), pp. 130–131 and Brecht's fascinating 'Notes on the Folk Play': 'The big cities moved with the times, progressing from the folk play to the revue. Revue is to the folk play as a song-hit to a folksong...More recently the revue has been taken up as a literary form. Wangenheim of Germany, Abell of Denmark, Blitzstein of the USA and Auden of England have written interesting plays in the form of revues, plays that are neither crude nor humble. Their plays have something of the poetry of the old folk play but absolutely nothing of its naivety. They avoid its conventional situations and schematized characters....Their situations are grotesque and at bottom they hardly have characters, barely even parts for the actors. The linear story has been thrown on the scrap heap....Their performance demands virtuosity—they cannot be played by amateurs—but it is the virtuosity of the cabaret.' Bertolt Brecht, 'Notes on the Folk Play', in John Willett (trans. and ed.), *Brecht on Theatre: The Development of an Aesthetic* (London: Bloomsbury, 2013), 153–157 (p. 153).

[84] Isherwood, *Goodbye to Berlin*, in *The Berlin Novels* (London: Vintage, 1999), p. 258.

they have an audience; Herr Nowak's dinnertime stories are accompanied by macabre pantomime as he relays the events of an innocent man's execution in the Wilhelmine empire. The story 'On Ruegen Island' focusses on play-acted arguments fuelled by jealousy in an unacknowledged *ménage-à-trois*. Isherwood later returned to this episode in *Christopher and His Kind*, writing that 'even when Christopher felt genuinely jealous, genuinely furious with Otto, he *continued to play* for Stephen's amusement. Otto, being *a natural actor*, knew this instinctively and entered into the *performance*; he didn't object to *taking the unsympathetic role*.'[85]

The nightclub singer Sally Bowles, perhaps Isherwood's most famous creation, never stops performing. During a police interview, she gives a 'comic-opera' performance to the delight of two policemen and Isherwood's narrator.[86] When simply meeting for a drink with friends, they enjoy 'watching her, like a performance at the theatre'.[87] Similar to the narrator of *Vile Bodies*, the 'Christopher' who narrates his Berlin life cultivates intimacy and familiarity with his readers through aside remarks and a confessional tone. The 'Christopher Isherwood' of *Goodbye to Berlin*, *Prater Violet*, and *Down There on a Visit* is a narrator–participant who is variously known as 'Chris', 'Herr Christoph', 'Herr Issyvoo', 'Mr Kreestoffer Ischervood', and 'Christopher'. He compères the episodes of his life, accompanied by what amounts to a musical cast: the nightclub singer Sally, the pianist Klaus, and the music-hall performer Frl. Mayr who eventually embarks on a 'cabaret-tour' through the Netherlands.[88] The world of theatre offers both 'Christopher' as narrator and Isherwood as author a way of representing life. The garden party at Bernhard Landauer's lake house is 'the dress-rehearsal of a disaster'[89] while, according to Isherwood, the narrator in *Mr Norris Changes Trains* had to be restrained so as not to 'upstag[e] Norris's performance as the star'.[90] In Christopher's world, there are mostly 'crude dialogues' and 'absurd costumes' while the mothers know when one 'needs a cue line'.[91] Isherwood's prose consistently borrows metaphors and language from the stage with characters engaged in deliberate acts of putting on a show for the benefit of others.

Isherwood's engagement with stage entertainment throughout the 1930s, both as keen theatregoer and, together with W. H. Auden, as dramatist,

---

[85] Isherwood, *Christopher and His Kind* (London: Vintage, 2012), pp. 45–46, my emphasis.
[86] Isherwood, *Goodbye to Berlin*, p. 328.   [87] Isherwood, *Goodbye to Berlin*, p. 269.
[88] Isherwood, *Goodbye to Berlin*, p. 465.   [89] Isherwood, *Goodbye to Berlin*, p. 453.
[90] Isherwood, *Christopher and His Kind*, p. 191.
[91] Christopher Isherwood, *Prater Violet* (London: Vintage, 2012), pp. 120–121 and p. 3.

## 70 LITERATURE AND SOUND FILM IN MID-CENTURY BRITAIN

becomes palpable in *The Berlin Novels*' style and focus on character. In a series of lectures given at the University of California, Santa Barbara, in 1960, Isherwood relates his own experiences of theatre, both professionally and privately, to his practice as a writer:

> The thing that I learned from working in what one might call the professional theater—the theater of the good playwright, of the craftsman, as opposed to the theater of the expressionist, of the poet—was that the thing that matters supremely is not plot or situation, but it is character....Once an audience is really interested in the character, the audience will forget about the weaknesses of the structure of the play.[92]

'A Writer and the Theatre' provides important insight into Isherwood's thinking about the affordances of stage performance, literary text, and film. On his account, structural shortcomings—lack of coherence or fragmentation—in stage performance can be balanced out by character and the context of live performance. Theatre, according to Isherwood, 'is a box, a place of imprisonment in which the audience is shut up with the actors'.[93] The conditions of live performance are particular to the theatre and not something that can be replicated by film: 'the frontal human drama of really having live actors on the stage is something in which the cinema does not and cannot attempt to deal'.[94] While Isherwood notes in a further lecture titled 'A Writer and the Films' that film's key functions comprised of 'bringing to the masses all kinds of material which hitherto had been inaccessible to them, of turning stage plays into a canned film version, and of presenting the fascinating creatures known as the stars', this does not change the fact that theatre is a wholly different medium that thrives and relies on transient live performance and audience response.[95] Although theatre forms an important and frequent source for film, the conditions of performance and reception are fundamentally different. While Isherwood describes theatre as a 'box', cinema is 'a window through which you look outside'.[96] Theatre relies heavily on speech and sound whereas cinema is 'dominate[d] by

---

[92] Christopher Isherwood, 'A Writer and the Theatre', in James J. Berg (ed.), *Isherwood on Writing* (Minneapolis: University of Minnesota Press, 2007), 84–98 (p. 90).

[93] Isherwood, 'A Writer and the Theatre', p. 91.

[94] Isherwood, 'A Writer and the Theatre', p. 91.

[95] Christopher Isherwood, 'A Writer and the Films', in James J. Berg (ed.), *Isherwood on Writing* (Minneapolis: University of Minnesota Press, 2007), 99–113 (p. 104).

[96] Isherwood, 'A Writer and the Theatre', p. 91.

ADAPTING AUDIO-VISION 71

image and movement'; 'in the theater you can remain perfectly still and deliver speeches which cover four or five pages, and, if you know your business as an actor, and if the speech is of real quality, people will listen to you.'[97]

These retrospective reflections on the relation between theatre and film also help reframe the reading of Isherwood's literary works. As noted in Chapter 1, Isherwood himself drew attention to the fact that most of his literary works were produced either after or alongside his career as dramatist and scriptwriter for film.[98] Thinking through the affordances of theatre, film, and literary text was, in short, part and parcel of his entire writing career. *Mr Norris Changes Trains* and *Goodbye to Berlin*, in particular, reflect Isherwood's interest as well as professional preoccupation with stage performance, which is directly related not merely to the sustained semantics of theatre and performance throughout *Goodbye to Berlin*, but also speaks to the text's consistent focus on character presentation. In these regards, Isherwood, like Waugh, engages in transmediation; those elements which he considers central to successful theatre performance are adapted for his prose texts.

At the same time, there are elements of direct media representation, especially of sound film, that can be found throughout Isherwood's work. Like Waugh's *Vile Bodies*, Isherwood adopts in his work an ambivalent, critical stance towards early sound film despite his own involvement in the film industry. In *Goodbye to Berlin*, readers find some subtle hints to the superficiality and danger of the film industry: Sally is abandoned by her boyfriend Klaus 'who leaves his gig at *The Lady Windermere* for a job synchronizing music for the films'. She is then conned by a young man pretending to be a European agent for Metro-Goldwyn-Mayer on the lookout for an English actress speaking German. The conman succeeds, not least due to his convincing shoptalk: 'he told me how they make sound-effects and how they do the trick-work'.[99] Following *Goodbye to Berlin*'s cursory commentary on the film industry, Isherwood's *Prater Violet* (1945) looks back to the early 1930s and addresses the pitfalls of sound film production, in which a musical film not only fails to suitably adapt a stage show, but, more importantly, also fails to appropriately address the political and social

---

[97] Isherwood, 'A Writer and the Theatre', p. 93.

[98] Christopher Isherwood, 'Isherwood on Hollywood' (1968), Interview with Charles Higham, in James J. Berg and Chris Freeman (eds), *Conversations with Christopher Isherwood* (Jackson: University Press of Mississippi, 2001), 45–51 (pp. 47–48).

[99] Isherwood, *Goodbye to Berlin*, p. 323.

## 72 LITERATURE AND SOUND FILM IN MID-CENTURY BRITAIN

concerns of its time. Based on Isherwood's work as a screenwriter for Berthold Viertel's *Little Friend, Prater Violet* is the story of 'Christopher' being invited to write scenes and dialogue for a musical film set in Vienna and produced by the British company 'Bulldog Pictures' in 1933. The film's clichéd story is of the poor flower seller Toni who falls in love with a prince in disguise. Based on a fictional Blackpool stage show, the film offers little in the way of imagination or excitement, but is presented as a viable invest-ment for its producers because the musical elements of the stage show can be appropriated for the film: '[the stage show] folded up after three nights. But Mr. Chatsworth likes the music, and he thinks we can use most of the lyrics....'[100] A stab at the film industry in its early post-transition phase, the premise of *Prater Violet* picks up on the contemporary taste for musical and operetta films after successful Austro-German and American productions were released between 1929 and 1934. A few British operetta film produc-tions followed suit, for instance a film version of Noël Coward's *Bitter Sweet* (1933) and the immensely successful *Blossom Time* (1934), starring the popular Austrian tenor Richard Tauber.

As a critical consideration of sound, performance, and of the moral cor-ruption of the film industry, the novel centres on dialogue and the transmis-sion of sound, music, and speech via phone lines, cables, microphones, and personal conversations. The making of the sound film is portrayed in equal parts as 'symphony' and as 'infernal machine'.[101] Isherwood's story points readers towards the real-world circumstances and ramifications of the film industry's move to sound, describing the 'great barn-like sound-stage' and the complications of working with early recording equipment and hyper-sensitive microphones on set:

> Mr Watts and the camera operator are discussing how to avoid the mike shadow....On rare occasions, the microphone itself somehow manages to get into the shot, without anybody noticing it. There is something sinister about it, like Poe's Raven. It is always there, silently listening.[102]

As the microphone's sinister presence throws its shadow on the film image, it also keeps a close ear on the crew. Studio gossip has to be transmitted in the only soundproof (and therefore private) space available: the booth for

---

[100] Isherwood, *Prater Violet* (London: Vintage, 2012), p. 2.
[101] Isherwood, *Prater Violet*, p. 32 and p. 27.  [102] Isherwood, *Prater Violet*, p. 76.

sound editing on set.[103] The filming itself consists of a succession of musical numbers and their repeated rehearsals as the narrator 'can hear Anita practising [the theme song] now, with Pfeffer at the piano, somewhere behind the set: Spring wakes,/ Winter's dead./ Ice breaks,/ Frosts have fled.'[104] These rather uninspired lyrics are accompanied by a score 'as noisy as hell', which has become a necessity to mask the noise on set as 'the problem of camera noise is perpetual.'[105]

The finished film is successful in London, New York, and Vienna, but the narrator does not watch it. One of Christopher's acquaintances in Paris calls it 'a horrible British picture which, besides being an insult to the intelligence of a five-year-old child, is definitely counter-revolutionary and ought to be banned.'[106] In the novel, Christopher's friend Lawrence dismisses the operetta film as a reactionary fantasy. Indeed, operetta film productions of the 1930s were usually conservative, romantic fictions of the past: Warner Bros' *Viennese Nights* (1930) is the story of a woman caught between two men in early twentieth-century Vienna; *Blossom Time* is a fictionalized take on Franz Schubert's love life in nineteenth-century Vienna; *Waltzes from Vienna* (1934) tells the fictional story of Johann Strauss II's composition of *The Blue Danube Waltz*.

While 'Bulldog Pictures' is only concerned with producing its conservatively romantic *Prater Violet* in the relative safety of London, the film's director Bergmann learns that his family in Vienna is threatened by a local uprising of the Austrian Right as the Fascist grip on Berlin also tightens. Even though he agreed to directing the film, Bergmann despises everything the production embodies:

> The picture! I shit upon the picture! This heartless filth! This wretched, lying charade! To make such a picture at such a moment is definitely heartless. It is a crime. It definitely aids Dollfuss, and Starhemberg, and Fey and all their gangsters. It covers up the dirty syphilitic sore with rose leaves, with the petals of this hypocritical reactionary violet. It lies and declares that the pretty Danube is blue, when the water is red with blood...I am punished for assisting at this lie. We shall all be punished...[107]

---

[103] Isherwood, *Prater Violet*, p. 102.      [104] Isherwood, *Prater Violet*, pp. 79–80.
[105] Isherwood, *Prater Violet*, p. 59 and p. 75.      [106] Isherwood, *Prater Violet*, p. 122.
[107] Isherwood, *Prater Violet*, p. 91.

74 LITERATURE AND SOUND FILM IN MID-CENTURY BRITAIN

Although the success of *Prater Violet* ultimately enables Bergmann and his family to leave Austria for Hollywood, his comments are an indictment of the sound film and of an industry that propagates romanticized, nostalgic visions of nineteenth-century Europe and feeds the public with reactionary fairy tales of singing flower girls who become operatic princesses as the world wavers on the brink of disaster. While Waugh's fictional treatment of sound film is a vision of technological failure and lost financial assets, Isherwood's *Prater Violet* portrays sound film as mindless, reactionary escapism with considerable political danger.

Both Waugh and Isherwood's critical treatment of early sound film discloses their ambivalent stance, not least because the new medium was rather excessively drawing on stage forms including revue, cabaret, and operetta for its plots, music, and performers. The 'all talking', 'all singing', and 'all dancing' motion picture occupied a singular position in the media system of the 1930s, because it raised the questions of what a sound film should be and how it might relate to its neighbours, the theatre and the silent film. This chapter has traced the ways in which Evelyn Waugh and Christopher Isherwood were not silent observers to this process, but actively participated in questioning the affordances of theatre, film, and literature. By drawing on features of stage revue and cabaret shows, adapting them for the literary text in a process of transmediation, they show the literary text's own capacity to become mediatized in the age of audio-vision. Waugh and Isherwood also take this opportunity to comment directly on the shortfalls of early sound film, thereby insisting on literature's ability to remain current in an audio-visual media ecology.

*Literature and Sound Film in Mid-Century Britain.* Lara Ehrenfried, Oxford University Press.
© Lara Ehrenfried 2025. DOI: 10.1093/9780198950790.003.0003

# 3
# Dialogue and Intelligibility

One of the most significant changes that sound technology brought to film was of course the possibility of synchronized dialogue: it led to a complete reappraisal of the roles played by voice and speech for designing filmic action, characterization, and storytelling. Even before the advent of synchronized sound film, the mid-century media ecology was uniquely tuned in to matters of speech: telephony and radio broadcasting, for instance, had already put speech and voice on the map of public discourse in Britain.[1] In the light of such developments, discussions of mid-century writing often note the apparent interest in talk in much of the period's literature. In 1990, David Lodge's seminal work 'Dialogue in the Modern Novel' examined the works of Evelyn Waugh, Henry Green, and Ivy Compton-Burnett for its apparent, new-found interest in dialogue. 'The thirties novel', Lodge wrote, 'is characteristically about social and verbal interaction, presented objectively and externally. The stream of consciousness gives way to a stream of talk, but it is talk without the reassuring gloss of the classic novel's authorial voice.'[2] Similarly, Laura Marcus noted that 'much fiction and poetry of the 1930s is intensely productive of "talk" and "talking" and of gossip and the overheard'.[3] The ubiquity of spoken conversation in the media ecology drew writers to an in-depth examination of dialogue: they 'developed an interest in using fiction as a way of analysing talk', as John Mepham argues with reference to the works of Patrick Hamilton and Elizabeth Bowen.[4]

---

[1] See, for example, Richard Menke, 'Literature and Telecommunication', in James Purdon (ed.), *British Literature in Transition, 1900–1920: A New Age?* (Cambridge: Cambridge University Press, 2021), 192–208; Simon Potter, *This is the BBC: Entertaining the Nation, Speaking for Britain? 1922–2022* (Oxford: Oxford University Press, 2022).

[2] David Lodge, 'Dialogue in the Modern Novel', *After Bakhtin: Essays on Fiction and Criticism* (London: Routledge, 1990), 75–86 (p. 81).

[3] Laura Marcus, 'Talking Films', in Benjamin Kohlmann and Matthew Taunton (eds), *A History of 1930s British Literature* (Cambridge: Cambridge University Press, 2019), 177–193 (p. 178).

[4] John Mepham, 'Varieties of Modernism, Varieties of Incomprehension: Patrick Hamilton and Elizabeth Bowen', *British Fiction after Modernism: The Novel at Mid-Century* (Basingstoke: Palgrave Macmillan, 2007), 59–76 (p. 60).

## 76 LITERATURE AND SOUND FILM IN MID-CENTURY BRITAIN

This chapter expands such existing lines of enquiry regarding the work of Bowen, Green, and Compton-Burnett and directly engages with mid-century literature's pronounced interest in talk by relating it to the film industry's developing practices surrounding film dialogue. I argue that film and literature's growing proximity can be detected quite clearly if viewed from the vantage point of dialogue. I suggest that it is not merely speech or voice that become foregrounded in both media, but, rather, that film and literature increasingly conceive of dialogue and speech audio-visually. Both media forms construct new, audio-visual approaches to dialogue. In what follows, I examine the emergence of such an audio-visual conception of dialogue in the film industry, discussing Alexander Korda's *The Divorce of Lady X* (1938) as a case study. I then turn to the essays, broadcasts, and fiction of Bowen, Green, and Compton-Burnett to show how their conceptions of dialogue illustrate mid-century literature's move to a more mediatized, performative textuality that intersects significantly with the sound film's audio-visual approach to dialogue.

## Screen Talk

By the mid-1930s, production practices in the film industry had become increasingly geared towards foregrounding dialogue and improving the intelligibility of the speaking voice.[5] Dialogue became a key tool for structuring filmic action, characterization, and pace. Matters of synchronization, too, were nowhere more prominently present (and more masterfully concealed) than in film dialogue: synchronized speech, as Donnelly observes, forms one of the key synch points around which a sound film builds its illusion of the causal relationship between image and sound, between visual action and voice.[6] A synch point is constituted, for instance, by the combination of audible speech and visible lip-synchronization in a film. This overlap of hearing speech and seeing a character's lips move sustains the impression that sound is produced directly by the film image.

As shown in Chapters 1 and 2, film studios and industry professionals initially conceived of synchronized sound as a mere technological addition

---

[5] Helen Hanson, *Hollywood Soundscapes: Film Sound Style, Craft and Production in the Classical Era* (London: BFI, 2017).

[6] K. J. Donnelly, *Occult Aesthetics: Synchronization in Sound Film* (Oxford: Oxford University Press, 2014), p. 4.

to cinema that could be incorporated relatively easily into already existing production practices during the early sound years. As a result of this initial approach, sound was treated analogously to the film image: 'the recording of speech [was] modeled upon the way cinematography record[ed] visible material, and the treatment of music and sound effect [was] modeled upon the editing and laboratory work applied to the visual track'.[7] As outlined by James Lastra, developments in applying synchronized sound to film production were shaped by two progressive models of sound recording. The film industry first followed a 'perceptual fidelity' model that was based on principles of phonographic sound reproduction and enabled by early sound-on-disc systems, such as Vitaphone, which was used for early sound films including *The Jazz Singer* (1927).[8] The perceptual fidelity model presupposed that 'the camera be the eye and the microphone the ear of an imaginary person viewing the scene'.[9] The aim was to record a perfect replica of the live event of performance in the film studio and filmic space was to be created visually and acoustically through, for instance, volume regulation that would appear proportionate to the specific shot taking place.[10] This process 'privilege[d] the original sound event over all other considerations'.[11] However, while this approach recorded a copy of the original studio performance, it did not, in fact, produce the desired effect of tonal complexity, intelligible speech, and plausible spatial depth for audiences in the cinema.

Inspired by improvements in sound transmission in telephony, an alternative idea also began to emerge within the film industry in the early 1930s. Lastra describes this as a new model focussed on 'intelligibility' rather than 'perceptual fidelity': the intelligibility model was considerably more concerned with the outcome and the effect of the recording process for cinema audiences, which often required '"exaggerating" [sound] in order to "attract attention." Artificiality in order to produce the *effect* of naturalism. Directionality to produce the *effect* of attention'.[12] The intelligibility approach privileged recording and editing work that would produce the desired effects of realism and spatial depth in the cinema.[13] By being less

---

[7] David Bordwell, 'The Introduction of Sound', *The Classical Hollywood Cinema: Film Style & Mode of Production to 1960* (London: Routledge, 2002), pp. 298–308 (p. 301).

[8] Lastra, *Sound Technology and the American Cinema* (New York: Columbia University Press, 2000), p. 195.

[9] Lastra, *Sound Technology*, p. 183.

[10] Bordwell, 'The Introduction of Sound', p. 302.     [11] Lastra, *Sound Technology*, p. 182.

[12] Lastra, *Sound Technology*, p. 193.     [13] Lastra, *Sound Technology*, pp. 181–183.

78  LITERATURE AND SOUND FILM IN MID-CENTURY BRITAIN

faithful to the actual live performance in the film studio, sound recording and editing could enhance the illusion of filmic realism to an ever-greater degree. Helped along by technological innovation throughout the 1930s, this kind of curated intelligibility became more widely applied in the film industry. Lastra summarizes that 'it became the norm not to match visual and acoustic "scale", not to locate the microphone with the camera...and not to offer a perceptually based "coherent point of audition"'; rather, the emerging alternative approach focussed on 'enhancing intelligibility through close miking and soundproofing'.[14]

By 1935, it had become much easier to work with sound on a film set: the directional microphone, the development of the microphone boom, and reduced recording noise through the use of optical film all helped to make sound film more mobile on set, improved the volume range and intelligibility of the recorded voice, and gave studios greater flexibility in post-production editing.[15] As a consequence of these technological innovations and the industry's greater focus on curated intelligibility (as opposed to perceptual fidelity), synchronized dialogue was firmly established as the main element of 1930s commercial film production. Both Bordwell and Lastra suggest that, by the end of the transition phase, synchronized dialogue had become more than an attractive add-on to film. From about 1932, it was the key feature of film. Dialogue became 'the sound assumed to be most important to the narration' and to story progression.[16] Although Lastra rightly cautions that the 'dialogue track' could also contain sounds other than speech (for example, gun shots or a telephone ringing), it did mainly capture recorded speech. The dialogue track would take priority over other elements of film sound and 'the sonic background, described again and again as the very essence of sonic realism, [was] now effectively reduced to a generic *loop* that repeat[ed] endlessly, in the service of the dialogue track'.[17] Technological innovation and the practical experience of studios and industry professionals had led to the creation of well-modulated soundtracks which would largely be structured by applying the principle of the primacy of dialogue.[18] In the hierarchy of sound production, the dialogue track came to carry the highest

---

[14] Lastra, *Sound Technology*, p. 188.

[15] See Bordwell, pp. 300–302; Lea Jacobs, *Film Rhythm after Sound: Technology, Music, and Performance* (Oakland, CA: University of California Press, 2015), p. 166; Lastra, *Sound Technology*, p. 188.

[16] Lastra, *Sound Technology*, p. 187.      [17] Lastra, *Sound Technology*, p. 210.

[18] Hanson, *Hollywood Soundscapes*, p. 17.

significance for the development of character and story.[19] Recordists and editors would be tasked with placing dialogue and speech in the foreground of the soundtrack whereas sound effects, ambient noise, or music would become part of the sonic background. To improve intelligibility of the dialogue track, other sounds, even if they were natural to the setting or scene, sometimes had to be eliminated or pared down substantially while the 'importance of having the dialog [*sic*] always clearly understandable [went] without saying'.[20]

In addition to the dominant role taken by dialogue during the production process, spoken interaction on screen also became key to maintaining the audience's experience of synchronicity and thereby also vital to marketing sound film's greatest asset. Dialogue offered filmmakers the most important and most frequent synch points that could create and sustain the illusion of speech emanating from the image. As Donnelly notes, such 'coalescence is taken by the audience as an assumption of relationship, an admittance of direct connection. This is essentially a psychological process'.[21] Sarah Kozloff further considers the function of film dialogue in relation to the film image. Dialogue, she rightly notes, serves multiple purposes beyond a mere communication of filmic narrative or characterization. Indeed, film dialogue fulfils aesthetic, commercial, and ideological functions.[22] The technological conditions outlined by Donnelly, such as the frequent use of dialogue as synch points of sound and image, are key to film's ability to establish its diegetic world, to assert the impression of filmic realism, and to construct causality.[23] The sound–image interplay facilitated by synchronized dialogue allows film to offer an ideological or aesthetic meta-commentary on the action that is shown. Synchronized sound–image connections are also especially suited to the commercial exploitation of what Kozloff describes as 'star turns'.[24] These points will be illustrated further in the following discussion of Alexander Korda's peculiarly British take on screwball comedy, *The Divorce of Lady X*.

---

[19] Lastra reminds readers that the dialogue track could also contain non-verbal sound that would be considered key to developing the filmic narrative (e.g., the sound of a bomb exploding, a telephone ringing, a gunshot). However, speech was the primary component of the dialogue track.

[20] Lastra, *Sound Technology*, p. 204.     [21] Donnelly, *Occult Aesthetics*, p. 43.

[22] Sarah Kozloff, *Overhearing Film Dialogue* (Berkely, CA: University of California Press, 2000), pp. 33–34.

[23] See Kozloff, *Film Dialogue*, p. 33.     [24] Kozloff, *Film Dialogue*, p. 34.

# 80 LITERATURE AND SOUND FILM IN MID-CENTURY BRITAIN

The 1930s were a great period of experimentation during which directors and actors discovered how film dialogue could influence pace and mood of individual scenes and whole films. Lea Jacobs, for instance, argues convincingly that many scenes of Howard Hawks's films are 'organized around a "word score"', which allowed the director increasing 'rhythmic control' over film.[25] 'The structure of dialogue', Jacobs writes further, 'fulfills several rhythmic functions without the benefit of a beat. Speech allows control of duration at a very refined level—to fractions of a second.'[26] Jacobs's illuminating discussion of dialogue's role in film rhythm highlights the importance of speech for filmic pace. It also points to how image–sound interaction is shaped by careful and deliberate editing. There are at least four major categories of designing image–sound interaction which all entail a different type of synchronization: a 'dialogue-based' approach, a 'sound effects-based' approach, sound as 'punctuation', and the widely known principle of 'mickey-mousing'.[27]

In the dialogue-based approach, the visual image of characters talking is closely matched to the recorded speech; here, synch points are formed by the film image showing a character's mouth movements and matching up these movements to appear 'consistent with the sounds of the words' that audiences hear on the soundtrack.[28] Donnelly calls this dialogue-based approach the 'degree zero style' of sound film.[29] It is in these moments of visible lip synch that sound and image give the impression of their closest coherence. In this form of synchronization, sound is firmly anchored in the visual diegesis as voices are presented as directly emanating from the characters that audiences see on screen.

The sound effects-based approach works similarly in that audiences 'see and hear activities that occur simultaneously' (for example, a telephone ringing or a gunshot firing).[30] Mickey-mousing describes the matching of music to visual activities on screen, whereby the music seems to either mimic or enhance the rhythm of visual action. Jacobs evocatively describes this process as a 'synchronization between movement and/or cutting and the beat'.[31] The dialogue-based approach to image–sound interaction leads to the perceptual experience of tightly aligned synchronicity and is the most naturally applicable to this chapter's analysis of dialogue in sound film and

---

[25] Lea Jacobs, *Film Rhythm after Sound: Technology, Music, and Performance* (Oakland, CA: University of California Press, 2015), p. 216.

[26] Jacobs, *Film Rhythm*, p. 216.  [27] Donnelly, *Occult Aesthetics*, pp. 32–33.

[28] Donnelly, *Occult Aesthetics*, p. 4.  [29] Donnelly, *Occult Aesthetics*, p. 32.

[30] Donnelly, *Occult Aesthetics*, p. 32.  [31] Jacobs, *Film Rhythm*, p. 58.

# DIALOGUE AND INTELLIGIBILITY   81

mid-century fiction. However, the idea of sound as a means of 'punctuation' proves equally fruitful: both Donnelly and Michel Chion have theorized sound as a means of punctuation in cinema. Sound as punctuation means that

> there are sonic emphases on an element such as a cut, a piece of dialogue (such as a revelation), a particular shot, or dramatic camera movement. The impetus is from narration rather than representation and consequently it often (although not always) takes place in the non-diegetic music and tends to 'underline' narrative activity.[32]

Such 'punctuative use of sound in relation to the visuals' forms an element of 'auditory setting';[33] sound as punctuation 'creates and defines film space' and serves as a sonic guide to visual rhythm and narration. The punctuative use of sound can complement, support, or undercut dialogue–image interaction. It can function as a counterpoint to the image, as proposed in Eisenstein's theory of montage, but can equally form a sonic emphasis and enhance the visuals.[34]

In light of the narrative and aesthetic opportunities offered by dialogue–image interaction, it is hardly surprising that the film industry of the 1930s became increasingly concerned with a number of key factors involved in screen talk: first, the actor's delivery of lines; and, second, the timbre or tonal quality of the speaking voice itself. The transition to sound film created a new, expansive market for voice coaches, and major studios such as MGM and Paramount set up vocal training departments for their actors due to the widespread belief that the voice could be trained and shaped to fit the new requirements of the talking picture.[35] As early as 1931, voice was considered an essential element of filmic characterization, scene-setting, and typecasting. An actor's 'vocal style had to be intelligible and intelligent, fit the character and dramatic situation, and, most important, convey a sense of illusionistic "presence"'.[36] The speaking voice, married to the film image, became a central feature of a film character's individuality and also a

---

[32] Donnelly, *Occult Aesthetics*, p. 32.   [33] Chion, *Audio-Vision*, p. 48 and pp. 54–55.

[34] On Eisenstein's theory of montage and the possibility of using sound as counterpoint, see Sergei Eisenstein, W. I. Pudovkin, and G. V. Alexandrov, 'Statement on Sound', in Richard Taylor (ed.), *The Eisenstein Reader* (London: BFI, 1998), pp. 80–81. An excellent discussion of early theories of sound as counterpoint can be found in Kristin Thompson, 'Early Sound Counterpoint', *Yale French Studies* 60 (1980), 115–140.

[35] Donald Crafton, *The Talkies: American Cinema's Transition to Sound, 1926–1931* (New York: Scribner, 1997), pp. 445–479.

[36] Crafton, *The Talkies*, p. 459.

82  LITERATURE AND SOUND FILM IN MID-CENTURY BRITAIN

mark of distinction for an actor's public persona. The tonal quality of the voice, in combination with looks and accent, notably shaped public image and informed filmic typecasting on the basis of both vocal capacity and looks. Fans, the press, and producers often commented on performers' vocal abilities and accents. As noted by Crafton, Surrey-born Ronald Colman, for instance, came to personify the ideal English gentleman in Hollywood films of the 1930s and 1940s due to his clear diction, British accent, and the warm timbre of his speaking voice.[37] In Britain, Jessie Matthews took elocution lessons to shape her pronunciation into a distinctive upper-class accent.[38] Her well-trained voice and 'posh' accent, coupled with her doll-shaped face and graceful, fluid movements as a dancer, made her the perfect choice for playing stylish, elegant women in a number of successful musical comedies, including *Evergreen* (1934), *First A Girl* (1935), and *Sailing Along* (1938). In contrast to Matthews's elegant persona, Gracie Fields's Lancashire accent and her impressive vocal range as a singer were her trademark features. Fields's distinctive accent was her asset, but it also meant that she was mostly typecast as a working-class or lower-middle-class character and her roles usually involved music-hall and comedy elements as exemplified by films such as *Sally in Our Alley* (1931), *This Week of Grace* (1933), and *Sing as We Go* (1934). Voice and accent, alongside looks, determined the casting of these women: while Matthews was marketed as the elegant, feminine 'dancing divinity', Fields's accent and voice typified her as the down-to-earth Lancashire 'lass'.[39]

This same mechanism of typecasting on the basis of voice, accent, and looks is also at work in Alexander Korda's *The Divorce of Lady X*, starring Merle Oberon and Laurence Olivier. In a letter dated 21 July 1938, a young London typist outlines why she enjoyed Korda's film, noting that 'the voices in it weren't particularly affected, and Oberon's voice is beautiful I think.... I have always liked Oberon...because she hasn't gone Hollywood and doesn't indulge in giving a lot of tripey interviews.'[40] By 1938, Merle Oberon was a popular actress both in Britain and in Hollywood. Her rapid rise to

---

[37] Crafton, *The Talkies*, pp. 460–461.

[38] Sarah Street, '"Got to Dance my Way to Heaven": Jessie Matthews, Art Deco and the British Musical of the 1930s', *Studies in European Cinema*, 2.1 (2005), 19–30 (p. 21).

[39] For further discussion of both Fields and Matthews, see chapters 10 and 12 of Jeffrey Richards, *The Age of the Dream Palace: Cinema and Society in 1930s Britain,* revd edn (London: Tauris, 2009).

[40] Betty M. Swallow and Helen Bradley, *Dear Helen: Wartime Letters from a Londoner to her American Pen Pal,* ed. Russell M. Jones and John H. Swanson (Columbia, MO: University of Missouri Press, 2009), pp. 37–38.

stardom began when Korda gave her the part of Anne Boleyn in *The Private Life of Henry VIII* (1933). Upon being discovered by Korda, she 'threw herself into intensive voice training; she was aware that she still had a hint of the odd, almost Welsh lilt of Anglo-Indian speech.'[41] Throughout her career, Oberon concealed that she had been born in 1911 in British India and, instead, pretended to have been born in Tasmania.[42] Likely fearing possible stigmatization due to her family history, ethnicity, and accent, she created a public persona whose 'whiteness' would not be questioned. Her photogenic beauty, coupled with her relentless voice training, made her an extremely successful and sought-after performer in mid-1930s Britain. Olivier, by 1938, had already made his name as a Shakespeare actor—not least due to his studies at The Royal Central School of Speech and Drama, where Elsie Fogerty was teaching the 'voice beautiful' approach to aspiring actors. This approach trained 'a highly articulated and resonant performance voice that made use of a heightened and aestheticised version of RP.'[43] Olivier, known for his impeccable speaking voice, ideally represented the type of the sophisticated and well-educated educated upper-class gentleman. In *The Divorce of Lady X*, Olivier and Oberon were paired to great effect.

## *The Divorce of Lady X* (1938)

*The Divorce of Lady X* was directed by Tim Whelan and must be considered a vital part of British cinema history as one of only seven feature-length film productions in Technicolor in Britain before the Second World War.[44] The production is a British take on the genre of screwball comedy, featuring engaging verbal sparring matches and an entertaining battle of the sexes. Olivier plays the divorce lawyer Everard Logan who ends up involuntarily sharing a hotel room with Oberon's Leslie Steele as dense London fog

---

[41] Charles Higham and Roy Moseley, *Princess Merle: The Romantic Life of Merle Oberon* (New York: Pocket Books, 1952), p. 52. Oberon's voice training has also been discussed more recently in Babli Sinha, 'A "Strangely Un-English Actress": Race, Legibility, and the Films of Merle Oberon', *Journal of Popular Film and Television* 44.4 (2016), 220–226 (p. 223).

[42] Angela Woollacott, 'Colonial Origins and Audience Collusion: The Merle Oberon Story in 1930s Australia', in Desley Deacon, Penny Russell, and Angela Woollacott (eds), *Transnational Lives: Biographies of Global Modernity, 1700–Present* (London: Palgrave Macmillan, 2010), 96–108.

[43] Maggie Inchley, *Voice and New Writing, 1997–2007* (London: Palgrave Macmillan, 2015), pp. 49–50.

[44] Sarah Street, *Colour Films in Britain: The Negotiation of Innovation, 1900–1955* (London: Bloomsbury, 2019), p. 68.

## 84  LITERATURE AND SOUND FILM IN MID-CENTURY BRITAIN

prevents their respective journeys home late one night. Much to his dismay, and entirely against his better judgement, Logan is smitten with the confident, witty Leslie, but because she refuses to give him her name, he falsely concludes that she must be the cheating wife of his latest, wealthy client, Lord Mere, in an unfolding high-profile divorce case. The film cleverly uses dialogue, speech patterns, and voice–image interaction to characterize Logan and Leslie and to facilitate narrative progression. In a fascinating inversion of the 'fast-talking dames' of American screwball comedy, *The Divorce of Lady X* effectively positions Oberon's Leslie as the substantially calmer, more collected character whilst Olivier's Logan often hectically delivers line after line.[45] The more flustered his speech becomes, the calmer Leslie responds to his verbal outbursts. Consider, for instance, the following scene just after Leslie, in need of a bed for the night in the overcrowded hotel, has 'crept' into Logan's opulent hotel suite, which he refuses to share with anyone else:

LOGAN: May I ask when you propose to creep out again?

LESLIE: [Pause] Oh, after the usual eight hours and breakfast.

LOGAN: Oh really? So we're going to bunk in together, are we?

LESLIE: [Pause] There are two rooms. One for each of us.

LOGAN: Yes, but both beds are in here.

LESLIE: There's a couch in there. You can have the couch. [she walks to the dresser by the bed]

LOGAN: What? [screeches] Of all the shameless impudence was there ever anything more female? And you actually thought you could get away with it!

LESLIE: If you had any decent feelings, you'd insist on turning out.

LOGAN: Did you or did you not hear what I said to the manager?

LESLIE: Naturally I overheard some of it.

LOGAN: Yes, with so little feeling that you pinched my bed from under my very nose knowing perfectly well that I've been up for two nights and I've got a hard day's work tomorrow assuming I can't resist your fascination. [Pause] [sighs] I'm really very sleepy, will you please go?

LESLIE: You don't really mean that. You're much too nice to turn me out.

---

[45] On women in American screwball comedy, see Maria DiBattista, *Fast-Talking Dames* (Yale: Yale University Press, 2001) and the first chapter of Heidi Wilkins's *Talkies, Road Movies and Chick Flicks: Gender, Genre and Film Sound in American Cinema* (Edinburgh: Edinburgh University Press, 2016).

# DIALOGUE AND INTELLIGIBILITY    85

LOGAN: Nice? I'm glad that you don't know me. The trouble with me is that I'm weak. A charming young girl like you could bear anything over on me in five minutes, but at least I know my weakness so I force myself to be rude. Sometimes even brutal.

LESLIE: You do like talking about yourself, don't you?

LOGAN: Why yes, most men do. But at least they know the truth about themselves. Women don't. They only know the truth about each other.

LESLIE: Well, we'll have a nice long talk about you some other time. Now, as you're so very tired, I won't keep you up. So, good night. [she walks to the bed]

LOGAN: What did you say?

LESLIE: I said 'good night'.

LOGAN: Quite, yes, I heard you say 'good night', but what do you mean by saying 'good night'? You can't come here saying things like that. Look here, [stammers] I'm I'm I'm very very tired would you please go?

LESLIE: You don't mean that.

LOGAN: Oh yes, I do. I've met too many women like you before. Conceited, sure of yourself, and sure of your power over men, utterly unscrupulous, ruthless, conceited, spoilt. [pointing his finger at her]

LESLIE: Don't do that. [she grabs the hand pointing at her]

LOGAN: Married aren't you?

LESLIE: [Pause] Yes.

LOGAN: Yes, yes, I knew. There's a poor wretched husband waiting for you, sitting at home, wondering where you are, hoping against hope that his worst fears aren't justified. And this time for once they aren't, this time you're with a man who isn't the least bit stirred by your charms. Now, I must repeat, will you please…

LESLIE: How do you know so much about women?

LOGAN: Because in my profession I have to be able to see what's behind those lovely deceiving lips.

LESLIE: Are you a dentist?[46]

Leslie communicates mostly in confident one-liners. Her voice remains steady and calm and does not significantly change in pitch or tone throughout this conversation. Her brief matter-of-fact replies are the composed

---

[46] *The Divorce of Lady X*, featuring Laurence Olivier and Merle Oberon, produced by Alexander Korda, directed by Tim Whelan (London Films, 1938). Typescript of this dialogue scene by the author, including notes on character movement, intonation, and pauses.

## 86 LITERATURE AND SOUND FILM IN MID-CENTURY BRITAIN

repartee to Logan's increasingly flustered demeanour. He repeats himself, even giving the impression of a brief stutter. His speech indicates that he is fighting for his composure as he tries to navigate Leslie out of his room. Not only does he have more lines than Leslie, he also speaks much quicker than she does, so that some of his syllables are swallowed and the end of one sentence merges into the beginning of another: 'You can't come here saying things like that. Look here...'. On average, Logan speaks about four to five words per second while Leslie articulates only about two to three words per second in this scene. Logan thus delivers his lines approximately at double the speed than Leslie. In addition, Logan makes use of a fuller range of pitch and volume. His voice hits much higher notes ('What did you say?') and his speaking volume clearly increases, for instance when he lectures Leslie on his personal catalogue of the faults of women.

In this scene, film dialogue is essential to narrative development and to the characterization of Logan and Leslie. The rhythm and delivery of their speeches establishes their relationship and sets the pace. The speed and intonation of each sentence creates what Elizabeth Bowen, in relation to literary fiction, would later describe as the 'psychological materialization of the characters'.[47] Audiences learn that Logan is a fast talker—professionally and privately. They also learn that he struggles to control his temper when being challenged and that he becomes flustered when a situation can no longer be controlled (either physically or verbally) by himself. In contrast, Leslie appears more playful, confident, and unconventional. She uses pauses and draws out her short sentences to deliberately throw Logan off-balance. Audiences quickly learn that she has the upper hand on Logan in this battle of the sexes. In this first encounter, both their accents and word play suggest that they are wealthy, educated upper-class characters (Leslie is, in fact, the daughter of a judge with a genteel family background).

The performers' differing speeds of delivery set an interesting filmic pace in this scene which oscillates between slowing down and speeding up, creating tension and keeping audiences on their toes. The conversation demonstrates dialogue's potential to create opposition and tension between the characters whose resolution (or, at least, tempering) will form the driving force of the story in a classic 'will they or won't they' narrative. As such, the dialogue is functional in a number of ways: it sets in motion filmic action, it introduces elements of characterization and psychological motivation;

---

[47] Elizabeth Bowen, 'Notes on Writing a Novel', in Hermione Lee (ed.), *The Mulberry Tree: Writings of Elizabeth Bowen* (London: Vintage, 1999), 35–48 (p. 41).

it also contributes to audiences' understanding of characters; and it creates tension by contrasting differing speech patterns that reflect the underlying screwball comedy theme of 'opposites attract'.

This sequence of the film uses tight, dialogue-based synchronization, aligning mouth movements with the words that are spoken. The dialogue is mainly filmed in a classic shot-reverse shot sequence which usually shows the character talking in a medium shot or upper-body shot. In addition, there are sound effects based synch sequences, such as the sound of footsteps on the floorboards as Leslie and Logan are walking around the room. In addition, the sequence uses sound cues as punctuation marks to emphasize key actions. As Leslie walks towards Logan's hotel room door, her walk is accompanied by non-diegetic music. When she then moves to take the 'Do not disturb' sign off his hotel room door, her action is accompanied by high-pitched, plucked strings that draw attention to her action. The non-diegetic music continues as Leslie enters the room, where Logan is on the phone and initially does not notice her. When she begins talking to him and he finally becomes aware of her presence in the room, the non-diegetic music stops completely. There is a moment of silence as the two characters are taking each other in (this is conveyed through shot-reverse shot filming). The absence of non-diegetic music or sound is then maintained for the duration of the two characters' dialogue. This, of course, allows audiences to focus on the spoken exchange, but, from a technical point, it also improves intelligibility. As Logan, after much discussion, finally agrees to let Leslie stay in his room, Leslie jumps at him to give him a brief hug, exclaiming 'Yes!' At this precise point, the non-diegetic music starts up again with a flourish as she is jumping to hug him. Here, the musical flourish provides a further punctuative use of sound: it marks the end of this initial spoken interaction, the end of the 'meet-cute', but it also emphasizes the sudden physical contact between the characters who have previously been circling around each other in the hotel bedroom.

## Elizabeth Bowen on Dialogue

'Plot', Elizabeth Bowen wrote in 1945, 'is diction. Action of language, language of action.'[48] Throughout her career as a writer, Bowen commented repeatedly, in different essays and broadcasts, on the relationship between

---

[48] Bowen, 'Notes on Writing a Novel', p. 35.

88  LITERATURE AND SOUND FILM IN MID-CENTURY BRITAIN

dialogue, diction, and the mechanics of storytelling, amounting to what Allan Hepburn describes as 'a practitioner's theory of the novel.'[49] Much of Bowen's 'theory' is doubtlessly influenced not merely by cinema, but also by her experience of writing and speaking for radio. As Hepburn notes, Bowen became a 'regular contributor' to the BBC's radio programme from the early 1940s to the 1970s.[50] She became familiar with the demands radio placed on the writer, such as the requirement for sound and voice to convey action, character, and location. Bowen wrote broadcasts, such as *New Judgement: Elizabeth Bowen on Jane Austen* (which aired in March 1942) and *London Revisited: As Seen by Fanny Burney* (which aired in November 1942).[51] She also gave speeches, interviews, and participated in the BBC series 'Book Talk: New and Recent Fiction'.

In her 'Notes on Writing a Novel', which were first published in *Orion* in 1945, Bowen addresses 'Plot', 'Characters', 'Scene', 'Dialogue', 'Angle', 'Advance', and 'Relevance' in literary fiction. In these sections, Bowen articulates an audio-visual understanding of literary fiction that is significantly shaped both by her experience of working in radio and her pronounced interest in film. Indeed, she closely aligns the role of the novelist with that of a film director: 'the cinema, with its actual camera-work, is interesting study for the novelist. In a good film, the camera's movement, angle and distance have all worked towards one thing—the fullest possible realization of the director's idea.'[52] However, it is not *merely* camera-work or visual imagination that ought to guide the work of the novelist-director. According to Bowen, it is dialogue that is at the heart of the novelist's craft. Bowen grounds her analysis in the complementarity of audio-vision. Dialogue, she writes, is at once the most important and the most demanding element of literary fiction: it

> must appear realistic without being so. Actual realism—the lifting, as it were, of passages from a stenographer's take-down of a 'real life' conversation—would be disruptive. Of what? Of the illusion of the novel.... What must novel dialogue, behind [the] mask of these faked realistic qualities, really be and do? It must be pointed, intentional, relevant.

---

[49] Allan Hepburn, 'The Heroic Today: Elizabeth Bowen and the Technique of the Novel', *Irish University Review*, 51.1 (2021), 57–71 (p. 57).

[50] Allan Hepburn (ed.), 'Introduction', in *Listening In: Broadcasts, Speeches, and Interviews by Elizabeth Bowen* (Edinburgh: Edinburgh University Press, 2010), 1–23 (p. 1).

[51] The broadcasts and plays are included in Hepburn's collection *Listening In: Broadcasts, Speeches, and Interviews by Elizabeth Bowen*, pp. 39–62.

[52] Bowen, 'Notes on Writing a Novel', p. 43.

It must crystallise situation. It must express character. It must advance plot.... Dialogue provides means for the psychological materialization of the characters.... Every sentence in dialogue should be descriptive of the character who is speaking. Idiom, tempo, and shape of each spoken sentence should be calculated by [the] novelist, towards this descriptive end.... Failure in any one piece of dialogue is a loss, at once to the continuity and the comprehensibility of the novel.[53]

Dialogue had to fulfil a number of different functions: the textual mediation of different features of speech, such as idiom and tempo, could distil a situation and develop character and plot for the reader. Interestingly, Bowen notes that dialogue must *appear* 'realistic without being so', that a mere 'stenographic' fidelity to real-life conversation is not suitable for achieving the desired effect of an 'illusion' of real life in the novel.

These ideas, at their core, are of course closely related to the experience Bowen had drawn from radio (attention to sound, vocal intelligibility, expressiveness of voice); but they can be equally aligned with the film industry's fidelity/intelligibility debate as outlined by James Lastra, whereby realistic sound–image interaction for cinema audiences was not produced through the faithful recording and reproduction of action on the sound stage, but by artificial addition and enhancement of dialogue and sound effects as well as careful editing. Furthermore, Bowen presents dialogue as a means of multi-dimensional representation in the novel: 'every sentence' needs to be 'descriptive of the character who is speaking' and 'crystallize situation' in addition to serving as the 'psychological materialization' of the novel's cast of characters. If dialogue fails, it is a 'loss of continuity and comprehensibility'.[54] While these are reflections stemming from Bowen's own literary practice, they may be equally instructive to her fellow novelists and contemporary filmmakers. In her 'Notes', Bowen asserts the crucial importance of dialogue for the novelist and points to speech as a key element for establishing 'relevance' and meaning: dialogue is 'illustrative' of character but also a 'part of action, a means of advancing plot'.[55] In effect, these thoughts on the audio-visuality of dialogue within literary fiction share a great deal with the evolving principle of the primacy of dialogue in mid-century film.

---

[53] Bowen, 'Notes on Writing a Novel', pp. 41–42.
[54] Bowen, 'Notes on Writing a Novel', p. 42.
[55] Bowen, 'Notes on Writing a Novel', p. 47.

90  LITERATURE AND SOUND FILM IN MID-CENTURY BRITAIN

Bowen's short stories exemplify her interest in interaction and conversation from different angles. 'Oh, Madam...' (1941) is arguably one of Bowen's most overt experiments in exploring the nature of literary dialogue with reference to its underlying audio-visual dimensions. This story, inspired by Katherine Mansfield's 'The Lady's Maid' (1920), consists entirely of a housemaid's conversation with her mistress on the morning following a German air raid which destroyed parts of their house and a nearby cinema in London. The story is written as a one-sided dialogue, which gives readers solely the maid's speech while her employer's responses and interjections can only be inferred from the maid's answers. This approach allows Bowen to focus entirely on one character's speech patterns and to demonstrate the productivity of dialogue for stimulating visual scene-setting and for developing characterization, action, narrative space, and psychological complexity:

> The drawing-room? Oh, *madam*...Very well...*There!*
>
> I don't know what to say: really...You know, madam, I'd rather last night again than have to show you all this. [...] It used to sort of sparkle, didn't it, in its way...As it is—why, look, madam: just this rub with my apron and the cabinet starts to come up again, doesn't it? Like a mirror—look—as though nothing had happened...If I could get started in here—but what am I talking about! The windows gone—it doesn't look decent, does it...Oh, I know, madam, I know: your satin curtains, madam! Torn and torn, like a maniac been at them. Well, he *is* a maniac, isn't he?...Yes, it did look worse—I swept up a bit in here. But I don't seem to have any head—I didn't know where to start.
>
> That's right, madam, go on the balcony. You won't see so much different from there. To look at the park, you wouldn't hardly believe...Sun shining...Well, it may do good, I suppose.[56]

The story uses a paragraph structure, which frequently indicates changes in scenery or spatial movement of the characters through the house. In this example, for instance, the paragraph structure follows a spatial and visual movement from the employer asking the maid to be taken to the drawing room, then being taken to the drawing room, and, finally, the employer stepping outside on the balcony. Each movement triggers a new line of conversation. Ellipses mainly suggest the interlocutor's responses and questions

---

[56] Elizabeth Bowen, 'Oh, Madam...', *The Collected Stories of Elizabeth Bowen* (London: Vintage, 1999), 647–652 (p. 649).

DIALOGUE AND INTELLIGIBILITY 91

to the maid's flow of speech, but may also indicate pauses, breaks, and hesitations in the dialogue as the two women make their way through the partially destroyed house. Punctuation and italicization function as markers of intonation and emphasis ('Oh, *madam…*Very well…*There!*'). In a move that appears parallel to the punctuative use of sound in film editing, which can serve to emphasize cuts, camera movements, or particular actions, textual formatting and punctuation highlight the visual and haptic experience of the bombed home and form a textual visualization of intonation and emphasis in conversation.

Dashes, italicization, and ellipses gain importance as the story progresses. The employer communicates her decision to have the house closed down and to retire to 'her ladyship's house' in the countryside.[57] The maid is distraught:

No such great hurry?—I don't understand—I—you—why, madam? *Wouldn't* you wish—? Why, no, I suppose not, madam…I hadn't thought. You feel you don't really…Not after all this. *But you couldn't ever, not this beautiful house!* You couldn't ever…I know many ladies *are*. I know many ladies feel it is for the best. You can't but notice all those good houses shut. But, madam, this seemed so much your home—[58]

The employer's decision to abandon the house is met with shock and panic. Repetition ('you couldn't ever…') conveys both disbelief and despair at the situation. While the maid previously communicated mostly in full sentences, giving an impression of relative composure, her state of emotional upheaval is now indicated by speech dissolving into fragments. Bowen's story is thus constructed solely out of one half of an extended piece of dialogue between two women. She would later reprise this narrative strategy in her novel *The Heat of the Day* (1948), in which the protagonist Stella is interrogated on the possibility of her (now deceased) lover Robert Kelway having been a Nazi spy.[59] Here, as in 'Oh, Madam…', the one-sided dialogue reflects a character's response to authority (the maid answering her employer, Stella having to supply answers to the coroner's court), whereby 'situation' is created by the narrator without any kind of narratorial description. In both cases, dialogue (even of the one-sided kind) uniquely explores the capacity of written speech to move beyond mere characterization. In 'Oh, Madam…',

---

[57] Bowen, 'Oh, Madam…', p. 651.    [58] Bowen, 'Oh, Madam…', pp. 650–651.
[59] Elizabeth Bowen, *The Heat of the Day* (New York: Anchor, 2002), pp. 340–344.

92  LITERATURE AND SOUND FILM IN MID-CENTURY BRITAIN

readers experience situation and the imaginary, visual movement through the narrative space of the bombed house as well as the psychological consequences of an air raid mediated purely through speech.

The exploration of different dimensions and functions of dialogue continues in much of Bowen's wartime fiction, notably 'Careless Talk', which was first published in October 1941 in *The New Yorker* as 'Everything's Frightfully Interesting'.[60] The story showcases what Hepburn describes as key components of Bowen's aesthetic, namely her talent for conveying 'impression', her sensitivity 'to atmosphere and place', and her ability to 'render visually' places in terms 'of light and image'.[61] As in the previous example of 'Oh Madam,…', Bowen's gift for conveying the visual and the atmospheric is, in effect, an audio-visual matter: in this story, the text creates and sustains atmosphere and 'crystallizes situation' largely through speech. 'Careless Talk' follows a conversation between four characters (Joanna, Mary, Eric, and Ponsonby) over lunch at a busy restaurant in wartime London. In the space of just over four pages, the story combines vacuous Home Front conversation between acquaintances with the pressures of wartime rationing. As Céline Magot observes, the story suggests that, in wartime, 'words lose their substance' and 'dialogue becomes a denial of exchange'.[62] Mary's speeches, especially, are marked by repetition and an inflationary use of adverbs and adjectives, a 'word shortage', as noted by Magot: 'How good, how kind, *how* thoughtful!'[63] Interaction between characters is vague throughout the story and, in keeping with this impression of superficial conversation, there is frequent repetition of verbs and nouns that do not denote a specific, defined object or activity ('happen', 'thing', 'matter'). The story uses ellipses, italics, and dashes more sparingly than 'Oh, Madam…', but it relies heavily on indefinite pronouns ('something', 'everything', 'anything'), further suggesting indeterminacy.[64] 'Careless Talk' derives its plot purely from vacuous conversation, demonstrating the emptiness of character interaction.

In 'Songs My Father Sang Me' (1944), a young woman on a date tells the story of her father leaving her on her seventh birthday. The interaction

---

[60] The story was retitled as a reference to the British Ministry of Information propaganda campaign 'Careless Talk Costs Lives', launched in 1942.

[61] Allan Hepburn, 'Introduction', Allan Hepburn (ed.), *People, Places, Things: Essays by Elizabeth Bowen* (Edinburgh: Edinburgh University Press, 2008), 1–23 (p. 7).

[62] Céline Magot, '"Careless Talk": Word Shortage in Elizabeth Bowen's Wartime Writing', *Miranda*, 2 (2010), 3 July 2010. http://journals.openedition.org/miranda/1189 (accessed 8 April 2022).

[63] Bowen, 'Careless Talk', *The Collected Stories of Elizabeth Bowen*, pp. 750–754 (p. 750).

[64] Bowen, 'Careless Talk', p. 752.

DIALOGUE AND INTELLIGIBILITY  93

between the woman and her partner functions as a frame narrative to an embedded story of abandonment. The frame dialogue is short and snappy:

> 'Then anything isn't really the matter, then?'
> 'This tune, this song, is the matter.'
> 'Oh—shall we dance?'
> 'No.'…It's what they are playing—this tune.'
> 'It's pre-war', he said knowledgeably.
> 'It's last war.'
> 'Well, last war's pre-war.'[65]

In contrast to these short, stichomythic sentences and the quick back-and-forth between the two speakers in the frame narrative, the woman's story of abandonment is delivered in long, monologic speeches which focus on her childhood experience of loss. The more words the woman uses in her attempt to convey the events of her seventh birthday, the less she appears to comprehend her father's decision to leave his family:[66]

> 'I licked pastry-crumbs off my chin and began on chocolate. By this time my father lay on his back, with his fingers thatched together over his eyes: he talked, but more to the sky than me. None of the things he was saying now went anywhere near my brain—a child's brain, how could they?—his actual words are gone as though I had never heard them, but his meaning lodged itself in some part of my inside and is still there and has grown up with me. He talked about war and how he had once felt, and about leaves and love and dancing and going back to the war, then the birth of me.'[67]

The story constructs two timelines: one for the frame narrative and one for the embedded narrative drawing on her memories. The distinction between the two timelines hinges on setting up two different speech patterns for the woman. While the frame narrative is characterized by brief and, at times, dismissive exchanges with her partner, the re-told experience of the seventh birthday is a long, monologic narrative that contains fragments of remembered conversation with her father.

---

[65] Bowen, 'Songs My Father Sang Me', *The Collected Stories of Elizabeth Bowen*, pp. 730–742 (p. 730).
[66] Neil Corcoran, *Elizabeth Bowen: The Enforced Return* (Oxford: Oxford University Press, 2004), p. 157.
[67] Bowen, 'Songs My Father Sang Me', p. 739.

## 94  LITERATURE AND SOUND FILM IN MID-CENTURY BRITAIN

These brief examples illustrate some of Bowen's theoretical reflections on literary dialogue, its grounding in the audio-visual imagination, and the possibilities offered by a mediatized textuality: speech facilitates characterization, relationships, and plot development; it 'crystallizes' and 'materializes' narrative situation. 'Oh, Madam...', although only containing one speaker's side of dialogue, aptly captures emphasis, pauses, and hesitations whilst also indicating the speaker's increasing anxiety and emotional exhaustion. Even in 'Careless Talk', where the interaction between all characters seems neither to the point nor particularly meaningful, the dialogue visualizes the scene and circumstances as diction becomes action. 'Careless Talk' uniquely reflects on the problem of failed conversation, highlighting a superfluous use of language and illustrating how, in a wartime setting, words may become devoid of meaning. In 'Songs My Father Sang Me', the contrast between the frame dialogue and the women's embedded recollections of her father's abandonment offers an in-depth psychological portrait but also an interweaving of narrative timelines that are brought to the reader's attention through a difference in style and speech patterns. Thus, Bowen's theoretical reflections on, as well as her writing of dialogue, strongly resonate with the period's evolving conventions for screen dialogue. The characteristics outlined by Bowen for literary dialogue—the idea of artifice to create the impression of realism, the prioritization of dialogue due to its capacity to facilitate plot development, the illusion of psychological causality, and the idea that a failure of dialogue also meant a failure of 'continuity'—equally hold for the principles of synchronized sound film with its focus on curated intelligibility.

## Henry Green on Speech and Vision

Henry Green's essays, reviews, and radio broadcasts equally offer insightful remarks on the relationship between writing and conversation: in a broadcast piece titled 'A Novelist to his Readers', Green asserts that the 'best way for the novelist to communicate with his readers' is through (literary) dialogue and that the printed text presented the most 'direct' channel to communicate 'with the imagination of his readers'.[68] In a review of James Sutherland's *The Oxford Book of English Talk* (1953), Green commented that 'no anthology

---

[68]  Henry Green, 'A Novelist to his Readers', Matthew Yorke (ed.), *Surviving: The Uncollected Writings of Henry Green* (London: Harvill, 1993), 136–142 (p. 137).

DIALOGUE AND INTELLIGIBILITY    95

can be as successful as a gramophone record made off a concealed microphone and possibly nothing would be more untypical or boring than such a record. Art must intrude.'[69] He proceeds to ask whether the novelist can actually produce 'an accurate rendering of contemporary speech' since 'the whole difficulty, which anyone who writes dialogue knows only too well—[is] that written dialogue is not like the real thing, and can never be'.[70] While he believes that the spoken word is 'the great source of our language' and that fictional dialogue, as outlined by Bowen, is indeed 'the first case of the novelist's need for notation from real life', Green is also adamant that the real-life repetitions, pauses, and mannerisms of speech 'will never do in print'.[71] Instead, Green aims to construct writing that is 'non-representational',[72] meaning it is not an accurate transcription of what real life looks and sounds like, but an individual and stylized approximation that is nevertheless designed to produce an intended effect in the reader. It is especially dialogue that Green is interested in. In order to 'create life, of a kind, in the reader', literature had to resort to dialogue: 'Because we do not write letters any more, we ring up on the telephone instead. The communication between human beings has now come to be almost entirely conducted by conversation'.[73] The kind of writing, the kind of dialogue, that is required though, is 'non-representational'—it is not 'an exact record of the way people talk'.[74] Green adds that it is often the 'tone…which carries the meaning' and that 'what is left unsaid…gives us food for thought'.[75] He is interested in how fictional dialogue might convey, in writing, tone and emphasis as well as the hidden meanings and visual-behavioural clues surrounding spoken interaction that one often encounters in real life. Much of Green's writing seems to 'surrender all the conventionalities of fiction—plot, authorial explanation, descriptive detail—to the drift of pure speech', creating, as James Wood remarks, 'apparently aimless conversations'.[76]

Green's view of writing dialogue as a 'non-representational' act that must be geared towards producing a certain effect in the reader strongly

---

[69] Henry Green, 'The Spoken Word as Written', *Surviving: The Uncollected Writings of Henry Green* (London: Harvill, 1993), pp. 170–173 (p. 170).

[70] Green, 'The Spoken Word as Written', p. 171.

[71] Green, 'The Spoken Word as Written', p. 173; Bowen, 'Notes on Writing a Novel', p. 42.

[72] Green, 'A Novelist to his Readers', p. 137.

[73] Green, 'A Novelist to his Readers', p. 137.

[74] Green, 'A Novelist to his Readers', p. 137.

[75] Henry Green, 'A Novelist to his Readers', p. 141.

[76] James Wood, 'A Plausible Magic', Marina MacKay and Lyndsey Stonebridge (eds), *British Fiction after Modernism: The Novel at Mid-Century* (Basingstoke: Palgrave Macmillan, 2007), 50–58 (p. 53).

# 96 LITERATURE AND SOUND FILM IN MID-CENTURY BRITAIN

resonates with Bowen's reflections on dialogue as artifice as well as with sound film's privileging of intelligibility over perceptual fidelity. Green explicitly states elsewhere that non-representational means 'to represent a picture which was *not* a photograph...nor, in dialogue, a tape-recording.[77] As a novelist, he is not interested in producing transcriptions of real-life conversations or descriptions that approximate photographic images as he believes that either would lose their effect in writing. Rather, the novelist is responsible for the creation of fictional dialogues and matching descriptions which are suited to their medium, text, to produce the desired effect or illusion for the reader. In short, the writer's task is to create and sustain the illusion of intelligible, meaningful speech and evocative images in literary fiction.

His focus on dialogue in order to develop character and story is evident from his earliest works in the late 1920s: *Living* (1929), his second novel, is mostly structured into episodic scenes that highlight dialogic exchanges between characters. These scenes are juxtaposed to move the story along. Green himself wrote of *Living* that the book was conceived in 'a very condensed kind of way in short paragraphs [...] a kind of very disconnected cinema film.[78] The novel moves between the family of Birmingham factory owner Mr Dupret and his son, young Dupret, and the lives of their working-class employees. The novel avoids articles and conjunctions and there is only minimal description, which is often presented in an elliptic style: 'Evening. Was Spring. Heavy blue clouds stayed over above.[79] The novel pays particular attention to mediating the difference in accents between the upper-middle-class Dupret family and their working-class employees: while Mrs Dupret and her son speak in full sentences, their employees' idiom and accent is markedly different in spoken interaction:

'Yes I'm goin' to Orstrylia' 'e said' said Aaron Connolly to Mr Eames, 'I'm goin' to Orstrylia, don't care what no one says but I'm goin', 'e said. And I told 'im not be 'asty but to bide 'is time, that's what I told 'im—'it am a grand country for one that 'as some money', I said, 'but it am a 'ard bleeder for one that ain't.'[80]

---

[77] Henry Green, 'The Art of Fiction', *Surviving: The Uncollected Writings of Henry Green* (London: Harvill, 1993), 234–250 (p. 239).

[78] D. J. Taylor, *Bright Young People: The Rise and Fall of a Generation, 1918–1940* (London: Vintage, 2008), p. 253.

[79] Henry Green, *Living*, in *Loving, Living, Party Going* (London: Vintage, 2005), p. 213.

[80] Green, *Living*, p. 223.

In addition to such class-based differences in accent and idiom, Green's text uses flexible punctuation and also omits punctuation to indicate either pauses and hesitations or 'flow' when writing speech.[81] Young Dupret, for instance, is intent on making his non-availability clear to his mother. There are no commas or full stops that might indicate, in writing, a pause in conversation or a measured delivery. Instead, the sentences run into each other without a stop, as if there were a particular rush to communicate and insist on his prior engagement: 'No I can't manage Tuesday fortnight I'm dining with the Masons for their dance.'[82] Minimum description—often elliptic— serves to illustrate the scene of conversation with a high degree of textual immediacy. There is no superfluous or elaborate narratorial, descriptive comment. Instead, the novel focusses on the creation of dialogue scenes and what readers might perceive as a level of verbal or textual immediacy in the novel's approach to scene-setting.

Following the publication of *Living*, Green's writing began to include more overt references to intonation and emphasis, often coupled with short descriptions of the scene or environment in which characters find themselves. Green's later fiction often suggests a preoccupation not so much with *what* characters say, but *how* they say it and how this verbal interaction can be framed by a character's behaviour, tone, and social or physical environment. It is especially *Party Going* (1939), with its more overtly omniscient narrator, which interweaves this verbal interaction and textual scene-setting. The novel focusses on a group of upper-class socialites who are stranded in a London hotel when dense fog prevents their departure by train to a house party in France. The novel devotes much attention to describing voices with a view to at least three features: tone and pitch, emphasis, and accent:

'No', and Alex was now speaking in his high voice he used when he was upset, 'that's not the point.'[83]

'Isn't someone going to ask me what I'd like to drink?' and she put emphasis on the someone.[84]

'She were mortal bad I reckon when I see her took upstairs', this strange man said, speaking now in Brummagem. 'Now don't misunderstand me',

---

[81] On Green's use of punctuation, see Lodge, 'Dialogue in the Modern Novel', p. 82.
[82] Green, *Living*, p. 226.
[83] Henry Green, *Party Going*, in *Loving, Living, Party Going* (London: Vintage, 2005), p. 419.
[84] Green, *Party Going*, p. 447.

he said. 'I don't mean any harm, just a civil inquiry, that's all. You see I was sitting nigh her when she was taken bad', and by now he was speaking ordinarily, 'and I think I'll just ask after her.'[85]

Throughout the novel, describing a speaker's tone and emphasis takes precedence over describing the characters themselves.[86] *Party Going* reveals the superficiality, even dysfunctionality, of talk as characters constantly misunderstand each other as well as the implications of each other's tone, facial expression, posture, and movement. Both audio-vision and synchronicity come into play here, as observed by Ingo Berensmeyer in an extensive analysis of Green's novel: 'there is a close match between story time and discourse time: events are unfolded in the narrative as they occur. Especially at the beginning, the narrator stresses that events happen simultaneously as the narrative shifts from one scene to the next.'[87]

The nuanced descriptions of voice in Green's works resonate with the film industry's preoccupation with voice as a direct result of the transition to sound. As technological advances were made to enhance the intelligibility of the voice over background music and sound effects in film, descriptions of tone and emphasis became equally central to Green's literary dialogue.[88] Paradoxically, Green himself frequently referred to his poor hearing as a source of inspiration for writing dialogue. In an interview with Terry Southern, originally published in *The Paris Review* in 1958, Green further explains his conception of 'non-representational' dialogue:

non-representational was meant to represent a picture which was not a photograph, [...] nor, in dialogue, a tape-recording. For instance the very deaf, as I am, hear the most astounding things all round them, which have not, in fact, been said. This enlivens my replies until, through mishearing, a new level of communication is reached. [...] Thus when writing, I 'represent' very closely what I see (and I'm not seeing so well now) and what I hear (which is little) but I say it is 'non-representational' because it is not necessarily what others see and hear.[89]

---

[85] Green, *Party Going*, p. 477.    [86] Lodge, 'Dialogue in the Modern Novel', pp. 81–82.
[87] Ingo Berensmeyer, 'Henry Green, *Party Going* (1939)', in Christoph Reinfandt (ed.), *Handbook of the English Novel of the Twentieth and Twenty-First Centuries* (Berlin: De Gruyter, 2017), 232–251 (p. 241).
[88] Bordwell, 'The Introduction of Sound', p. 302.
[89] Henry Green, 'The Art of Fiction', *Surviving: The Uncollected Writings of Henry Green* (London: Harvill, 1993), pp. 234–250 (p. 239).

DIALOGUE AND INTELLIGIBILITY   99

Dialogue was not a direct transcription of speech overheard in real life, but a peculiar combination of hearing and mis-hearing, seeing and mis-seeing, paired with the idea of writing for effect to reach a 'new level of communication'. As in the case of Compton-Burnett and Bowen, Green's approach to writing literary dialogue is not one of perceptual literalism, but an artificial ('non-representational') curation that privileges the effect on the reader.

As such, Green's conception of 'non-representational' dialogue aligns closely with the fidelity/intelligibility debate that occupied the film industry in the 1930s as outlined by Lastra: film itself had of course reached a 'new level of communication' upon the introduction of synchronized sound and industry practices were increasingly geared towards the optimum use of sound recording and editing to foreground dialogue and to improve the intelligibility of speech and voice on screen. As emphasis was increasingly placed on the effects of sound–image interaction for audiences, intelligibility and the illusions of spatial depth and filmic realism became central to the industry's careful curation of sound. Artificial layering of sounds could enhance the impression of filmic realism while microphone placement, editing, and volume adjustment could steer the viewer's attention and produce a sense of three-dimensional depth and directionality of sound.

## Dialogue and Scenic Narration in the Novels of Ivy Compton-Burnett

The novels of Ivy Compton-Burnett are a prominent case study for Lodge's idea that mid-century fiction moves from the interiority of modernist stream-of-consciousness narration to the social world and the dynamics of 'talk'. Indeed, Compton-Burnett's fiction appears to push conversation to an elaborate extreme as all thought and emotion becomes externalized through speech.[90] In keeping with such an assessment, Brian McFarlane remarks that Compton-Burnett 'rarely tells the reader anything other than what the characters say to each other, so that one sometimes wonders if her true métier was the radio play'.[91] While these assessments certainly direct readers'

---

[90] Lodge writes that in Compton-Burnett, 'everything that is thought is spoken aloud, or rather, nothing that is not spoken aloud can be known'. Lodge, 'Dialogue in the Modern Novel', p. 83.

[91] Brian McFarlane, 'Reading Film and Literature', in Deborah Cartmell and Imelda Whelehan (eds), *The Cambridge Companion to Literature on Screen* (Cambridge: Cambridge University Press, 2007), 15–28 (p. 23).

# 100 LITERATURE AND SOUND FILM IN MID-CENTURY BRITAIN

attention to the productivity of speech in Compton-Burnett's oeuvre, they also solely interpret her works as pieces of 'radiophonic' or sound-centred fiction. From the perspective of an increasingly mediatized textuality, I suggest here that Compton-Burnett's novelistic technique, in fact, extends beyond a pure focus on speech or sound to the interplay of dialogue and scenic presentation of events. Precisely by approaching her subjects through talk, and by combining character interaction with scenic narration, Compton-Burnett creates novels of social interaction that work at the intersection of speech and image and may thus be viewed more accurately as producing audio-visual (rather than purely radiophonic) effects. Readers may understand her 'scenic narration' as describing two interlinked elements; first, the 'scene' in the sense of Genette's categories of duration, whereby story time equals or very closely approximates discourse time; and, second, 'scenic' as an externalized point of view, a form of external focalization, that encourages readers to inhabit a position similar to a camera-eye observer to narrated events. The 'scenic' features of Compton-Burnett's fiction were also noted by her contemporary Bowen in two detailed reviews of *Parents and Children* and *Elders and Betters* in 1941 and 1944. On the scenic quality of Compton-Burnett's dialogue, for instance, Bowen writes: 'the dialogue, in less than half of a phrase, in the click of a camera-shutter, shifts from place to place.... Scenes...are played out without mercy.'[92]

Beginning with the novel *Pastors and Masters* in 1925, Compton-Burnett applied a dialogue-oriented style to her fiction that would, throughout her career, prompt questions from friends, reviewers, and interviewers as to whether she ought to be writing stage plays rather than prose fiction. Compton-Burnett herself did not think much of 'exposition and description' and preferred her stories to be carried extensively by characters' voices.[93] Like Elizabeth Bowen and Henry Green, she was not interested in 'creating

---

[92] See Elizabeth Bowen, 'Parents and Children by Ivy Compton-Burnett', Review in the *New Statesman*, 24 May 1941. Reprinted in *The Mulberry Tree: Writings of Elizabeth Bowen*, ed. Hermione Lee (London: Vintage, 1999), 160–163 (p. 162).

[93] Charles Burkhart (ed.), 'I. Compton-Burnett and M. Jourdain: A Conversation', in *The Art of I. Compton-Burnett: A Collection of Critical Essays* (London: Gollancz, 1972), 21–31 (p. 21): 'I do not see why exposition and description are a necessary part of a novel. They are not of a play, and both deal with imaginary human beings and their lives. I have been told that I ought to write plays, but cannot see myself making the transition. I read plays with especial pleasure, and in reading novels I am disappointed if a scene is carried through in the voice of the author rather than the voices of the characters. I think that I simply follow my natural bent.'

DIALOGUE AND INTELLIGIBILITY 101

the illusion of actual speech' in a literary text.[94] In a conversation with her close friend and confidante Margaret Jourdain in 1945, Compton-Burnett reflected on her writing of dialogue, saying that 'I think that my writing does not seem to me as "stylised" as it apparently is, though I do not attempt to make my characters use the words of actual life.'[95] Instead, she considered her writing a mixture between a novel and a play in which all characters had an elaborate and sophisticated command of language.[96] Her novels privilege refined dialogue in order to develop plot and to show character relationships. It is key to note Compton-Burnett's own assessment of her work as a mix of novels and stage plays. This idea gives expression to the dialogue-oriented nature of her work, but it also conveys the importance of scenic representation, of putting readers into the position of an audience that can watch, listen, and read at the same time. Novels like *A House and its Head* (1935), *Parents and Children* (1941), and *Manservant and Maidservant* (1947) indicate the novel's move towards a mediatized textuality that explores the multi-dimensional expressivity of written conversation.

Compton-Burnett's novels are confined to the households of well-to-do families in the late Victorian and Edwardian era. Her characters usually speak in full and grammatically correct sentences that are carefully constructed, underlining artificiality rather than naturalism. *A House and Its Head* (1935), for instance, begins as follows:

'So the children are not down yet?' said Ellen Edgeworth. Her husband gave her a glance, and turned his eyes towards the window. 'So the children are not down yet?' she said on a note of question. Mr. Edgeworth put his finger down his collar, and settled his neck. 'So you are down first, Duncan?' said his wife, as though putting her observation in a more acceptable form.... 'So you are down first of all, Duncan', said Ellen, employing a note of propitiation, as if it would serve its purpose. Her husband implied by lifting his shoulders that he could hardly deny it. 'The children are late, are they not?' said Ellen, to whom speech clearly ranked above silence.[97]

[94] Lodge, 'Dialogue in the Modern Novel', p. 83.
[95] Burkhart, 'I. Compton-Burnett and M. Jourdain: A Conversation', p. 22.
[96] John Bowen, 'An Interview with Ivy Compton-Burnett' (BBC Home Programme, 17 September 1960), *Twentieth Century Literature*, 25.2 (Summer 1979), 165–172 (pp. 165–167).
[97] Ivy Compton-Burnett, *A House and Its Head* (New York: New York Review of Books, 2001), pp. 3–4.

## 102  LITERATURE AND SOUND FILM IN MID-CENTURY BRITAIN

Ellen's question is repeated five times, but her husband Duncan, the *pater familias*, remains largely silent and dismissive. Ellen's attempts at moving Duncan to an answer turn more desperate with each repetition. The first, 'So the children are not down yet?', is simply a statement with a question mark. The repetition of this statement 'on a note of question' points readers to Ellen's altered intonation to elicit an answer from Duncan. The following 'So you are down first of all, Duncan?' turns to a direct address which also makes him, rather than the children, the subject of the question. Ellen repeats this phrase again, 'on a note of propitiation', but even this reverent and submissive demeanour will not move Duncan to speak. Duncan's prolonged silence, his refusal to participate in a conversation with his wife on the morning of Christmas Day, indicates a level of cruelty and coercive control that will only become more apparent over the course of the novel. Crucially, in the space of only a few questions and some short descriptive passages, Compton-Burnett has already revealed to her readers almost everything they need to know about Ellen, Duncan, and the state of their relationship.

Whilst the dialogue is strongly indicative of character relationships, this example from *A House and Its Head* also shows Compton-Burnett's preference for a scenic presentation of events that combines character speech and a stance of externalized observation of events: discourse time and story time align and the one-sided interaction between Ellen and Duncan is presented by a narrator who remains largely covert. The reader is given an external point of view with some selective moments of omniscient narration (such as the narrator's knowledge of Duncan's own view of himself as 'tall'; the narrator's comment on 'later additions' to the Victorian country house). Yet, the narrator offers a predominantly external perspective on the scene; a description of the space and the characters as viewed by an outside observer to events. It is as if readers were looking through a window onto the scene that is unfolding on this Christmas morning in 1885. This impression is enhanced by the use of verbs such as 'seem', 'appear', 'indicate', and conditional constructions ('as though', 'as if it would'). All of these phrases, taken together, create a sense of externalized presentation, of a scene that is observed from the outside by an entity that cannot (for the most part) interpret or know these characters' intentions and emotions with certainty. The narrator creates a diegetic space through observation, minimal description, and dialogue that reminds readers of Christopher Isherwood's programmatic statement 'I am a camera with its shutter open, quite passive, recording, not thinking.'[98] In other words, the narrator appears to function as a 'recording device' with minimal narratorial intrusion into the unfolding of events.[99] Alison Light suggests that the style puts the reader in the position of a 'voyeur', rather than a 'co-participant in the action'. In the world of Compton-Burnett's country houses, the reader is 'an observer not an actor in the charades of family life'.[100] Whilst Compton-Burnett's writing, like that of Bowen and Green, asserts the primacy and complexity of dialogue and spoken interaction, the scenic presentation of events and character interaction also puts the reader into an 'observer' position that suggests a concern with the audio-visual dimension, rather than a merely dialogue-oriented stance.

In *Manservant and Maidservant*, Compton-Burnett's dialogue has become even more focussed: here, the speech tags or speaker identifiers ('he said', 'she said') are used more sparsely than in the earlier *A House and Its Head*. The beginning of *Manservant and Maidservant* also contains less narrator intervention in order to set the scene: '"Is that fire smoking?" said Horace Lamb. "Yes, it appears to be, my dear boy." "I am not asking what it appears to be doing. I asked if it was smoking." "Appearances are not held to be a clue to the truth," said his cousin.'[101] In exchanges such as this, the characters refuse to participate in what Mepham, drawing on the work of Harold Garfinkel and Paul Grice, describes as 'maxims of cooperation in talk' or 'functional talk', namely conversation in which each speaker makes a concerted effort to understand the meaning of the other—an attitude of openness, shared horizons, and benevolence through which a mutual understanding or interpretation of the conversation is developed.[102] However, in Compton-Burnett's novel, nothing could be further from benevolence. Any careless or unreflective use of words is punished or, at the very least, drawn attention to. The need for intelligibility and the problem of language are foregrounded by the way in which Compton-Burnett's characters

---

[98] Christopher Isherwood, *Goodbye to Berlin,* in *The Berlin Novels* (London: Vintage, 1999), p. 243.

[99] On this point, see also Norman Page, *Speech in the English Novel* (Basingstoke: Macmillan, 1988), p. 138. Page makes similar observations on the novels of Henry Green.

[100] Alison Light, *Forever England: Femininity, Literature, and Conservatism Between the Wars* (Abingdon: Routledge, 2001), p. 22.

[101] Ivy Compton-Burnett, *Manservant and Maidservant* (New York: New York Review of Books, 2001), p. 3.

[102] Mepham, 'Varieties of Modernism', pp. 67–69. Mepham bases his discussion of functional talk and co-operation on the pragmatic principles of Harold Garfinkel and Paul Grice.

104  LITERATURE AND SOUND FILM IN MID-CENTURY BRITAIN

interpret (as well as deliberately misinterpret) each other's speeches. Often, characters take each other by their word and thereby show the problem (even impossibility) of 'literal' communication:

> Nance returned to the room. 'Mother does not feel any better. She thinks she will stay in bed.' 'She is not sure?' said Duncan. 'Yes, she is sure, Father. I might have put it differently.' Duncan glanced at her, and walked to the door. 'Ellen! Ellen! When are you coming down? Do you realise we are waiting? I don't seem to be able to get a message through.'[103]

Although completely different in outlook and subject matter, Compton-Burnett's narrative style may remind readers and audiences of the snappy screwball dialogue in Korda's *Divorce of Lady X*, which highlights the linguistic potential for comedy through the literal interpretation (or deliberate misinterpretation) of language. Kozloff rightly points out that screwball comedy derives its appeal from the 'disparity [that] exists between the literal meaning of the sentences and the inferences—ironic, extratextual, sexual—that the sophisticated viewer is supposed to perceive.'[104] Compton-Burnett's fictional dialogueputs this same principle to work in order to map characters against one another in a series of verbal sparring matches.

This chapter has shown that Elizabeth Bowen, Henry Green, and Ivy Compton-Burnett were concerned with the issue of how dialogue could distil character and plot, enhance psychological causality, and contribute to the 'continuity' of literary fiction. Compton-Burnett's novels present readers with a mixture of novel and play, chiefly carried by the voices of the characters, and working towards a combination of dialogue and scenic presentation. Henry Green's novels are especially attentive to nuances of intonation, pitch, and accent, centrally reflecting on written dialogue as 'non-representational'. Both Green and Bowen point out that written dialogue is not a mere textual transcription of conversations overheard in real life. While the novelist might take note of 'turns of phrase indicatory of class, age, degree of intellectual pretension...or acumen,'[105] the writer ultimately has to create fictional dialogue that appears realistic without actually being so, of curating intelligibility rather than relying on perceptual fidelity. The 'illusion of the novel' requires as much 'trickery' as the illusion of synchronized dialogue presented by the sound film. By examining developments in film dialogue

---

[103] Compton-Burnett, *A House and Its Head*, p. 50.
[104] Kozloff, *Film Dialogue*, p. 179.      [105] Bowen, 'Notes on Writing a Novel', p. 42.

alongside Bowen, Green, and Compton-Burnett's conceptions of dialogue, this chapter has outlined film and literature's growing proximity in their efforts to conceive of dialogue audio-visually. Such an audio-visual approach to spoken interaction became key to cinema, but it was equally characteristic of mid-century literature's wider move towards a more mediatized textuality.

*Literature and Sound Film in Mid-Century Britain*. Lara Ehrenfried, Oxford University Press.
© Lara Ehrenfried 2025. DOI: 10.1093/9780198950790.003.0004

# 4
# Documenting the Everyday

In response to the characteristic 'documentary impulse' of the 1930s, film and literary fiction pervasively questioned representational conventions, interrogating the roles played by image, sound, and text in recording the realities of life across the multi-national British state and the British Empire.[1] This chapter argues that this act of questioning undertaken by film and literature matters, because audio-vision and synchronicity, like the documentary itself, are never apolitical. As Michel Chion writes, the 'added value' that speech and synchronized sound add to film goes 'beyond the simple situation of a political opinion slapped onto images; added value engages the very structuring of vision — by rigorously framing it'.[2] There is no 'neutral way of speaking' and when, as is often the case in documentary or news reporting, 'the film or TV image seems to "speak" for itself, it is actually a ventriloquist's speech. When the shot of...three small airplanes in a blue sky declares "three small airplanes," it is a puppet animated by the anchorman's voice'.[3] The impossibility of 'neutral' representation thus poses a particular problem for those setting out to record (and write) 'actualities' in the 1930s. While silent documentaries, such as Robert Flaherty's *Nanook of the North* (1922), are of course no less 'neutral' or apolitical, audio-vision and synchronicity arguably raise the stakes: by producing the illusion of unmediated speech emanating from the image and by maintaining that sound is causally and temporally related to the image, technology seduces audiences into believing that they have direct or unmediated access to information when this remains an impossible feat. Documentary's claim to authenticity, and the products of documentary writing and filmmaking, 'are not just transparent windows on the "real world" of the people, but

---

[1] Leo Mellor, 'The Documentary Impulse', in Benjamin Kohlmann and Matthew Taunton (eds), *A History of 1930s British Literature* (Cambridge: Cambridge University Press, 2019), 257–270.
[2] Michel Chion, *Audio-Vision: Sound on Screen*, ed. and trans. Claudia Gorbman (New York: Columbia University Press, 1994), p. 7.
[3] Chion, *Audio-Vision*, p. 7.

DOCUMENTING THE EVERYDAY 107

encodings of meaning which actively construct the object of their gaze, as well as recording it.'[4]

The 'documentary impulse', Leo Mellor argues, is a 'cultural and creative reaction' to aesthetic influences, 'economic conditions', and technological innovation in the 1930s.[5] The work of Mass Observation (M-O), the activities of the Empire Marketing Board (EMB, 1928–1933) and the General Post Office (GPO, 1933–1940), new broadcasting formats launched by the BBC, and a plethora of non-fiction and travelogues of the decade can be viewed as responses to the period's heightened interest in documentary.[6] In some cases, literary fiction, too, sought to answer Storm Jameson's call for efforts to 'create the literary equivalent of the documentary film'.[7] The 1930s, as Laura Marcus writes, saw the emergence of new textual modes that appeared to bear a close relationship to the styles and narrative devices found in the documentary film: 'the documentary idea intersected different media [and] created new terms for an interdisciplinary synthesis'.[8] J. B. Priestley's *English Journey* (1934), John Sommerfield's *May Day* (1936), James Hanley's *Grey Children* (1937), Orwell's *The Road to Wigan Pier* (1937), and Auden and Isherwood's *Journey to a War* (1939) are important examples of the kinds of interactions described by Mellor and Marcus.

As this chapter will show, part of the sustained intersections between the GPO's documentary film practices and literary fiction is the question of audio-vision and the related problem of 'neutral' or unmediated representation. The case of George Orwell's early fiction of the 1930s is especially interesting in this regard as *A Clergyman's Daughter* (1935) and *Keep the Aspidistra Flying* (1936) are widely viewed (not least by Orwell himself) as 'silly potboiler[s]'.[9] However, the difficult nature of these works, and their apparent 'misfit' status in the Orwell canon, may be reframed if read from the vantage point of a writer seeking to devise textual responses to the impossibility of 'neutral' representation in a documentary-minded age. Similarly, Lewis Grassic Gibbon's *Sunset Song* (1932), although known as a

---

[4] John Baxendale and Christopher Pawling, *Narrating the Thirties* (Basingstoke: Macmillan, 1996), p. 20.

[5] Mellor, 'Documentary Impulse', pp. 257–258.

[6] Mellor, 'Documentary Impulse', pp. 258–259.

[7] Storm Jameson, 'New Documents', qtd. by Mellor in 'Documentary Impulse', p. 258.

[8] Laura Marcus, '"The Creative Treatment of Actuality": John Grierson, Documentary Cinema and "Fact" in the 1930s', in Kristin Bluemel (ed.), *Intermodernism* (Edinburgh: Edinburgh University Press, 2011), pp. 189–207 (p. 190).

[9] Nathan Waddell, 'Introduction', in George Orwell (ed.), *A Clergyman's Daughter* (Oxford: Oxford University Press, 2021), p. xi.

108  LITERATURE AND SOUND FILM IN MID-CENTURY BRITAIN

quintessential Scottish novel of the twentieth century, has not been framed as significant textual experiment addressing the problem of representation as it emerged in the 1930s. In what follows, the chapter traces how GPO documentary film and literary fiction by Orwell and Grassic Gibbon address the impossibility of neutral or unmediated representation through hybrid styles, juxtaposition, and temporal ruptures.

## Audio-Vision and Documentary Film in the 1930s

The camera and the microphone opened up new dimensions for the recording of actualities: sound and image technologies offered innovative means of gathering material for the portrayal of everyday life and for producing new kinds of social reportage in a documentary-minded decade. In 1934, for instance, the radio feature documentary emerged from the work of Laurence Gilliam, Olive Shapley, and Lance Sieveking at the BBC. Gilliam, who was responsible for special features at the BBC, was the driving force behind *'opping 'oliday*, a documentary broadcast which used interviews, singing, and fragments of dialogue, all recorded on location with a mobile recording van.[10] The radio programme followed families and individuals travelling from London to Kent for seasonal hop-picking and was an early attempt to facilitate radio broadcasts that would put into practice the idea of people 'speaking for themselves' without script, direction, voice-of-god narration, and RP-speakers as dominant intermediaries.[11]

'Speak for Yourself' became an important slogan, especially in some retrospective accounts of the period's documentary movement, the activities of M-O, and the BBC's expanding broadcast programming. 'Speak for Yourself' expressed the belief that the British people at home and overseas had at their disposal the means to produce authentic representations of their everyday life and to give their own accounts, in their own voices, without interference.[12] As Simon Potter has shown in his impressive

---

[10] Some of the parallels between *'opping 'oliday* and Orwell's *A Clergyman's Daughter* are discussed by Tim Crook, 'George Orwell and the Radio Imagination', in Richard Lance Keeble (ed.), *George Orwell Now!* (New York: Peter Lang, 2015), pp. 193–208.

[11] Peter M. Lewis, '"A Claim to Be Heard": Voices of Ordinary People in BBC Radio Features', *Revue Française de Civilisation Britannique*, 26.1 (2021), pp. 1–13.

[12] This idea is expressed by a range of M-O publications, and in later accounts of British Documentary and M-O. See, for instance, *Speak for Yourself: A Mass-Observation Anthology, 1937–1949*, ed. Angus Calder and Dorothy Sheridan (London: Jonathan Cape, 1984); *The Rise and Fall of British Documentary*, ed. Elisabeth Sussex (Berkeley, CA: University of California

*Broadcasting Empire*, the BBC's radio programming was aimed at 'shaping' society and establishing transnational unity and community. Radio was viewed as a means of 'actively enforcing bonds of Empire' and as a form of 'cultural diplomacy' at home, in the dominions, and, to a lesser degree, in the dependent colonies.[13] Even broadcasts such as *'opping 'oliday* carried the BBC's mission as the programme educates listeners about seasonal work and constructs a communal experience out of the regional and linguistic differences presented by the programme.

While the radio feature documentary at the BBC was a new development in the 1930s, the documentary film had developed steadily over a period of about 35 years. The *cinématographe* devised by the Lumière brothers had been a portable device suited to location-filming, which was then used for the recording of *actualités* such as *La sortie des usines Lumière* (1895). Actuality referred to film's particular capacity for recording non-fictional everyday events.[14] Early Soviet film, especially the work of Dziga Vertov, further exerted a formative influence on British documentary.[15] Vertov had volunteered for the Cinema Committee in Moscow in 1917 and became responsible for the Soviet newsreel *Kino Nedelia*, which served as an intersection of non-fictional material, news reports, and propaganda in support of the Bolshevik revolution.[16] A third strand of influence emerged from the work of Flaherty: *Nanook of the North*, *Moana* (1926), and *Man of Aran* (1934) are amalgamations of travelogue, anthropological study, and fiction film.[17]

John Grierson, widely considered the founder of British documentary film, greatly admired Flaherty's work, famously commenting in a review of *Moana* on its 'documentary value' and thereby also giving rise to the term's frequent application to film.[18] Grierson had begun his career in film production as assistant films officer for the EMB in the late 1920s and subsequently took on the role of films officer for the GPO film unit in 1933. In this latter capacity, Grierson oversaw the activities of the GPO film unit and

---

Press, 1975); and Paul Rotha, *Documentary Diary: An Informal History of the British Documentary Film, 1928–1939* (London: Secker & Warburg, 1973).

[13] Simon Potter, *Broadcasting Empire* (Oxford: Oxford University Press, 2012), pp. 5–7.

[14] Erik Barnouw, *Documentary: A History of the Non-Fiction Film* (New York: Oxford University Press, 1974), pp. 6–7.

[15] Barnouw, *Documentary*, pp. 51–71, and Richard M. Barsam, *Non-Fiction Film: A Critical History* (Bloomington, IN: Indiana University Press, 1992), pp. 65–75.

[16] Barnouw, *Documentary*, pp. 52–55.     [17] Barnouw, *Documentary*, pp. 33–51.

[18] Brian Winston, *Claiming the Real: The Documentary Film Revisited* (London: BFI, 1995), p. 8. Valentine Cunningham suggests that travelogues were particularly important precursors to Grierson's concept of documentary. See Cunningham, *British Writers of the Thirties* (Oxford: Oxford University Press, 1988), p. 341.

110　LITERATURE AND SOUND FILM IN MID-CENTURY BRITAIN

significantly shaped British documentary film production in the 1930s. He began his career with an openness towards avant-garde and experimental cinema, as shown by his own early documentary film *Drifters* (1929), which was influenced by Flaherty's travelogues and Eisenstein's *Battleship Potemkin* (1925).[19] Yet, as the 1930s progressed, Grierson became more dismissive of formal experiment and, as Marcus notes, 'alienated from concepts of "film art"'.[20]

In 1934, just as the BBC began experimenting with more actuality material for its radio broadcasts, Grierson's film unit at the GPO acquired sound equipment and began their work on documentaries and public relations films with synchronized sound.[21] Reflecting on the short film *6.30 Collection* (1934), a brief account of West London's Sorting Office containing some ambient noise, a commentary spoken by Stuart Legg, and title music by Walter Leigh, Grierson commended the unit's first experiments with 'authentic sound': 'the natural noises and the overheard comments, orders, calls and conversations, created a new and curious relationship between the audience and the screen. The distance was broken down in a certain intimate delight.'[22] Sound equipment, which according to Grierson facilitated 'eavesdropping' for the audience, enhanced the filmmakers' approach to everyday life and created a new kind of 'intimacy' in conjunction with the film image.[23] The microphone, Grierson noted elsewhere, had 'the power to bring to the hands of the creative artist a thousand and one vernacular elements, and the million and one sounds which ordinarily attend the working of the world'.[24] In this capacity, the creative 'power' of the microphone matched and complemented the creative power of the camera.[25] The endeavour to record and report 'the working of the world' united the British documentary filmmakers despite their divergent approaches to audio-vision. As James Mansell rightly points out, the filmmakers around Grierson

---

[19] Marcus, '"The Creative Treatment of Actuality"', p. 191. See also Ian Aitken, 'Introduction', *The Documentary Film Movement: An Anthology* (Edinburgh: Edinburgh University Press, 2008), 1–68 (p. 10): *Drifters* 'was a poetic montage documentary, which drew heavily on the filmmaking styles of Sergei Eisenstein and Robert Flaherty, and on Grierson's understanding of avant-garde aesthetics. Grierson later described it as an "imagist" film, because it added "poetic reference" to "symphonic form".'

[20] Marcus, '"The Creative Treatment of Actuality"', p. 192.

[21] John Grierson, 'The GPO Gets Sound', *Cinema Quarterly*, 2.4 (Summer 1934), pp. 215–221.

[22] Grierson, 'The GPO Gets Sound', p. 217.

[23] Grierson, 'The GPO Gets Sound', p. 217.

[24] John Grierson, 'Creative Use of Sound', in Forsyth Hardy (ed.), *Grierson on Documentary* (New York: Harcourt, Brace & Co., 1947), 112–118 (p. 113).

[25] Grierson, 'Creative Use of Sound', p. 113.

'were motivated by a desire to represent the realities of everyday social life...as well as to harness film's potential to enhance democratic citizenship'; they were also, however, part of a government-sponsored public relations unit with the directive to 'project and produce a sense of shared British identity'.[26] In this regard, the GPO and the BBC had common goals: both were intended to 'foster transnational British identity' and to educate their respective audiences.[27]

One of the GPO's significant experiments with sound–image interaction was *The Song of Ceylon* (1934), a film which questions, repeatedly, its own representational conventions and its status as documentary or actuality film. The production addresses the impossibility of any neutral or unmediated representation of its subjects by framing itself as an aesthetic object, inspired by the 'city symphonies' of the 1920s. The film had emerged from a commission to create four travelogues for the Ceylon Tea Propaganda Board with the intention of marketing trade with the colonies and, specifically, to show audiences the tea trade.[28] It is a problematic production, not least because it avoids any direct mention of the imperial exploitation of labour and resources in present day Sri Lanka.[29] The image material for the film was shot on location in 1933 by Basil Wright prior to the GPO's acquisition of sound equipment. The soundtrack, recorded with Visatone Marconi equipment, was created and edited at Blackheath studios after location filming had concluded.[30]

Under the guidance of Alberto Cavalcanti, who had been invited to join the GPO by Grierson in 1933, the British documentary filmmakers began to construct more creative approaches to asynchronous and synchronous image–sound relationships. As William Guynn remarks, 'Cavalcanti was there advocating a freer relationship between sound and image than the typical fiction film or documentary, with its voice-of-god commentary, had permitted.'[31] The GPO filmmakers' training in sound practices by Cavalcanti

---

[26] James G. Mansell, *The Age of Noise in Britain: Hearing Modernity* (Urbana, IL: University of Illinois Press, 2017), p. 136.

[27] Potter, *Broadcasting Empire*, pp. 5–6.

[28] Ian Aitken (ed.), 'Ceylon Tea Propaganda Board', *Encyclopedia of the Documentary Film*, Vol. 1 (New York: Routledge, 2006), 194–195 (p. 194).

[29] Stuart Hood, 'John Grierson and the Documentary Film Movement', in James Curran and Vincent Porter (eds), *British Cinema History* (London: Weidenfeld & Nicholson, 1983), p. 101.

[30] William Guynn, 'The Art of National Projection: Basil Wright's *Song of Ceylon*', in Barry Keith Grant and Jeannette Sloniowski (eds), *Documenting the Documentary: Close Readings of Documentary Film and Video* (Detroit: Wayne State University Press, 2013), pp. 64–80 (p. 67).

[31] Guynn, 'The Art of National Projection', p. 67.

112　LITERATURE AND SOUND FILM IN MID-CENTURY BRITAIN

shows its impact clearly in *Song of Ceylon*. The film contains four parts: 'The Buddha', 'The Virgin Island', 'The Voices of Commerce', and 'The Apparel of a God'. As the title implies, *Song of Ceylon* conceptually emphasizes sound over image and points to the ways in which sound here structures the image track.

The film's composer Walter Leigh described the role of sound or the film as

a sound-score which has a definite shape, and not only is an accompaniment to the visuals, but adds an element which they do not contain. The film has, in fact, been cut throughout with an eye to the sound-score. Its form is musically conceived; an analysis of its four movements would read like that of a symphony. Each sound has been selected for its seeming inevitability, as harmonies are in music. Even the commentary is calculated as an effect and not as a necessary nuisance. The chief aims of the sound-score are simplicity and clarity.[32]

This 'symphonic' approach described by Leigh aligns *Song of Ceylon* with the popular 'city symphonies' of the 1920s, including Walther Ruttmann's *Berlin—Die Sinfonie der Großstadt* (1927) and Cavalcanti's own evocative portrait of Paris in *Rien que les heures* (1926).[33] 'Simplicity', 'clarity', and harmony are created through the combination of images and sounds; the film's visuals are framed by sound. Leigh's description also contains clear reference to the film's wholly curated nature: the soundtrack is based on the selection of sounds that *seem* 'inevitable'; commentary is produced for 'calculated...effect'. This is not a neutral representation of a place and its people, but a highly mediated composition for a Western European audience. Indeed, audiences in Britain lauded the film for its coherent aesthetic and its stringent adherence to principles of montage when the film was released in 1934. Graham Greene, for instance, praised the film's 'perfect construction' and 'perfect application of montage'.[34] In 1935, *The Song of Ceylon* also won the first prize for best film overall at the International Film

---

[32] Walter Leigh, 'The Musician and the Film', *Cinema Quarterly*, 3.2 (1935), 70–74 (p. 74).

[33] Guynn, 'The Art of National Projection', pp. 68–75. Grierson himself had also cited the city symphonies as inspiration for his own production of *Drifters* (1929). See Marcus, '"The Creative Treatment of Actuality"', pp. 191–192.

[34] Graham Greene, 'Song of Ceylon', *The Spectator*, 4 October 1935, in John Russell Taylor (ed.), *The Pleasure Dome: Graham Greene—The Collected Film Criticism, 1935–40* (Oxford: Oxford University Press, 1980), pp. 25–26.

DOCUMENTING THE EVERYDAY    113

Festival in Brussels.[35] This critical success in Britain and Western Europe was likely grounded in the GPO's agenda of combining commercially sponsored marketing and public relations film with a pursuit of artistic expression. The film reflects an implicit 'emphasis on high culture' in its 'symphonic' approach.[36] At the same time, this approach is also a clear, self-referential form of *mise-en-scène*, whereby the film steps away from a claim to 'neutral' reporting or unmediated representation. The filmmakers' conception of the production is primarily grounded in aesthetics, not in actuality.

The film's voiceover commentary is derived from excerpts of Robert Knox's *An Historical Relation of the Island Ceylon*, a seventeenth-century report of Knox's life in the Kingdom of Kandy (located in parts of central and East Sri Lanka). Knox, who was a sailor for the British East India Company, spent about twenty years (c. 1659–1679) on the island. *Song of Ceylon* borrows liberally from Knox's text, taking cues and inspiration from his account of island life. By borrowing Knox's seventeenth-century words for the voiceover commentary, the island and its inhabitants are simultaneously placed within and outside of chronological historical time. The commentary begins, for instance, by clearly and problematically exoticizing the island location and describing it as 'dark', 'monstrous', and dangerous whilst the screen remains black: 'in ancient times, all the low parts of this land were covered with dark and monstrous forests through which no man might pass without peril.'[37] Only as the voiceover commentary moves to the next sentence does the image track slowly begin to fade in, showing close-ups of plants and foliage. Knox's words and Wright's images continue to form an uneasy combination: 'Wright, like Knox, is yet another European recording his account of the island....the narration demonstrates the ongoing colonial presence of Europeans and their ability to speak for the island and its people.'[38]

The second and third parts of the film form important counterpoints to the first part that begins with Knox's seventeenth-century words as voiceover narration. The second half of the film, and especially part three, 'The Voices

[35] James Chapman, *A New History of British Documentary* (Basingstoke: Palgrave Macmillan, 2015), p. 71.
[36] Potter, *Broadcasting Empire*, p. 10. Potter notes this 'emphasis on high culture' for the BBC's broadcast programming.
[37] *The Song of Ceylon*, dir. Basil Wright, prod. John Grierson (GPO Film Unit, 1934).
[38] Jon Hoare, 'Song of Ceylon: Analysis,' *Colonial Film: Moving Images of the British Empire*, 2010, www.colonialfilm.org.uk/node/486 (accessed 8 May 2023).

of Commerce', contrasts its visual material with the soundtrack. Images of local agricultural activities, such as harvesting coconuts and vegetables, are underscored by seemingly unrelated vox pops, performing readings of everyday consumer interactions in English, such as the acknowledgement of a receipt for payment and a female voice reading out a shopping list. There are sound effects of telephone exchanges and the beeping and whirring of modern communications technologies. The sounds and voices of Western European everyday commercial activity are juxtaposed with the images of daily agricultural labour in South Asia. The clash of sound and image creates a marked contrast between West and East, industry and agriculture, and, ultimately, between colonizer and colonized. The film's frequent use of such contrapuntal sounds aligns closely with Eisenstein's concept of the contrapuntal use of sound in montage. The image track, for instance, shows an elephant felling a tree, while the soundtrack underscores these visuals by loud, metallic and industrial soundscapes: a gong produced through hitting a vibrating sheet of metal and the sound of a train running across tracks, followed by the noise of telephones and morse signals. In a feature for *Cinema Quarterly*, Herbert Read praised *Song of Ceylon* alongside Cavalcanti's *Pett and Pott: A Fairy Story of the Suburbs* (1934) as exciting experiments in counterpoint.[39] The soundtrack defamiliarizes the image and, by using counterpoint and montage, negates its own claim to presenting unmediated actuality.

Walter Leigh notes that *The Song of Ceylon* uses different kinds of music as well as a combination of synchronized and non-synchronized elements to achieve audio-visual juxtaposition. The film's 'chief claim' to success, Leigh argues, is that 'it shows examples of a few of the possibilities offered by an entirely new approach to the whole problem of sound' and of sound's relation to the image in documentary.[40] Paul Rotha echoed this approach more broadly, when he commented that 'sound and picture working together permit more than one idea to be expressed at the same time'.[41] The use of sonic counterpoint in *The Song of Ceylon* expands and contrasts the film's visual dimension and invites audiences to question the visual representation of the island and its people. This does not exempt the film from its attitude of white British superiority and its problematic exoticization of

---

[39] Herbert Read, 'Experiments in Counterpoint', *Cinema Quarterly*, 3.1 (1934), pp. 17–21.

[40] Walter Leigh, 'The Musician and the Film', *Cinema Quarterly*, 3.2 (1935), 70–74 (p. 74).

[41] Paul Rotha, *The Documentary Film* (London: Faber, 1936), p. 199. Quoted in Mellor, 'Documentary Impulse', p. 258.

present-day Sri Lanka, but it shows the film's questioning of representational conventions and at least a degree of awareness for the impossibility of neutral or unmediated representation of its subject matter.

Following *The Song of Ceylon,* the GPO continued their work with *Pett and Pott, Housing Problems* (1935), *Coal Face* (1935), *Enough to Eat?* (1936), and *Night Mail* (1936). The possibility of synchronizing the soundtrack with the film image sparked a number of different ideas within the film unit, which often stood in opposition to Grierson's own evolving vision for GPO film.[42] Cavalcanti, who was strongly influenced by surrealism and Soviet theories of film sound, saw its primary function in creating a stimulating counterpoint to the image rather than as a feature that would contribute to the illusion of realism.[43] To this end, Cavalcanti much preferred music and sound effects over prolonged sequences of recorded dialogue and argued that film benefitted from a more creative use of sound effects, an idea he applied consistently in his *Pett and Pott.*[44] Looking back on the early sound years, the director Edgar Anstey also reflected that many members of the GPO 'looked with contempt on dialogue because of the kind of thing they had in Hollywood films.... Our first approach to sound was to use it in a kind of abstract way...to try to take sounds and orchestrate them.'[45] Orchestrating sound and using it as counterpoint was one means by which the impression of a causal relation between image and soundtrack could be broken. Apart from Grierson himself, not many members of the GPO were interested in enhancing filmic realism.

In contrast to Cavalcanti and Anstey, who advocated for the contrapuntal and even abstract use of sound, the chief sound engineer, Ken Cameron, had a more pragmatic and functional view of sound that was more in line with the self-effacing ideals of classical narrative cinema: 'just as the perfect colour-film, the colour should not be noticed, so in the perfect sound film, the actual sound should be so perfectly wedded with the picture that the illusion of reality is complete.'[46] Cameron's perspective as a sound professional is

---

[42] The differences in approaches towards sound between Cavalcanti, Jennings, Rotha, and Grierson are discussed in greater detail by James G. Mansell in 'Rhythm, Modernity and the Politics of Sound', in Scott Anthony and James G. Mansell (eds), *The Projection of Britain: A History of the GPO Film Unit* (London: BFI, 2011), pp. 161–167.

[43] Alberto Cavalcanti, 'Sound in Films', in Elisabeth Weis and John Belton (eds), *Film Sound: Theory and Practice* (New York: Columbia University Press, 1985), pp. 98–111 (p. 102).

[44] *Pett and Pott: A Fairy Story of the Suburbs,* dir. by Alberto Cavalcanti, produced by John Grierson (GPO, 1934).

[45] Sussex, *The Rise and Fall of British Documentary,* p. 46.

[46] Ken Cameron, *Sound in the Documentary Film* (London: Pitman & Sons, 1947), p. 1.

# 116 LITERATURE AND SOUND FILM IN MID-CENTURY BRITAIN

considerably closer to Grierson's own aims for sound in the documentary film. In 'The GPO Gets Sound', Grierson frames the acquisition of recording equipment as a cost-saving measure which, incidentally, would also contribute to a greater 'authenticity' of the filmic work and remove the interference of a 'professional' (RP) accent:

> We do the job ourselves if we want a commentary, and save...the quite unendurable detachment of the professional accent. Better still, if we are showing workmen at work, we get the workmen on the job to do their own commentary, with idiom and accent complete. It makes for intimacy and authenticity....[47]

Grierson's comments on the value of having workers speaking their own commentary reflects a broader concern with pursuing the 'authentic' voices of the people and also returns to the period's wider idea of letting people 'speak for themselves'. This included a move away from BBC English and RP-inflected voice-of-god narration. Grierson's documentary project, much like the BBC's radio feature documentaries, set out to record local dialects and accents that would amount to portraits of local difference and variety with the broader aim of constructing an image of national unity. As Potter notes in relation to the BBC, 'voice' was never an uncontested site: to some parties, BBC English was 'a marker of quality and authority'; to other listeners, the same voice and accent could signify 'privilege, hierarchy, and the narrow interests of Britain's elite'.[48] The question of voice and accent, both in radio broadcasts but also in documentary film, was thus an important element that would determine audience engagement (or a lack thereof). The GPO documentaries *Housing Problems* and *Enough to Eat?*, for instance, use their soundtracks in an effort to evoke the kind of 'authenticity' and 'intimacy' called for by Grierson by including various forms of local and regional speech. While these films adhere to standard practices of sound–image synchronization, these films move away from straightforward voiceover narration by one authoritative RP speaker. Instead, these productions use multiple narrators alongside interviews and vox pops to introduce sociolinguistic variety.

However, these apparently more realist productions carry with themselves, yet again, the problem of representation. The films frame their speakers and

---

[47] Grierson, 'The GPO Gets Sound', p. 216.      [48] Potter, *Broadcasting Empire*, p. 11.

interviewees as objects of the camera's gaze; their living conditions and personal circumstances, especially in *Housing Problems*, become the material of voyeuristic exploration. As Marsha Bryant notes, while the documentary filmmakers 'sought to establish contact across class and national boundaries [and] [t]heir presence at coal mines, factories, slums…attested to their genuine desire to understand and intervene in the social problems of their day', their efforts of filming and observation 'were often blind to the imperial male politics of their own representations'.[49] Form and mode certainly play a role in either complicating or alleviating the problem of representation. Realist approaches to documentary run the risk of providing the illusion of direct representation, while more experimental productions show that neutral representation and unmediated access are unattainable conceits.

Following *The Song of Ceylon*, the GPO continued its work on more experimental films: *Coal Face* and *Night Mail*, both of which contain considerable engagement with montage, counterpoint, and image–sound juxtaposition.[50] *Coal Face*, a film about the British mining industry, uses voiceover commentary, piano and drum music by Benjamin Britten, a sound montage spoken by male and female voices, and the short poem 'O Lurcher Loving Collier' by W. H. Auden. The film's mixture of poetry, commentary, and choir song does not aim at a naturalistic portrayal of coal mining, but produces a montage that praises the workers' heroic effort and bravery in the face of their dangerous and challenging work.[51] The film was also, as Cavalcanti reports, an important rehearsal for many elements featured in the following production of *Night Mail*, the GPO's most successful documentary film.[52]

*Night Mail*, directed by Harry Watt, continued the GPO's creative collaboration with Britten and Auden. It is a short film about a postal train from London to Glasgow which collected and distributed letters and parcels as an overnight service during the 1930s. The film stars workers of the post office and records their nightly activities on the train. In the second

---

[49] Marsha Bryant, *Auden and Documentary in the 1930s* (Charlottesville: University Press of Virginia, 1997), p. 172.

[50] *Coal Face*, dir. Alberto Cavalcanti (GPO Film Unit, 1935), and *Night Mail*, dir. Basil Wright and Harry Watt (GPO Film Unit, 1936).

[51] For the short poem used in *Coal Face*, see W. H. Auden, 'O Lurcher Loving Collier', in Edward Mendelson (ed.), *The English Auden: Poems, Essays and Dramatic Writings 1927–1939* (London: Faber & Faber, 1977), p. 290. The poem was written in June 1935.

[52] See Elizabeth Sussex, 'Cavalcanti in England', in Ian Aitken (ed.), *The Documentary Film Movement: An Anthology* (Edinburgh: Edinburgh University Press, 2008), 181–202 (pp. 182–183).

## 118 LITERATURE AND SOUND FILM IN MID-CENTURY BRITAIN

half of *Night Mail*, the authoritative voiceover narration turns into a verse commentary written by W. H. Auden and underscored by experimental music composed by Benjamin Britten. The poetry is spoken with changes in rhythm and tone to match Britten's music: 'This is the Night Mail crossing the border, / bringing the cheque and the postal order, / Letters for the rich, letters for the poor, / the shop at the corner and the girl next door.'[53] In his diary, Britten described the complicated process of recording the music and verse for the film to ensure their synchronism in time:

> The music I wrote really comes off well—&, for what is wanted, creates quite a lot of sensation! The whole trouble, & what takes so much time is that over the music has to be spoken a verse—kind of patter—written by Auden—in strict rhythm with the music. To represent the train noises. There is too much to be spoken in a single breath by the one voice (it is essential to keep to the same voice and to have no breaks) so we have to record separately—me, having to conduct both from an improvised visual metronome—flashes on the screen—a very difficult job! [Stuart] Legg speaks the stuff splendidly tho.'[54]

Verse and music are intended to keep to the rhythm of the moving train to represent the 'train noises.'[55] The commentary's function is to mimic acoustically the forward movement and rhythm of the train and to provide an aural impression of the working environment for the staff on the train. Speech and sound contribute to a syncopated soundtrack. The fusion of music, narration, and poetry is aligned with images of the train's motion.

The use of sound effects in *Night Mail* equally combines innovative experiment with the attempt to create a rendition of the train's soundscape: sound close-ups and sound effects are used throughout to construct the illusion of the running train. When, for instance, one of the heavy bags filled with letters and parcels intended for a station needs to be dropped off, one of the workers asks when exactly to perform the task. A more experienced member of staff advises 'you need to wait two bridges and forty-five

---

[53] W. H. Auden, 'Night Mail', in Edward Mendelson (ed.), *The English Auden: Poems, Essays and Dramatic Writings 1927–1939* (London: Faber & Faber, 1977), pp. 290–292. Auden wrote the poem in July 1935. It is grouped with his 'Fragments for Film'.

[54] Benjamin Britten, Diary Entry for 'Wednesday 15 January 1936', in John Evans (ed.), *Journeying Boy: The Diaries of the Young Benjamin Britten 1928–1938* (London: Faber & Faber, 2009), pp. 326–327.

[55] On this point, see also Marcus, 'The Creative Treatment of Actuality', p. 198.

DOCUMENTING THE EVERYDAY    119

beats' before the intended station will be reached. While the camera focusses on the inside of the train with the worker counting the appropriate number of bridges and beats, the soundtrack elevates the sounds outside of the carriage, which the worker inside is so intent on hearing. First, the sound of the train driving through two tunnels (the bridges) is heard. This is achieved by a change in reverberation of the train running over its tracks. Then the soundtrack audibly foregrounds the train running over its tracks by means of sound close-ups. The characteristic sound of a train crossing the joints of a track is counted as a 'beat' by the worker. Initially, the recording team were unable to get this particular sound close-up from the recording of a real train: 'our microphones were not selective enough to get the "clickity-clack"—the general overall roar of the train drowned it out'.[56] Instead, the recording team used a model to achieve the desired effect: 'Off we went to...the model train makers, and got a class-six engine, made to perfect scale....We pushed our tiny train by hand backwards and forwards...until we were in synchronism with the picture and then recorded it'.[57] The result enables audiences to hear the train running over its tracks and to understand how the workers use this sonic feature as an indication of direction and timing.

This unique combination of image and sound, coupled with the integration of Auden's poetry and Britten's music, creates new forms of audio-visual representation that neither authoritatively survey nor wholly romanticize their subject matter. *Song of Ceylon*, *Coal Face*, and *Night Mail* demonstrate the GPO's creative engagement with the representational conventions of sound film. At the heart of these documentary films lies an audio-visual approach that mixes modes of commentary, such as scientific lecture, social reportage, direct interview, vox pops, and poetry alongside the image material. Audio-visual combination and juxtaposition, as found in *Song of Ceylon* and *Night Mail*, uses the montage of image and sound with the aim of attaining a closer approximation of lived experience, but also of defamiliarizing its actuality material.

The impossibility of neutral representation is a recurrent problem in these films. However, it is a problem that is addressed directly, especially in some of the more experimental productions considered here. The GPO documentaries rely on montage, juxtaposition, and the combination of poetry, prose, and song to confront audiences with the impossibility of an

---

[56]  Harry Watt, *Don't Look at the Camera* (London: Paul Elek, 1974), p. 90.
[57]  Watt, *Don't Look at the Camera*, p. 91.

120 LITERATURE AND SOUND FILM IN MID-CENTURY BRITAIN

objective viewpoint or unmediated representation. Instead, montage and mixed modes draw attention to the films as aesthetic products. Audio-visual devices explicitly and clearly frame the material. *Mise-en-scène* is not self-effacing, but noticeably present in the techniques of juxtaposition applied by the filmmakers. There are also some ruptures in the alignment of sound and image: perfect synchronism and apparently causal image–sound relations are sometimes completely undercut by soundtracks that clash with the visuals. Some of the GPO's documentary films thus disrupt the notion of providing unmediated or 'neutral' access to their subject matter. As the remainder of this chapter will show, the literary works of Lewis Grassic Gibbon and George Orwell, while responding to the call of the 1930s 'documentary impulse', are similarly concerned with delineating quite explicitly the impossibility of neutral or unmediated representation.

### *Sunset Song* as Documentary Experiment

Lewis Grassic Gibbon's novel *Sunset Song* was published in 1932 and reissued posthumously as the first part of the trilogy *A Scot's Quair* (1946). *Sunset Song* follows the life of Chris Guthrie, a young woman from the rural North East of Scotland. As a backdrop to Chris's coming-of-age story in a patriarchal and rural society (her father dies, she marries, has a son, and is widowed in the First World War), *Sunset Song* traces the decline of Scottish farming communities over the first two decades of the twentieth century. The novel reflects the 1930s interest in the 'regional' and 'rural' of the nation: as Kristin Bluemel notes, 'some of the decade's most successful writers took readers to the cultural peripheries and physical borderlands…they helped extend popular imaginings of the nation beyond any sense of an essential or singular Englishness.'[58] In terms of its content and focus, *Sunset Song* is as far removed from the Southern English 'centre' as possible; yet, its form and language is overtly experimental and perhaps closer to the tastes of the intellectual avant-garde of the interwar years than one might expect. The novel repeatedly foregrounds the materiality and mediality of language; it develops a hybrid narrative style composed of different, localized forms of speech; and it presents time and lived experience as simultaneously

---

[58] Kristin Bluemel, 'Beyond Englishness: The Regional and Rural Novel in the 1930s', in Benjamin Kohlmann and Matthew Taunton (eds), *A History of 1930s British Literature* (Cambridge: Cambridge University Press, 2019), 17–30 (p. 17).

DOCUMENTING THE EVERYDAY    121

historical, communal, and individual. Examining the ways in which *Sunset Song* tests the novel's representational capacities in the age of audio-vision opens up a new view of Grassic Gibbon's work, which has traditionally been read either as a work of uncompromising realism and Scottish nationalism or as a formative work of Scottish modernism.[59]

Structurally, *Sunset Song* draws on music and the temporal dimensions of agriculture as a way of ordering the passing of time: the novel begins with a 'Prelude', ends with an 'Epilude', and contains 'The Song' in its middle. This musical structure is further divided into sub-sections that move along 'the cyclical rhythm of agricultural labour':[60] beginning and ending with 'The Unfurrowed Field' and, in the middle, containing the chapters 'Ploughing', 'Drilling', 'Seed-Time', and 'Harvest' in their chronological order. This double form of structuring is the first indication of the novel's characteristic mixture of realist and surrealist practices of portraying everyday life, which Nick Hubble and Benjamin Kohlmann have separately discussed as key features of 1930s literature and culture.[61] Ben Highmore suggests that surrealist 'collage (or montage) provides a persistent methodology for attending to everyday life'. In confronting and contrasting 'disparate elements', collage lends new 'visibility' to everyday life by 'making the ordinary strange through transferring it to surprising contexts and placing it in unusual combinations'.[62] In this vein, *Sunset Song* juxtaposes musical structure and the temporal order of agricultural labour to present daily life in the North-East of Scotland and to simultaneously render strange, exciting, and new this historically and locally specific form of lived experience. The combination of art and agricultural labour is co-constitutive of the novel's narration and structure.

This approach of unlikely juxtaposition and collage is maintained throughout the text as *Sunset Song* curates its own characteristic idiom and

---

[59] For accounts that foreground the novel's realism and nationalism see, for instance, Hanne Tange, 'Grassic Gibbon's Art of Community: *A Scots Quair* and the Condition of Scotland', *Studies in Scottish Literature*, 33.1 (2004), 247–262; Hanne Tange, 'Language, Class and Social Power in *A Scots Quair*', in Scott Lyall (ed.), *The International Companion to Lewis Grassic Gibbon* (Glasgow: Association for Scottish Literary Studies, 2015), 22–32; on modernism, see Morag Shiach, 'Lewis Grassic Gibbon and Modernism', in Scott Lyall (ed.), *The International Companion to Lewis Grassic Gibbon* (Glasgow: Association for Scottish Literary Studies, 2015), 9–21.

[60] Shiach, 'Lewis Grassic Gibbon and Modernism', p. 13.

[61] Nick Hubble, *Mass-Observation and Everyday Life* (Basingstoke: Palgrave Macmillan, 2006), pp. 79–90, and Benjamin Kohlmann, *Committed Styles: Modernism, Politics, and Left-wing Literature in the 1930s* (Oxford: Oxford University Press, 2014), pp. 90–160.

[62] Ben Highmore, *Everyday Life and Cultural Theory* (London: Routledge, 2002), p. 46.

# 122 LITERATURE AND SOUND FILM IN MID-CENTURY BRITAIN

style. The novel synthesizes Doric Scots, a dialect spoken in the North-East of Scotland, and written standard (Southern) English. While nineteenth and twentieth-century works of fiction set in Scotland or featuring Scottish characters frequently use Scots for direct speech and Standard English as narrative voice (as done, for instance, in Walter Scott's *Waverley* of 1814), such a distinction also implies 'assumptions (intended or not) about the authority of standard English, with additionally implied class distinctions between the author and his characters'.[63] By contrast, Grassic Gibbon develops a new narrative voice for his novel by merging English and Scots into a hybrid style, thereby creating forms of expression and rhythm that appear to abolish sociolinguistic distinctions.[64] While the novel's style thus presents a fusion of standard English and Doric Scots, the novel's syntax is also inflected with the rhythm and order of spoken language: 'there was such speak and stir as Kinraddie hadn't known for long'.[65] Grassic Gibbon's style has been characterized as 'lightly Scoticized English' which prioritizes readability over some more complex approaches to the use of Scots in prose and poetry by artists of the Scottish Renaissance, such as Hugh MacDiarmid.[66] The effect of this montage style of Scots and English is to build and present community and belonging and to deconstruct sociolinguistic difference.[67]

The novel further omits quotation marks for direct speech and, instead, italicizes spoken interaction, thereby visually minimizing punctuation marks that separate the narrator's voice from the voices of characters:

---

[63] Roderick Watson, 'Alien Voices from the Street: Demotic Modernism in Modern Scots Writing', *Yearbook of English Studies*, 25 (1995), 141–155 (p. 147).

[64] Ian Carter, 'Lewis Grassic Gibbon, *A Scot's Quair*, and the Peasantry', *History Workshop Journal*, 6 (1978), 169–185 (p. 174).

[65] Lewis Grassic Gibbon, *Sunset Song* (Edinburgh: Canongate, 2020), p. 189.

[66] William R. Malcolm, *A Blasphemer & Reformer. A Study of James Leslie Mitchell/Lewis Grassic Gibbon* (Aberdeen: Aberdeen University Press, 1984), p. 127. Other writers associated with the Scottish Renaissance include Neill Gunn, Nan Shepherd, Naomi Mitchison, and Edwin and Willa Muir. See Scott Lyall, '"That Ancient Self": Scottish Modernism's Counter-Renaissance', *European Journal of English Studies*, 18.1 (2014), 73–85.

[67] Grassic Gibbon's endeavour to mediate regional dialect is certainly not a new strategy: Emily Brontë (*Wuthering Heights*, 1847), Elizabeth Gaskell (*Mary Barton,* 1848; *North and South,* 1855), and Charles Dickens (*Great Expectations,* 1861) all textually represent local dialects in the Victorian novel. However, in these novels, dialect tends to be a device for demonstrating class and socioeconomic difference while *Sunset Song* uses language to deconstruct sociolinguistic difference. On this point, see Charles Ferrall, 'From Wells to John Berger: The Social Democratic Era of the Novel', in Robert L. Caserio and Clement Hawes (eds), *The Cambridge History of the English Novel* (Cambridge: Cambridge University Press, 2012), 807–822 (p. 812).

DOCUMENTING THE EVERYDAY **123**

So when the minister came on him and cried out right heartily *Well, you'll be my neighbour Guthrie, man?* father cocked his red beard at the minister and glinted at him like an icicle and said *Ay, MISTER Gibbon, I'll be that.* So the minister held out his hand and changed his tune right quick and said quiet-like *You've a fine-kept farm here, Mr. Guthrie, trig and trim, though I hear you've sat down a bare six months.*[68]

Through repetitive idiomatic expressions, such as 'folk said that…' or 'they said', the narrator reports and relays information circulating in the local community, rather than appearing to superimpose a 'voice-of-god' narration. At the same time, the unspecific 'folk' or 'they' also raises the question of who speaks and who is spoken to. There is vagueness and ambiguity, as well as an oral (and aural) quality to the narration that ensures the reader's continued awareness of the story as *told* and *framed* by other voices. *Sunset Song* 'mixes…an internalised and colloquial narrative style in which Chris Guthrie's personal voice and the voice of her community and the impersonal authorial voice are all contained'.[69] The novel's idiom and syntax create a polyphonic community voice that, as Alastair Cording comments, at times personifies 'local gossip and rumour, satire, comedy and commentary. It is simultaneously perceptive, plain-spoken, intimate, ignorant and untrustworthy'.[70]

The 'Epilude' demonstrates the novel's interest in the sensory materiality and mediality of language and music: when Chris's husband, Ewan Tavendale, is shot as a deserter in the First World War, Chris and her local community are attending a service of remembrance at which a memorial for the fallen soldiers is unveiled. The narrator of the 'Epilude' pauses here to include the inscription on the memorial, in capital letters, followed by the minister's full sermon at the unveiling of the memorial—a long speech printed in italics.[71] The 'Epilude' then also integrates an image of musical notation to record what is heard by the congregation at the memorial service (see Figure 4.1).[72] The text thus draws attention to the sensory, and specifically audio-visual, nature of lived experience. The narration includes

---

[68] Grassic Gibbon, *Sunset Song*, p. 59.    [69] Watson, 'Alien Voices', p. 146.

[70] Alastair Cording, 'Adapting *Sunset Song* for the Stage: Notes by Alastair Cording', in *Lewis Grassic Gibbon's Sunset Song*, dramatized by Alastair Cording (London: Nick Hern, 2004), xiii–xxi (p. xix).

[71] Grassic Gibbon, *Sunset Song*, pp. 252–253.

[72] Grassic Gibbon, *Sunset Song*, pp. 253–254.

your hair and was eerie and uncanny, the *Flowers of the Forest* as he played it:

It rose and rose and wept and cried, that crying for the men that fell in battle, and there was Kirsty Strachan weeping quietly and others with her, and the young ploughmen they stood with glum, white faces, they'd no understanding or caring, it was something that vexed and tore at them, it belonged to times they had no knowing of.

He fair could play, the piper, he tore at your heart marching there with the tune leaping up the moor and echoing across the loch, folk said that Chris Tavendale alone shed never a tear, she stood quiet, holding her boy by the hand, looking down on Blawearie's fields till the playing was over. And syne folk saw that the dark had come and began to stream down the hill, leaving her there, some were uncertain and looked them back. But they saw the minister was standing behind her, waiting for her, they'd the last of the light with them up there, and maybe they didn't need it or heed it, you can do without the day if you've a lamp quiet-lighted and kind in your heart.

**Figure 4.1** Excerpt from the final page of Lewis Grassic Gibbon's *Sunset Song* (1932).

the lettering on the memorial, as first seen by the congregation, the minister's sermon, as heard by the congregation, and the music experienced by the characters. The integration of musical notation at the end of the novel forms the culmination of a wider textual preoccupation with music that is maintained throughout: popular folk songs feature regularly in the everyday life of the community. There is singing and dancing at special occasions, such as Chris and Ewan's wedding, but also everyday music as Chris is singing to

DOCUMENTING THE EVERYDAY   125

herself while performing her daily tasks at the farm.[73] Scottish folk songs, such as the seventeenth-century 'The Bonnie House o' Airlie' and the eighteenth-century 'Auld Robin Gray' are referenced by the text and performed by characters of the community in Kinraddie.[74]

There are some significant parallels between the novel's textual manoeuvres in the Epilude and interwar avant-garde writing. Hope Mirrlees's expansive 600-line poem *Paris*, first printed in 1920 by the Hogarth Press, similarly integrates some bars of musical notation and mimics the style, layout, and typesetting of posters and plaques encountered by the poem's speaker on her wanderings through the French capital.[75] Nina Enemark and Sofia Permiakova suggest that Mirrlees's poem simultaneously draws on visual and sonic dimensions; it must be read aloud and yet also considered as text and typeface set on paper to fully account for its visual and acoustic features.[76] The musical notation, an excerpt from Handel's opera *Rinaldo* (1711), as noted by Julia Briggs, is introduced by the poem as 'The Seventeenth Century lies exquisitely dying.../ Hu s s s h'. The following two lines then contain the excerpt from Handel's opera, a sequence requiring 'diminuendo' from the performer.[77] Text, image, and sound intersect in the poem to create multisensory and multi-medial effects. The musical notation, and its implied soundscape, become part of the poem's textual dimension while simultaneously pushing the limits of what might be considered as forms of 'text' or 'textual representation' in the poem.

Grassic Gibbon's *Sunset Song* similarly embeds the musical notation into the text, which first describes the player and then moves on to the song: 'Highlandman McIvor tuned up his pipes and began to step slow round the stone circle by Blawearie Loch...*the Flowers of the Forest* as he played it.'[78] The musical notation shows the duple metre (a 2/4 time signature), which indicates the melody be played as lament. The musical notation alters the reading experience: it transforms the novel by adding further visual and sonic dimensions to the printed text. The musical notation can be 'read' and

[73] Grassic Gibbon, *Sunset Song*, pp. 156–157, 161–163, 229.
[74] Grassic Gibbon, *Sunset Song*, pp. 162–163.
[75] Hope Mirrlees, *Paris: A Poem* (London: Faber & Faber, 2020).
[76] See Sofia Permiakova, '*Paris: A Poem* by Hope Mirrlees: The Liminal World of Paris in 1919', *Journal of European Studies*, 51.3/4 (2021), 192–203 (p. 199); Nina Enemark, 'Antiquarian Magic: Jane Harrison's Ritual Theory and Hope Mirrlees's Antiquarianism in *Paris*', in Elizabeth Anderson et al. (eds), *Modernist Women Writers and Spirituality* (London: Palgrave Macmillan, 2006), 115–33 (pp. 126–127).
[77] Mirrlees, *Paris*, p. 17, and Julia Briggs, 'Commentary on *Paris*', in Hope Mirrlees, *Collected Poems*, ed. Sandeep Parmar (Manchester: Carcanet, 2011), 254–283 (p. 274).
[78] Grassic Gibbon, *Sunset Song*, pp. 253–254.

126  LITERATURE AND SOUND FILM IN MID-CENTURY BRITAIN

invites the possibility of thinking of the action described here as performance. The musical score itself, as A. J. Carruthers notes, can 'transform,
interrupt or structure the textual field'.[79] The key difference between Grassic
Gibbon and Mirrlees's texts is of course form and genre. The musical score
in Mirrlees's poetry interacts differently with the lines of verse surrounding
it than the interaction found between musical notation and Grassic
Gibbon's narrative prose text. Indeed, the novel's integration of the musical
lament raises fundamental questions about the capacities of narrative prose
to stretch beyond its textual, typographical form, and to offer a sensory,
affective reading experience that highlights the novel's Epilude as a key
moment of mourning: not merely Chris's mourning for her husband, or the
community's for their fallen men, but also a mourning for the end of a way
of life that can hardly be conveyed in words. The musical notation crucially
entails a questioning of the novel's limits and capacities as a literary form
and asks readers to consider the combination of text, image, and sound as
mediatized forms of textual expression.

If read in conjunction with *The Song of Ceylon*, important intersections
emerge between the documentary film and Grassic Gibbon's novel. Both the
novel and the documentary film draw attention to their status as curated,
aesthetic objects whose framing inevitably shapes the presentation of their
subject matter. Both also question the representational conventions of their
media form in different ways. In response to such questions, both structure
themselves around music and merge forms of musical, visual, and textual
representation—either in the style of a 'symphonic composition' or folk
song. The visual, aural, and textual cues in both works defamiliarize their
subject matter and renew the 'visibility' of that which is presented while
also insisting on the impossibility of direct or unmediated access to their
material.

## George Orwell and the Limits of the Novel

George Orwell's early prose fiction connects in surprising ways with the
hybrid narration constructed by Grassic Gibbon's *Sunset Song*. Orwell's
success in the 1930s largely derived from his journalism and 'stimulating'
non-fiction works such as *Down and Out in Paris and London* (1933),

---

[79] A. J. Carruthers, *Notational Experiments in North American Long Poems, 1961–2011*
(Cham: Palgrave Macmillan, 2017), p. xiv.

DOCUMENTING THE EVERYDAY 127

*The Road to Wigan Pier* (1937), and *Homage to Catalonia* (1938).[80] By contrast, his early novels have been judged as 'false starts towards the triumphs of *Animal Farm* and *Nineteen Eighty-Four*' and as 'try-outs by an apprentice' who had not yet found his own distinctive voice.[81] However, Orwell's novels of the 1930s rehearse a variety of experimental textual approaches, including scenic and episodic narration and dramatic dialogue, to construct narrative texts that question the representational conventions of the novel and the limits of prose narrative. Despite its reputation as a 'bad' novel, *A Clergyman's Daughter* (1935), for instance, ought to be viewed as a key text in Orwell's oeuvre because it forms 'a valuable record of Orwell trying his hand at episodic storytelling'. Nathan Waddell cites one of Orwell's letters to Henry Miller, in which Orwell himself writes that the novel contains some valuable literary 'experiments'.[82]

Orwell's work of the 1930s, as Keith Williams observes, both turns towards and simultaneously criticizes 'the documentary mode of [his] time from within'.[83] The 'inconsistencies' and 'political difficulties' that David Dwan notes as characteristic of Orwell's oeuvre, then, materialize in the creation of clashes and discontinuities on the level of narrative form in these early novels.[84] *A Clergyman's Daughter* and *Keep the Aspidistra Flying* are instructive texts for they reveal Orwell's own interrogation of practices of (textual) representation and address the impossibility of unmediated access to lived experience following his first novel *Burmese Days* (1934).

*A Clergyman's Daughter* traces a moment of crisis in the life of its protagonist, Dorothy Hare, who is the daughter of an impoverished rector in the fictional English town of Knype Hill. Dorothy dutifully performs the work of a housekeeper to her father but she constantly worries about incoming bills as her father refuses to acknowledge the family's debts and financial precarity. Suddenly, one day, Dorothy finds herself homeless in London

---

[80] Q. D. Leavis called Orwell's non-fiction 'stimulating' while finding his novels of the 1930s 'dreary' and 'dull'. See Q. D. Leavis, 'The Literary Life Respectable: Reviews of Edwin Muir and George Orwell', in G. Singh (ed.), *Collected Essays. Vol. 3: The Novel of Religious Controversy* (Cambridge: Cambridge University Press, 1989), pp. 283–289. The review was first published in *Scrutiny*, 9.2 (September 1940).

[81] Michael Levenson, 'The Fictional Realist: Novels of the 1930s', in John Rodden (ed.), *The Cambridge Companion to George Orwell* (Cambridge: Cambridge University Press, 2007), 59–75 (p. 59); Roger Fowler, *The Language of George Orwell* (Basingstoke: Macmillan, 1995), p. 60.

[82] Waddell, 'Introduction', p. xi.

[83] Keith Williams, '"The Unpaid Agitator": Joyce's Influence on George Orwell and James Agee', *James Joyce Quarterly*, 36.4 (1999), 729–763 (p. 729).

[84] David Dwan, *Liberty, Equality, and Humbug: Orwell's Political Ideals* (Oxford: Oxford University Press, 2018), p. 206.

128 LITERATURE AND SOUND FILM IN MID-CENTURY BRITAIN

suffering from amnesia. The sudden shift in Dorothy's circumstances and her amnesia stem from her having been assaulted by Mr Warburton, a neighbour in her father's community of Knype Hill. Unable to remember her name and identity, Dorothy's Christian faith is tested in the face of pressing worldly concerns such as money, food, and shelter, before she ultimately returns to her former life at her father's rectory. Although the original typescript of the novel has not survived, records of required changes show that the text had to be substantially altered before Victor Gollancz agreed to its publication.[85] *A Clergyman's Daughter* fosters immersion in the circumstances and environments of Dorothy's life by combining prose narrative, dramatic dialogue, and stage directions. Dorothy's crisis is also a narrative crisis, an interlude that disrupts narrative chronology and continuity. As with Grassic Gibbon's efforts to push the limits of the novel and to frame the text as a curated response to the period's 'documentary impulse', Orwell's novel strings together only loosely related sequences, which effectively echo what one might consider rather un-Orwellian forms of avant-garde writing.

The first part of chapter 1 begins *in medias res* with Dorothy being woken by her alarm clock. The second part of the chapter then 'zooms out' and provides a bird's eye view of Knype Hill: 'St Athelstan's Church stood at the highest point of Knype Hill, and if you chose to climb the tower you could see ten miles or so across the surrounding country...Immediately below you lay the town, with the High Street running east and west and dividing it unequally.'[86] The first chapter thus introduces readers to Dorothy's life and to the environments in which she moves. At the end of the chapter, she still sits at work after midnight. Tired, she 'worked on, mechanically...and pinching herself every two minutes to counteract the hypnotic sound of the oil-stove singing.'[87] As chapter 2 then begins on the following page, the reader—as well as Dorothy—are suddenly shaken out of the assumption of narrative continuity: 'Out of a black, dreamless sleep, with the sense of being drawn upwards through an enormous and gradually lightening abysses Dorothy awoke to a species of consciousness.'[88] Dorothy is no longer at home; she is on a bench, somewhere in an (as of yet) unidentified town. Before Dorothy even realizes that she cannot remember her own name, the novel makes a point of narrating the lack of connection between

---

[85] Peter Davies, 'Note on the Text', *A Clergyman's Daughter* (London: Penguin, 2000), pp. v–viii.

[86] George Orwell, *A Clergyman's Daughter* (London: Penguin, 2000), p. 11.

[87] Orwell, *Clergyman's Daughter*, p. 84.     [88] Orwell, *Clergyman's Daughter*, p. 85.

DOCUMENTING THE EVERYDAY **129**

sensory perception and cognitive faculties of interpreting and contextualizing this perception: 'as yet it could not properly be said that she was *looking*. For the things she saw were not apprehended...they were not even apprehended as things moving; not even as *things*.'[89] The reader is taken from the familiar context of Dorothy's housework routine to a narrative episode that focusses on disorientation and the disjoint between sensory perception and cognitive processing. Although Dorothy slowly regains her ability to connect perception and cognition, she now lives without any recollection of who she is and where she came from. It is only at the end of the novel's final chapter that Dorothy finds herself back at the rectory and working in her usual routine, creating costumes for a play performed by the parish's children.[90]

Structurally, *A Clergyman's Daughter* adapts the order of a five-act play, or, of a screen play. In its turn to a performative, audio-visual structure, it actually shares some surprising features with Waugh's adaptation of stage revues for *Vile Bodies* that were discussed in Chapter 2. In Orwell's novel, there are five chapters (five acts), each of which is subdivided into a minimum of two subsections (scenes). Chapter 1 functions as an exposition whereas chapter 2 then outlines the sudden complication in the form of Dorothy's amnesia and homelessness. The novel further establishes the link between prose narrative and drama or screen play by adding dramatic dialogue to its repertoire, thereby framing parts of the text as a script for performance. A rehearsal for a play on *Charles I* with a group of children is partially rendered in dramatic dialogue in chapter 1 and mixes spoken lines of the rehearsal with surrounding verbal exchanges taking place off-stage: '*A girl*: "Please, Miss, Mother said as I was to tell you, Miss—" /*Dorothy*: "Keep still, Percy! For goodness sake keep still!" /*Cromwell*: "'Alt! I 'old a pistol in my 'and!".'[91] Later, in the climactic chapter 3, the novel returns to this strategy to convey Dorothy's experience of homelessness in London. The first part of chapter 3 is written entirely as a piece of dramatic or scripted dialogue that covers more than thirty pages of the novel:

(*Scene*: Trafalgar Square. Dimly visible through the mist, a dozen people, Dorothy among them, are grouped about one of the benches near the north parapet.)

*Charlie* (singing): "Ail Mary, 'ail Mary, 'a-il Ma-ary—'

---

[89] Orwell, *Clergyman's Daughter*, p. 85.
[90] Orwell, *Clergyman's Daughter*, pp. 286–297.
[91] Orwell, *Clergyman's Daughter*, p. 60.

130  LITERATURE AND SOUND FILM IN MID-CENTURY BRITAIN

(Big Ben strikes ten.)

*Snouter* (mimicking the noise): 'Ding dong, ding dong! Shut your—noise, can't you? Seven more hours of it on this—square before we got the chance of a set-down and a bit of sleep! Cripes!'

*Mr Tallboys* (to himself): '*Non sum qualis eram boni sub regno Edwardi!...*'[92]

While this chapter specifically recalls episode fifteen, 'Circe', of James Joyce's *Ulysses* (1922), Orwell adapts the model of Joyce's modernist text to present a cacophony of homeless voices encountered by Dorothy in Trafalgar Square.[93] She meets Mr Tallboys, who used to be a rector, Snouter who tries to sleep, and the old Mrs Wayne who tells Dorothy that she knows what it means to 'come down in the world'. There is little interaction between characters and, in most instances, they are taking turns speaking to themselves and to the reader. There are scripted directions, which specify the manner of delivery: 'singing', 'chanting', 'sotto voce', 'double marking time', 'beating an imaginary drum and singing', 'declaiming'.[94] The scene produces a 'polyphonic discourse'.[95] While this part of the novel may of course be viewed as an early expression of Orwell's 'radiophonic' style, such a reading arguably neglects the audio-visual dimension of this scripted performance, which entails directions regarding gestures, body language, and props.[96] The 'Trafalgar Square' episode outlines movements and activities of the characters and provides some guidance on their feelings and behaviour.[97] This part of the novel also describes in great detail the setting in which the characters move. It is possible that the integration of scripted (or dramatic) dialogue and these more extensive stage directions were, at least in part, inspired by Orwell's attempts to write a play in the 1920s while living in Burma.[98] However, by taking inspiration from Joyce's *Ulysses*, the 'Trafalgar Square' episode also juxtaposes prose narration and screen play or drama, which self-consciously tests the limits of the novel's representational conventions.

---

[92] Orwell, *Clergyman's Daughter*, p. 151.

[93] Orwell's fraught relationship with modernism is discussed by Patricia Rae, 'Mr. Charrington's Junk Shop: T. S. Eliot and Modernist Poetics in *Nineteen Eighty-Four*', *Twentieth-Century Literature*, 43.2 (1997), 196–220.

[94] Orwell, *Clergyman's Daughter*, pp. 151–184.

[95] Lorraine Saunders, *The Unsung Artistry of George Orwell: The Novels from Burmese Days to Nineteen Eighty-Four* (London: Taylor & Francis, 2016), p. 31.

[96] The novel is read as a 'radiophonic' piece with direct links to Orwell's proven interest in radio by, for instance, Tim Crook in 'George Orwell and the Radio Imagination', pp. 193–208.

[97] See Orwell, *Clergyman's Daughter*, pp. 171, 174, 177–178.

[98] On this point, see Peter Davison, *George Orwell: A Literary Life* (Basingstoke: Macmillan, 1996), pp. 23–24.

DOCUMENTING THE EVERYDAY 131

Some of the language here is inspired by Orwell's own 'documentary' activities in the summer and autumn of 1931: from August to October that year, he had spent some time tramping and hop-picking, keeping a diary on his travels and including some notes on phrases and idioms he had overheard amongst the workers. Having lived amongst the seasonal labourers, he comments, for instance, on their 'Rhyming Slang. I thought this was extinct, but it is far from it. The hop-pickers used these expressions freely: A dig in the grave, meaning a shave. The hot cross bun, meaning the sun. Greengages, meaning wages.'[99] In *A Clergyman's Daughter*, Orwell then incorporates these expressions into the dialogue:

> *Ginger* (singing): '*There* they go—*in* their joy –
> 'Appy girl—*lu*cky boy –
> But 'ere am *I-I-I-*
> Broken—'*a-a-aa*rted!
> God, I ain't 'ad a dig in the grave for three days. 'Ow long since you washed your face, Snouter?'[100]

Some elements of the 'Trafalgar Square' episode, as well as Dorothy's work on a hop farm in chapter 2, thus appear to derive from Orwell's own work experiences and observations in the early 1930s; they also prefigure his research for *The Road to Wigan Pier*. As an observer–participant, Orwell acted and wrote in a manner not unlike those of M-O's volunteers and published a number of essays based on his experiences.[101] If, as Patricia Rae convincingly argues, Orwell's work on *The Road to Wigan Pier* forms a key example of what she terms 'modernist anthropology', Orwell's earlier work on *A Clergyman's Daughter* already acts as important, fictionalized precursor to this approach and ought to be read not as a 'failed novel', but as a literary experiment that tests the textual limits for combining prose narrative, scenic narration, and scripted dialogue alongside autobiographical experience to create this documentary novel.

Orwell's next novel, *Keep the Aspidistra Flying*, continues the trajectory of *A Clergyman's Daughter*, albeit more covertly. Like the previous story of Dorothy Hare, *Aspidistra* draws on Orwell's own biography, such as

---

[99] George Orwell, in Peter Davison (ed.), *Diaries* (London: Harvill Secker, 2009), pp. 2–22 (p. 21).
[100] Orwell, *Clergyman's Daughter*, p. 157.
[101] See Orwell, *Diaries,* pp. 2–22, and George Orwell, 'Hop-Picking', *New Statesman and Nation*, 17 October 1931.

## 132 LITERATURE AND SOUND FILM IN MID-CENTURY BRITAIN

working part-time in a bookshop in Hampstead.[102] Gordon Comstock, the novel's protagonist, is an aspiring poet who left his well-paid, full-time position as a copy writer for an advertising firm due to his contempt for both middle-class respectability and capitalism. Gordon wants to devote more time to his literary career and has therefore taken on a part-time position in a bookshop. However, his low income quickly ensures his descent into poverty which, in turn, hinders his creativity, destroys his sense of self, and negatively impacts his relationship with his love interest Rosemary. The lack of financial means severely limits his capacity to intellectually engage with his environment and existential worries dominate his life. Gordon bitterly concludes that there can be no writing without money and ultimately, when Rosemary falls pregnant, he abandons his hopes of becoming a poet, returns to full-time work as a copy writer, and marries her.[103]

*Aspidistra* spends much of its plot reflecting on the composition of poetry and integrating parts of Gordon's attempts at literary writing into the narrative text: 'the damp wind blew spitefully through the naked trees. *Sharply the menacing wind sweeps over.* The poem he had begun on Wednesday, of which six stanzas were now finished, came back into his mind.'[104] In part, the recurrent focus on poetry, and on the poet-figure, may reflect Orwell's admiration of T. S. Eliot, whom Orwell had asked to read *Down and Out in Paris and London* (1933) when he was looking for a publisher a few years earlier.[105] Graham Good even suggests that Gordon's poetry is 'heavily derivative from Eliot in vision, if not in versification.'[106]

---

[102] See Orwell's short essay, 'Bookshop Memories', which was first published in *Fortnightly* in November 1936, and reprinted in George Orwell, *Essays* (London: Penguin, 2000), pp. 25–29. See also John Rodden and John Rossi, *The Cambridge Introduction to George Orwell* (Cambridge: Cambridge University Press, 2012), p. 38.

[103] Orwell returns to this critical point in chapter 5 of *The Road to Wigan Pier*, where he asserts that 'there is no doubt about the deadening, debilitating effect of unemployment upon everybody…. The best intellects will not stand up against it. Once or twice it has happened to me to meet unemployed men of genuine literary ability; there are others whom I haven't met but whose work I occasionally see in the magazines. Now and again, at long intervals, these men will produce an article or a short story which is quite obviously better than most of the stuff that gets whooped up by the blurb-reviewers. Why, then, do they make so little use of their talents? They have all the leisure in the world; why don't they sit down and write books? Because to write books you need not only comfort and solitude—and solitude is never easy to attain in a working-class home—you also need peace of mind. You can't settle to anything, you can't command the spirit of hope in which anything has got to be created, with that dull evil cloud of unemployment hanging over you.' See George Orwell, *The Road to Wigan Pier* (London: Penguin, 2001), pp. 75–76.

[104] Orwell, *Aspidistra*, p. 110.

[105] Rae, 'T. S. Eliot and Modernist Poetics in *Nineteen Eighty-Four*', pp. 196–197.

[106] Graham Good, 'Orwell and Eliot: Politics, Poetry, Prose', in Peter Buitenhuis and Ira B. Nadel (eds), *George Orwell: A Reassessment* (London: Macmillan, 1988), 139–156 (p. 140).

DOCUMENTING THE EVERYDAY    133

*Aspidistra* is ultimately a novel that documents the writing process of a (failed) poet; the novel tests the ways in which narrative prose and poetry might be collated to mediate a writer's life.

As Ben Clarke notes, *Aspidistra* pursues 'as one of the central critical problems of the text, the need to actively inhabit and enjoy a society whilst recognizing its insufficiency and injustices'.[107] One might add here that the novel is equally interested in examining the problem of textual representation of this particular conflict. How might one present the disjoint between the intellectual labour of creating art and the real-world conditions for its making? Like *A Clergyman's Daughter*, *Aspidistra* is, at least in part, a literary experiment testing the ways in which a novel might address its subject matter. While *Clergyman's Daughter* is more overtly discontinuous and fragmented, lacking causal connections and a clear timeline due to Dorothy's amnesia, *Aspidistra*'s plot develops more slowly in a causally motivated chain of events. However, the perception of time, especially in relation to money, becomes a pertinent problem throughout this novel. From the very first page, Gordon's perception of time is tied to audio-visual, sensory experience: the striking and chiming of clocks and the ringing of the doorbell whenever a new customer enters the bookshop, structure the first chapter into discrete scenes that follow each other.[108] As he waits for customers, Gordon critically observes his surroundings and himself; he 'shortens the focus of his eyes' to view his reflection in a glass pane; his eyes then 'refocus themselves' on advertising posters across the street, before 'turning his eyes away' and becoming 'dull-eyed' at the sight of all the unsold, unwanted books in the shop.[109] This first chapter, like the first chapter of *Clergyman's Daughter*, establishes the protagonist in his surroundings and gives readers an impression of daily routine. It also establishes Gordon as the object of his own observation. Gordon is hyper-aware of himself, hyper-vigilant of his actions. While Dorothy's amnesia appears to render her more passive, Gordon is actively monitoring his actions and thoughts at all times.

Following this introduction, the novel turns to exploring problems of social alienation as well as creative and intellectual stasis as direct consequences of Gordon's lack of money. These specific issues are presented by the text as a problem of disjointed perception. Here, too, are parallels to the

---

[107] Ben Clarke, '"Beer and Cigarettes and a Girl to Flirt with": Orwell, Drinking and the Everyday', *English Studies*, 96.5 (2015), 541–561 (p. 544).

[108] George Orwell, *Keep the Aspidistra Flying* (London: Penguin, 2000), pp. 1, 9, 12, 16, 20.

[109] Orwell, *Aspidistra*, pp. 4, 5, 6, 7.

## 134 LITERATURE AND SOUND FILM IN MID-CENTURY BRITAIN

earlier *Clergyman's Daughter*: when Dorothy awakes, having lost her memory, the narrative reports this as a problem of synchronizing perception and cognition. In similar terms, Gordon's alienation is presented as a breakdown of audio-vision:

> He felt dreadfully thirsty already. It had been a mistake to let himself think of beer. As he approached the Crichton, he heard voices singing. The great garish pub seemed to be more brightly lighted than usual. There was a concert or something going on inside. Twenty ripe male voices were chanting in unison:
>
> 'Fo-or ree's a jorrigoo' fellow,
>
> For ree's a jorrigoo' fellow
>
> For ree's a jorrigoo fe-ELL-OW—
>
> And toori oori us!'
>
> At least, that was what it sounded like. Comstock drew nearer, pierced by ravishing thirst. The voices were so soggy, so infinitely beery. When you heard them you saw the scarlet faces of prosperous plumbers....He went round to the other side of the pub. The beer-choked voices followed him.[110]

Gordon hears the singing voices, but he does not see their source: the voices are acousmatic, their source and context a matter of assumption. Gordon can only assume that there is 'a concert going on'—but he cannot say this with certainty. Indeed, he imagines seeing the faces of those who sing, but he does not actually see them. When he has the opportunity to enter the pub (and thereby to see as well as hear the voices and their source in synchronism), he turns away as he cannot afford to buy a drink. Sound and vision are slowly uncoupled from one another; the experience of acousmatic voices conveys Gordon's sense of alienation. The link between vision and audition is broken when one cannot afford to participate in the social rituals of the everyday.[111]

The 'failure of acts and objects to realize their own possibilities', as Clarke notes, is a pervasive theme in Orwell's *Aspidistra*.[112] Yet, it is this particular failure which is also key to liberating objects and everyday acts from

---

[110] Orwell, *Aspidistra*, pp. 79–80.
[111] See Clarke, 'Orwell, Drinking and the Everyday', pp. 541–561.
[112] Clarke, 'Orwell, Drinking and the Everyday', p. 543.

DOCUMENTING THE EVERYDAY 135

habitual perception.[113] The textual form in which such 'failure of acts and objects' clearly emerges is the breakdown of audio-vision and recurrent ruptures of temporality, of clock time that runs counter to Gordon's subjective experience of time. For most of the novel, Gordon pursues his writing career by trying to compose a long narrative poem, *London Pleasures*: 'it was a huge, ambitious project—the kind of thing that should only be undertaken by people with endless leisure.'[114] But neither money nor leisure are at Gordon's disposal and so his creative efforts are constantly menaced by the march of time:

> Down in Mrs Wisbeach's lair the clock struck half past ten. You could always hear it striking at night. Ping-ping, ping-ping—a note of doom! The ticking of the alarm clock on the mantelpiece became audible to Gordon again, bringing with it the consciousness of the sinister passage of time. He looked about him. Another evening wasted. Hours, days, years slipping by.... In sheer self-punishment he dragged forth a wad of *London Pleasures*, spread out grimy sheets and looked at them as one looks at a skull for a *memento mori*.... The fruit (fruit, indeed!) of two years' work— that labyrinthine mess of words! And tonight's achievement—two lines crossed out; two lines backward instead of forward. The lamp made a sound like a tiny hiccup and went out.[115]

While clock time relentlessly moves forward, the process of writing and revising, and thereby also Gordon's subjective perception of time, moves backward. There is no sense of alignment or synchronism. It is precisely these moments of sensory and temporal rupture that bring into focus Gordon's 'lower-middle-class' existence and his feelings of isolation.[116]

This chapter has argued that some of the GPO's films and literary texts by Lewis Grassic Gibbon and George Orwell engage in a process of questioning representational conventions in response to the 'documentary impulse' of the

---

[113] Martin Heidegger's *Being and Time*, for instance, outlines two modes of engagement with objects: there is the practical use ('ready-to-hand') and a more detached engagement in those cases where one is suddenly confronted with the 'unusability' of an object or equipment, a kind of failure of the object to behave in the way that one expects it to in a given context: 'We discover its unusability, however, not by looking at it and establishing its properties, but rather by the circumspection of the dealings in which we use it. When its unusability is thus dis-covered, equipment becomes conspicuous. This conspicuousness presents the ready-to-hand equipment as in a certain un-readiness-to-hand.' Heidegger, *Being and Time*, trans. John Macquarrie and Edward Robinson (New York: Harper, 2008), pp. 102–103.
[114] Orwell, *Aspidistra*, pp. 32–33.    [115] Orwell, *Aspidistra*, p. 37.
[116] Orwell, *Aspidistra*, p. 23.

1930s. The works discussed here are attuned to the impossibility of granting unmediated access to their subjects. By framing themselves as the curated products of creative labour, these texts and films negate any possible claim to documentary realism. Rather, they test the limits of cinematic and novelistic representation and underline their own constructed nature. This matters at a time when technologies of vision and audition appear to facilitate 'direct' access to the everyday, when the difference between real and reel may become increasingly difficult to spot and even harder to maintain.

*Literature and Sound Film in Mid-Century Britain*. Lara Ehrenfried, Oxford University Press.
© Lara Ehrenfried 2025. DOI: 10.1093/9780198950790.003.0005

# 5
# Networks of Audio-Vision

This book began by discussing the altered roles played by sound, image, and text as a direct consequence of the rise of synchronized sound film. As part of the changes brought on by the consolidation of synchronized sound, I have further argued that new reflections on the affordances of media form became central to the paths of mid-century film and literature. Both the newly emerging conception of dialogue and the critical responses to the 'documentary impulse' of the 1930s evince the extent to which filmic as well as literary representation were reconfigured in the age of audio-vision. This chapter now turns to two further ideas: first, that audio-vision and synchronicity in film and literary fiction are networked phenomena, meaning that they build on a multi-media experience of vision and audition anchored in the wider media ecology. Second, I argue that these networks of audio-vision, grounded in multi-media experience, become key features of the thriller, one of the most popular genres in the 1930s and 1940s. I will show how some of the generic features of the thriller—suspense, violence, and crisis—fundamentally rely on audio-visual multi-media environments. I discuss Alfred Hitchcock's *The 39 Steps* (1935) and Thorold Dickinson's *Gaslight* (1940) and compare these films' audio-visual procedures to the textual strategies found in thrillers written by Eric Ambler and Graham Greene. The final section of the chapter then zooms out to suggest that the audio-visual conventions so commonly found in the thriller also circulate more widely in the mid-century mediascape: networks of audio-vision encode violence and crisis in the works of Jean Rhys and Patrick Hamilton, whose novels show the human's fundamental entanglement in these media networks. In a world that is increasingly (and threateningly) wired for audio-vision, characters themselves become mediatized and the human senses become part of the network.

## Thriller Sound

Between 1930 and 1939, the British film industry produced approximately 350 crime dramas and thrillers, making it one of the most successful and

# 138 LITERATURE AND SOUND FILM IN MID-CENTURY BRITAIN

productive genres of the period.[1] Many of these works reflect a sense of impending sociopolitical crisis in response to the rise of fascism, the events of the Spanish Civil War, and the global economic downturn.[2] The genre raised important questions about political and economic responsibilities, statelessness and exile, and could explore (in a fictional setting) new and rising threats to national and global security and infrastructure.[3] The thriller is also, as James Purdon notes, the 'characteristic genre of informatic identity'.[4] More than any other genre, it is concerned with collecting data and information, with tracing (and sometimes untracing) characters' movements and actions. In the thrillers of Eric Ambler and Graham Greene, but also in films such as *The 39 Steps* and *The Lady Vanishes* (1938), characters become, often involuntarily, entangled in the sinister machinations of foreign powers and secret organizations. The plots of these thrillers depend on networks of information and data collection, and on the characters' attempts to uncover or outrun such networks.[5]

The medium of sound film formally mirrors the thriller's topical interest in capturing and collecting information: the sound film's own physical processes of image and sound recording formally enact the thriller's genre-specific interest in data capture. The sound film creates and sustains audio-visual procedures for the thriller's generic features, thereby giving audio-visual form to some of the thriller's chief preoccupations.[6] In what follows, I examine some of the ways in which sound film establishes such audio-visual procedures for the thriller's representation of violence, crisis,

---

[1] See James Chapman, 'Celluloid Shockers', in Jeffrey Richards (ed.), *The Unknown 1930s: An Alternative History of the British Cinema, 1929–1939* (London: Tauris, 2000), 75–98.

[2] See W. H. Auden, *The Age of Anxiety: A Baroque Eclogue* (London: Faber & Faber 1948), and E. M. Forster, 'The 1939 State', *The New Statesman and Nation*, 10 June 1939, pp. 888–889. The period's sense of anxiety and war-dread has been addressed by literary critics: Steve Ellis, *British Writers and the Approach of World War II* (Cambridge: Cambridge University Press, 2015); Lyndsey Stonebridge, *The Writing of Anxiety: Imagining Wartime in Mid-Century British Culture* (Basingstoke: Palgrave Macmillan, 2007); Marina MacKay, 'Total War', in Benjamin Kohlmann and Matthew Taunton (eds), *A History of 1930s British Literature* (Cambridge: Cambridge University Press, 2019), 362–375.

[3] See, for instance, Wesley K. Wark (ed.), *Spy Fiction, Spy Films and Real Intelligence* (Abingdon: Routledge, 2006); Michael Denning, *Cover Stories: Narrative and Ideology in the British Spy Thriller* (Abingdon: Routledge, 2014); Brian Diemert, *Graham Greene's Thrillers and the 1930s* (Montreal & Kingston: McGill-Queens University Press, 1996); Phyllis Lassner, *Espionage and Exile: Fascism and Anti-Fascism in British Spy Fiction and Film* (Edinburgh: Edinburgh University Press, 2016).

[4] James Purdon, *Modernist Informatics* (Oxford: Oxford University Press, 2016), p. 81.

[5] Allan Hepburn, 'Thrillers', in Robert L. Caserio (ed.), *The Cambridge History of the English Novel* (Cambridge: Cambridge University Press, 2012), pp. 693–708, and David Trotter, *The Literature of Connection* (Oxford: Oxford University Press, 2020), pp. 198–205.

[6] On the genre conventions of the thriller, see Hepburn, 'Thrillers', pp. 695–696.

and suspense. For example, I discuss how the thriller film turns towards a more frequent use of diegetic sound and music and moves away from some of the non-diegetic scoring practices of Hollywood cinema. By placing new emphasis on the sound worlds of the diegesis, the thriller fosters the creation of new networks of sounds and signals, from which characters struggle to disentangle themselves. The thriller film further develops a sustained engagement with the possibilities of cinematic silence and shows a concerted interest in referencing, even representing, other media forms, thereby again highlighting the genre's interest in data capture and its embeddedness in the wider media ecology.

Diegetic and non-diegetic film scoring became key elements in the thriller's filmic representation of suspense and threat. Following the introduction of synchronized sound, scoring in narrative cinema had been predominantly orchestral, symphonic, and romantic in nature, especially in Hollywood cinema:

> the development of the classical Hollywood film score in the crucial decade of the thirties was dominated by a group of composers displaced from the musical idiom in which they had been trained. It was in Hollywood that they were able to reconstitute what John Williams has called 'the Vienna Opera House [in] the American West.'[7]

Hollywood's most prolific and successful composers were European émigrés: Max Steiner, Erich Wolfgang Korngold, and Franz Waxman. Their work was substantially influenced by opera and by the compositions of Gustav Mahler and Richard Strauss. Korngold's scoring style in particular focussed on developing recognizable, musical leitmotifs for characters, locations, and crucial plot points: 'nondissonant if mildly chromatic harmonies, monophonic textures, broad, sweeping melodies, and lush instrumentations were the order of the day', both because of the aesthetic proclivities of the "first wave" composers and because of the tastes of both studio and music department heads.'[8] Korngold's work on the swashbuckler *Captain Blood* (1935), for instance, shows this leitmotif-based approach to

---

[7] Kathryn Kalinak, *Settling the Score: Music and the Classical Hollywood Film* (Madison, WI: University of Wisconsin Press, 1992), p. 100. For a concise summary of classical Hollywood scoring practices, see also Carol Flinn, 'The Most Romantic Art of All: Music in the Classical Hollywood Cinema', *Cinema Journal*, 29.4 (1990), 35–50.

[8] Royal S. Brown, *Overtones and Undertones: Reading Film Music* (Berkeley, CA: University of California Press, 1994), p. 96.

140   LITERATURE AND SOUND FILM IN MID-CENTURY BRITAIN

film scoring, as noted by Kathryn Kalinak: the film contains musical 'leit-motifs for Peter Blood as well as for King James and King William; for all the important locations, Port Royal (also used to accompany the governor of Jamaica), Tortuga, Virgen Magra, England, and France; for the love between Peter Blood and Arabella Bishop'.[9] Classical Hollywood cinema of the Thirties and Forties largely relied on a combination of synchronized dialogue, some selected sound effects, and extensive, leitmotif-based music to create filmic continuity and coherence.

However, the thriller arguably took scoring practices into a different direction. Hitchcock's work on *Rebecca* (1940) and *Suspicion* (1941), for instance, shows some interesting Hollywood experiments with film music: the score for *Rebecca*, composed by Franz Waxman, sounds rich and romantic and appears to be more in line with the classical scoring principles popularized by Korngold. However, even a supposedly classical film score like *Rebecca* deploys elements of the thriller's audio-visual conventions to indicate the gradual eroding of the second Mrs de Winter's psyche. Waxman's composition makes frequent use of tremolos and glissandi. Glissandi are played as sliding movements from one pitch to another while tremolos produce, as the term indicates, an effect of 'trembling' or 'shaking' of the individual note.[10] These techniques might express an acoustic tipping point, a destabilization of pitch (and, sometimes, of volume), which sonically mimics a process of psychological or emotional crisis. In the case of *Rebecca*, viewers might experience the glissandi and tremolo as the acoustic marker of immanent psychological collapse or as markers of the constant threat of Rebecca's ghostly presence. Waxman's harp glissandi are treacherous, because they sound romantic and dream-like, recalling classical scoring practices while simultaneously subtly turning away from them.

Hitchcock's *Suspicion* takes this process of unravelling scoring practices a step further by using distorted variations of well-known music. The romantic waltz *Wiener Blut* by Johann Strauss II undergoes a makeover in this production: initially the waltz is played as diegetic music at a ball attended by Lina (Joan Fontaine) and Johnnie (Cary Grant). The waltz accompanies their first dance together and marks their falling in love. However, after their

---

[9] Kalinak, *Settling the Score*, p. 105.
[10] *Rebecca*, dir. Alfred Hitchcock, starring Joan Fontaine and Laurence Olivier (Selznick International Pictures, 1940); *Suspicion*, dir. Alfred Hitchcock, starring Joan Fontaine and Cary Grant (RKO Radio Pictures, 1941). For an evocative discussion of glissandi as an 'assault on pitch', see Mark Brownrigg, *Film Music and Film Genre*, Doctoral Dissertation (University of Stirling, 2003), pp. 118–119.

wedding, wealthy heiress Lina discovers that Johnnie is a penniless playboy with mounting debts who may have only married her for her money. Following this revelation, the waltz no longer functions as their love theme, but as an acoustic marker of distrust and danger as Lina begins to believe that Johnnie is scheming to kill her. Fragments of the waltz played by solo instruments, including oboe and violin, as well as variations of the waltz in a minor key recur as Lina's suspicions mount. The climactic scene of Johnnie carrying a glass of milk (which may or may not be poisoned) as he ascends a dark staircase is accompanied by strings and woodwinds playing sad fragments of the Strauss waltz in a minor key. The film establishes a network of musical cross-references, in which the waltz is first established as the lover's theme, only to be deconstructed and its meaning inverted.

Hitchcock's *The 39 Steps*, based on the novel by John Buchan (1915) and produced by Michael Balcon for Gaumont-British, tells the story of Richard Hannay who inadvertently becomes the target of a spy ring that is working to steal military secrets from the British government, when a counter-espionage agent seeks refuge and dies in Hannay's London flat.[11] The film presents, as David Trotter states, 'a significant advance into the network society'.[12] Its focus on the transmission and travel of (secret) information is typical for the thriller and becomes apparent in the ways in which the film taps into the media ecology of its time: newspapers and telephones play key roles, but so does the character of 'Mr Memory', who, as Trotter convincingly argues, functions as a human 'portable database', able to record and replay any piece of information he has encountered before.[13]

The film's soundtrack, anticipating those of *Suspicion* and *Rebecca*, abandons the melodic scoring practices of Hollywood cinema for prolonged sequences. The film's non-diegetic music largely employs horns, strings, and woodwinds that play dissonant and chromatic scales. There is also little in the way of a leitmotif-based approach to the music.[14] During Hannay's climactic escape both from the police and from the eponymous spy ring, he runs through the hilly terrain of the Scottish Lowlands. A variation of the film's opening theme accompanies the chase: horns and woodwinds play

---

[11] *The 39 Steps*, dir. Alfred Hitchcock, starring Robert Donat and Madeline Carroll (Gaumont-British, 1935). On the significant differences between Buchan's novel and Hitchcock's film, see David Trotter's excellent analysis in 'Mobility, Network, Message: Spy Fiction and Film in the Long 1930s', *Critical Quarterly*, 57.3 (2015), 10–21.

[12] Trotter, *Literature of Connection*, p. 199.

[13] Trotter, *Literature of Connection*, p. 199.

[14] Brown, *Overtones and Undertones*, pp. 96–97.

142 LITERATURE AND SOUND FILM IN MID-CENTURY BRITAIN

scales, winding up and down, thus sonically imitating Richard Hannay's movements through the mountainous scenery without drifting into mickey-mousing. The film's score largely withholds conventional melody. Instead, its soundtracks consist of musical scales, patterns, and fragments, combined with some chromatic writing, meaning a frequent use of halftones and notes outside the diatonic scale, which acoustically produce the impression of discord and dissonance. The move away from diatonic harmonies underscores the collapse of the perceived stability and orderliness of the diegetic world as experienced by the protagonist.[15]

*The 39 Steps* places sustained emphasis on diegetic sound effects and extensive use of silence to create tension and suspense for the audience. When Hannay takes the counter-espionage agent Annabelle Smith to his London flat, they both enter Hannay's sitting room in darkness and Smith asks him to refrain from switching on the lights. She moves through the dark room and presses herself against the wall between the windows to shield herself from view. The place lies in silence; there are no ambient sounds except for her audible footsteps on the floorboards. Once she has concealed herself from view, Hannay flips the light switch—another distinct sound that punctuates the silence for just a fraction of a second. When the telephone in Hannay's sitting room (another piercing sound effect) suddenly begins ringing incessantly, Smith begs him not to answer. They move to the kitchen, where Smith closes the blinds before Hannay switches on the light. The camera captures them in a medium-long shot as they stand a few feet away from each other. The telephone in the sitting room begins ringing again, cutting through the silence in the kitchen. As Hannay closes the kitchen door, the sound of the telephone is slightly muted, but remains audible through the closed door. The screen fades to black and a cut to an open window shows the curtains fluttering audibly in a medium-long shot. There is silence except for the distinct sound of the curtains moving in the breeze and noisily hitting against the wooden window frame. Another cut to Hannay's bedroom follows, where audiences can see him lying in his bed in darkness. The door bursts open and Smith enters, calling to him: 'Clear out, Hannay! They'll get you next!' She extends her hand towards him, coughs, and collapses on his bed with a knife stuck in her back. The telephone starts ringing again while the camera, for a second, shows a

---

[15] This tendency to employ more chromatic, atonal, and dissonant compositions increased further throughout the 1930s and 1940s and culminated in the development of the typical 'film noir' sound that combined chromaticism and dissonance with jazz elements. See Richard R. Ness, '"A Lotta Night Music": The Sound of Film Noir', *Cinema Journal*, 47.2 (Winter 2008), 52–73.

medium shot of Hannay sitting up in bed with the dead Smith collapsed over his lower body. Another cut moves the scene to the sitting room, showing a close-up of the telephone that is still ringing. The camera zooms out to bring Hannay into focus, who is moving towards the telephone, but does not pick up. There is silence in the room except for the shrill sound of the phone. The sound effect here simultaneously enforces and disrupts filmic silence. The oppressive stillness of Hannay's flat in the immediate aftermath of Smith's murder is conveyed through the interplay of camera focus (close-up followed by a zoom out) and sound editing to underscore the shrillness of the telephone and the absence of all other sounds as Hannay tries to fathom what has just happened in his home. The telephone, as in many other Hitchcock films, is used expertly to 'subject listeners to noise'.[16] These kinds of selective noises, however, work effectively to reinforce the audience's (and Hannay's) experience of silence.

'Silence', Bela Balázs notes, 'is an acoustic effect, but only where sounds can be heard. *The presentation of silence is one of the most specific dramatic effects of the sound film*.'[17] Balázs draws attention here to one of the most fundamental, but possibly also one of the most challenging aspects of synchronized sound film, namely, the fact that the sound film's interplay of sound, vision, and synchronization could facilitate new approaches to silence. Silence in the cinema, as outlined by Michel Chion, 'is never neutral emptiness. It is the negative of sound we've heard beforehand or imagined; it is the product of a contrast'.[18] Chion and Balázs both note that filmic silence does not mean that one 'hears nothing'; rather:

> [w]e feel the silence when we can hear the most distant sound or the slightest rustle near us. Silence is when the buzzing of a fly on the windowpane fills the whole room with sound and the ticking of a clock smashes time into fragments with sledgehammer blows. [...] A completely soundless space on the contrary never appears quite concrete, and quite real, to our perception; we feel it to be weightless...[19]

Thus, both critics point out that the technological and editorial possibilities of creating filmic silence (as well as the audience's phenomenological

---

[16] Chion, *Audio-Vision*, p. 57.
[17] Béla Balázs, 'Theory of the Film: Sound', in Elisabeth Weis and John Belton (eds), *Film Sound: Theory and Practice* (New York: Columbia University Press, 1985), 116–125 (p. 117, my emphasis).
[18] Chion, *Audio-Vision*, p. 57.
[19] Balázs, 'Theory of the Film: Sound', pp. 118–119.

# 144 LITERATURE AND SOUND FILM IN MID-CENTURY BRITAIN

experience of silence) are intricately tied to sound itself: a film can 'express silence' by 'subjecting the listener to...noise'.[20] Chion here refers to selective additions of diegetic sound that enhance perceived silence, 'because the only sound there is so intense, and heightened by the lack of other sounds, bringing out this emptiness in a terrible way'.[21] This might be achieved, for instance, by heightened volume or reverberation of a diegetic sound (the ringing of a door bell, footsteps on a staircase, the call of a bird or the ticking clock). Conversely, a total 'suppression of ambient sounds [in film] can create the sense that [audiences] are entering into the mind of a character absorbed by her or his personal story'.[22] On this view, the interplay of sound, image, and synchronization is key to facilitating the experience of silence in the sound film. *The 39 Steps* uses diegetic sound effects and deliberate, prolonged moments of filmic silence to create suspense.

*Gaslight*, based on Patrick Hamilton's successful stage play of the same name, explores the psychological manipulation and emotional abuse of a young woman by her criminal husband.[23] Richard Addinsell's score for *Gaslight* uses music primarily as a tool for conveying psychological anguish, anxiety, and instability. While the film generally contains more non-diegetic scoring than *The 39 Steps*, the film's key scenes heavily rely on diegetic music, silence, and diegetic sound effects. Similar to *The 39 Steps*, the opening credits begin with chromatic, high-pitched fanfares of brass instruments, followed by the film's theme music in a minor key. The first sequence of the film then shows the murder of Alice Barlow, an elderly woman who is killed in her London townhouse. Her belongings are searched by the perpetrator, who is hunting for the renowned 'Barlow Rubies'. The sequence is accompanied by non-diegetic music that mimics movements on screen (known as 'mickey-mousing'): the unidentified killer's walk up and down the stairs is underscored by ascending and descending scales and glissandi; the frantic search of drawers and other furniture is mimicked by screeching strings. Twenty years after the murder, a newlywed couple, Paul and Bella, move into the victim's house. Over the course of the film, it becomes evident that Paul (Anton Walbrook) is living a double life. He is actually Louis Bauer, a relative of Alice Barlow's, who has returned to the scene of the crime in order to continue his search for the Barlow rubies. He emotionally

---

[20] Chion, *Audio-Vision*, p. 57.    [21] Chion, *Audio-Vision*, p. 58.

[22] Chion, *Audio-Vision*, p. 89.

[23] *Gaslight*, dir. Thorold Dickinson, starring Diana Wynyard and Anton Walbrook (Anglo-American Film Corp., 1940). The film and Hamilton's stage play of the same name were released in the United States as *Angel Street*.

NETWORKS OF AUDIO-VISION 145

abuses and psychologically manipulates his young wife Bella (Diana Wynyard). Every night, Paul pretends to go out, but actually re-enters the attic of the house through an adjacent property in order to secretly continue his search for the gemstones.

The film uses the interplay of non-diegetic and diegetic music, sound effects, and silence to express Paul's manipulative and abusive behaviour while also conveying Bella's experience of fear and emotional distress. Whenever Paul continues his search for the rubies, he secretly walks in the attic over Bella's bedroom. These actions make her believe that she is imagining strange noises and footsteps in the house and slowly losing her mind. Paul's ascent to the attic through the neighbouring property is accompanied by non-diegetic music. When, however, he reaches the attic, the film cuts to Bella's bedroom and the music fades out. There is deafening silence, which is only broken by the diegetic sound of the footsteps; it is a dull noise of steps slowly falling on wooden floorboards over Bella's head. As Bella becomes desperate to mask the sound of the footsteps (and thus also the sound of what she believes to be a clear, acoustic sign of her loss of sanity), she plays a musical box in her bedroom to cover up the sound of the steps above her. The musical box is shown in a close-up and begins playing diegetic music. Meanwhile, the footsteps overhead continue to sound unnaturally loudly and appear to fall into rhythm with the beat of the music box. The enhanced volume of the steps and the rhythmic alignment of the steps with the diegetic music express Bella's heightened emotion and her inability to ignore the footsteps as her face's anxious expression is mirrored by the surface of the music box. Her reflection is captured in close-up by the camera (see Figure 5.1).

Although the film is set in Victorian London, it ties itself to a broader spectrum of media forms, and gestures to the audio-visual media ecology of its twentieth-century audiences. The music-box sequence is a brilliant moment of framed audio-vision in the film, which combines the close-up image of Bella's face with a layered diegetic soundtrack (the music, the footsteps in the attic). As Bella's face is reflected in the music box, audiences also get a view of the music box's interior: the technology behind the diegetic play of music is made apparent. It is the film's nod to its own processes of recording and to the technology and media networks attached to facilitating audio-vision.

In line with the turn away from romantic and melodic scoring practices, the film's use of non-diegetic music further underscores Paul's cruel manipulation of Bella. One of his gaslighting strategies is to make her

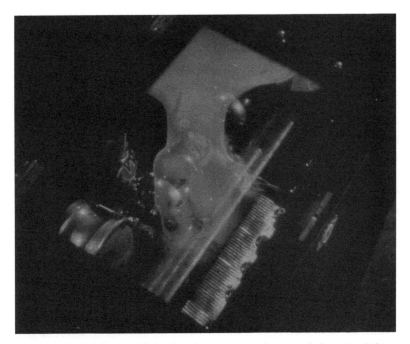

**Figure 5.1** Bella's face is reflected in the music box; frame grab from *Gaslight* (British National Films, 1940), directed by Thorold Dickinson.

believe that she is misplacing items around the house as well as stealing personal belongings from him. At a visit to a privately hosted concert, Paul accuses Bella of having taken his pocket watch. She denies the allegations, but breaks down when he insists that she has taken the watch. During the carriage ride home, non-diegetic music signals Bella's anguish and despair. High-pitched trumpets are followed by a repetitive string chord and high-pitched flutes that mix with the diegetic sound of clattering hooves on the pavement. As the flutes and trumpets work towards the upper limits of their range, the non-diegetic music acoustically reflects Bella's psyche and conveys the impression that her sanity is also pushed to its limits.

*Gaslight* deploys diegetic sound effects and silence to enhance tension and suspense while non-diegetic music, through high pitch, chromaticism, and fragmentation, indicates the breakdown of psychological stability. The film, although often overlooked in favour of its American remake with Ingrid Bergman and Joseph Cotten (1944), is a key achievement in the British film industry's candid exploration of domestic abuse and psychological manipulation. In contrast to *The 39 Steps*, which focusses on violence, threat, and suspense from a more externalized viewpoint, the intensely psychological focus of *Gaslight* is conveyed through its music, diegetic sound effects, and its nuanced use of silence. Despite their differences, these films use a set of audio-visual conventions to evoke the thriller's typical features of suspense, the threat of violence, and the experience of crisis. Both films also gesture towards their wider media ecology and the media networks in which they are firmly and fully embedded.

## Ambler's Silence and Greene's Audio-Vision

Eric Ambler is widely credited with revolutionizing the thriller in the 1930s by introducing complex protagonists to the genre. These protagonists are stateless civilians—exiles or émigrés—who become accidentally involved in the machinations of international intrigue and conspiracy. As the thriller depends on the 'secret flow of information',[24] silence, in Ambler's fiction, is often central to disrupting the transmissions of information. Silence is not merely 'the negative of sound', as Chion notes, but it is also a conscious means of delaying, momentarily pausing, or impeding the progression of narrative, thereby sustaining suspense for audiences and readers. In Ambler's works of the 1930s, silence appears as a multi-sensory, networked experience which is often, paradoxically, directly tied to sound. Taking up the ways in which sound film's audio-visual dimension facilitates silence, Ambler's protagonists usually perceive silence through selective noise and other sensory impressions. In *Uncommon Danger* (1937), Ambler's second novel, characters carry out actions in silence, interact with each other in silence, or find themselves caught up in moments of 'dead silence'.[25] Encounters with silence establish experiential connections between sound, vision, and touch:

> He found himself in a small and very dark courtyard. His eyes, however, were by now accustomed to the blackness, and he made for a pool of shadows which looked as though it might mark a way out. His right hand had touched a concrete wall and he was feeling his way along it when he heard a slight sound somewhere ahead of him. With a sinking heart he

---

[24] Hepburn, 'Thrillers', p. 695.
[25] The novel was published in the United States as *Background to Danger*. For moments of 'dead silence' in the novel, see Eric Ambler, *Uncommon Danger* (London: Penguin, 2009), p. 4 and p. 69.

148  LITERATURE AND SOUND FILM IN MID-CENTURY BRITAIN

stood still and listened. There was complete silence. He was still a trifle breathless and, as he strove to breathe noiselessly, the blood thumped in his head. He was beginning to think that the noise had been made by a rat, when it came again. This time it was more distinct—the scatch [*sic*] of shoe leather on a gritty surface.[26]

Silence and darkness are coupled to convey the experience of momentary disorientation: the narrator's descriptive comments create semantic networks of sound ('heard', 'listened', 'noise', 'thumped'), silence ('noiselessly', 'silence', 'still', 'breathless'), vision ('eyes', 'looked', 'dark', 'shadows'), and touch ('hand', 'touched', 'feeling', 'pool'). In another situation, as the protagonist Kenton enters the scene of a brutal murder, vision and sound merge to express the forceful sensation of shock and nausea:

In the silence of Room 25 in the Hotel Josef, however, death was no longer incidental. Here it was grotesque. Kenton found that he wanted to be sick and forced himself to look away. He knew that, useless though it might appear, he ought to find out if Sachs were still alive, and if he were, to go for a doctor. As he stood trying to overcome his nausea, he could hear the watch ticking on his wrist.[27]

The silences in Ambler's fiction are oppressive, conveying threat and fear. By taking recourse to visual, acoustic, and haptic sensory impressions, the protagonist's experience of silence anchors him phenomenologically in the diegetic world and mediates silence as multi-sensory experience. Similar to *The 39 Steps*, silence in Ambler's works is often punctuated and reinforced by sound: 'He was silent for a moment. There was no sound in the room *except* the ticking of the clocks and a faint hiss from the stove'; '*with the exception of* the sound of a train rumbling past in the distance, and the thin patter of rain on the roof, there was silence'.[28]

These descriptions by the narrator set the tone and atmosphere; they establish situation and convey suspense. The descriptions play to the cinematic idea of silence as a product of contrast as noted by Balázs and Chion: the characters experience silence and stillness *except for* the sound that breaks this silence. In *The Mask of Dimitrios* (1939), published in the United

---

[26] Ambler, *Uncommon Danger*, p. 45.     [27] Ambler, *Uncommon Danger*, p. 38.
[28] Ambler, *Uncommon Danger*, pp. 95, 202 (my emphasis).

States as *A Coffin for Dimitrios*, silence is not merely silence, but it can intensify and become more threatening and immersive as time progresses:

> They fell silent. Mr Peters began to trim his nails with a pair of pocket scissors. Except for the clicking of the scissors and the sound of Mr Peters' heavy breathing, the silence in the room was complete. To Latimer it seemed almost tangible; a dark grey fluid that oozed from the corners of the room. He began to hear the watch ticking on his wrist. He waited for what seemed an eternity before looking at it. When he did look it was ten minutes to nine. Another eternity. He tried to think of something to say to Mr Peters to pass the time. He tried counting the complete parallelograms in the pattern of the wallpaper between the wardrobe and the window. Now he thought he could hear Mr Peters' watch ticking. The muffled sound of someone moving a chair and walking about in the room overhead seemed to intensify the silence. Four minutes to nine.[29]

Sensing the intensification of silence precisely through the experience of sound is a technique also commonly found in the film thriller of the 1930s. Chion writes of such sequences in film that 'paradoxically we end up with an anxiety-producing impression of silence, all the stronger because the only sound…is so intense, and heightened by the lack of other sounds'.[30] Ambler adapts this filmic technique for the prose writer, creating multi-sensory soundscapes that denote silence precisely by drawing on selective noises that disrupt the notion of total stillness.

The works of Graham Greene display a similar approach to writing silence:

> All the way down the stairs he listened for Anna's screams, but only silence followed him. The snow was falling outside, quietening the wheels of cars, the tread of feet; but the silence up the stairs seemed to fall faster…[31]

> This was a modern building; the silence was admirable and disquieting. Instead of bells ringing, lights went off and on. One got the impression that all the time people were signalling news of great importance that couldn't wait.[32]

---

[29] Eric Ambler, *The Mask of Dimitrios* (London: Penguin, 2009), p. 199.
[30] Chion, *Audio-Vision*, p. 58.
[31] Graham Greene, *Stamboul Train* (London: Vintage, 2010), p. 79.
[32] Greene, *The Ministry of Fear*, p. 97.

150  LITERATURE AND SOUND FILM IN MID-CENTURY BRITAIN

There was silence again except for the tiny shifting of dust down the steps. Almost immediately a second bomb was under way. They waited in fixed photographic attitudes, sitting, squatting, standing: this bomb could not burst closer without destroying them. Then, it too passed, diminished, burst a little farther away.[33]

Here, Greene describes the types or modes of silence encountered by the characters more fully. Silence is given an array of attributes: it falls faster than snow; all-encompassing, it is more disconcerting and frightening than the screams the protagonist expects to hear. In the second example, the silence is characterized as 'admirable', 'disquieting', and 'sinister'. The third example returns readers to a technique also frequently found in Ambler's works: the idea of encountering silence *except for* the sound or noise that disrupts it. These silences do not simply create suspense or tension for the reader. They underscore deliberate, effectful intrusions of sound: the ringing of a telephone, the creak of a floorboard, the opening of a door, the shifting of dust particles. These silences also gesture towards the wider media ecology: they are part of a wider network of signals. In *The Ministry of Fear*, 'lights went on and off', which is framed by the text as a possible act of signalling, a visualized morse code that furthers secret communications. Elsewhere, the experience of being bombed is captured in 'fixed photographic attitude' before the sound of detonation hits. Silence is a fully mediatized event; one has to be plugged into the media network to perceive it and to understand its significance.

Published in 1938, Greene's *Brighton Rock*, with its examination of murder and corruption, establishes a network of audition, vision, and violence through different characters' encounters with microphones, photography, and sound recording—technologies, which the novel frames as symbolic inscriptions of violence. In the beginning of the novel, Hale meets the singer Ida (known to many characters in the text by her stage name Lily), or rather, Hale meets Ida's voice when 'somewhere out of sight a woman was singing, "When I came up from Brighton by the train": a rich Guinness voice, a voice from a public bar.'[34] Ida's alcohol-fuelled voice provides the soundtrack to Hale's gradual realization that his death at the hands of Pinkie and his henchmen is imminent: 'a wreath of orange blossoms,/ When next we met, she wore;/ The expression of her features / Was more thoughtful than

---

[33] Greene, *The Ministry of Fear*, p. 216.
[34] Graham Greene, *Brighton Rock* (London: Vintage, 2004), p. 4.

before.'[35] This initial link forged between violence and music continues when Hale is murdered while waiting for Ida outside a public washroom. Ida sings to herself in the mirror, 'softly this time, in her warm winey voice,'[36] and by the time she exits the bathroom, Hale is dead. While the reader only learns about Hale's murder after the fact, the novel retrospectively suggests a parallel timeline that effectively synchronizes Ida's song inside the women's washroom with Hale's gruesome death outside. *Brighton Rock's* 'cinematic' qualities stem from the novel's connections between sound, vision, and violence that, on multiple occasions, appear either 'synchronized' or following parallel timelines. The novel makes sound–image interaction one of its key narrative procedures: 'he stood with weak knees against the concrete wall with the blade advanced and watched the corner....the faintest sound of music bit, like an abscess, into his brain from the Palace Pier, the lights came out in the neat barren bourgeois road'.[37] Here, light and music are linked: the use of commas and short sub-clauses propels the narration forward and suggests that vision and audition happen simultaneously or, at the very least, in close succession. J. M. Coetzee notes the influence of film directors such as Alfred Hitchcock and Howards Hawks on *Brighton Rock's* treatment of violence; he derives such observations from Greene's own statement that his descriptions were 'capture[d]...with the moving eye of the cine-camera...I work with the camera, following my characters and their movements'.[38]

Greene's transitions between scenes in the novel translate for the literary text some of the processes of filmic continuity editing: there is, for instance, sound that travels from one place to the next, which helps the narrator transition from one scene to another. As filmic continuity editing often depends on sound to connect two scenes and to smooth over cuts, Greene applies a textual version of this strategy to *Brighton Rock*:

A scarlet racing model, a tiny rakish car...It was crammed tight: a woman sat on a man's knee, and another man clung on the running board as it swayed and hooted and cut in and out uphill towards the downs. The woman was singing, her voice faint and disjointed through the horns, something traditional about brides and bouquets, something which went

---

[35] Greene, *Brighton Rock*, p. 7.   [36] Greene, *Brighton Rock*, p. 18.
[37] Greene, *Brighton Rock*, p. 115.
[38] J. M. Coetzee, 'Introduction', in Graham Greene, *Brighton Rock* (London: Vintage, 2004), p. xi.

152 LITERATURE AND SOUND FILM IN MID-CENTURY BRITAIN

with Guinness and oysters and the old Leicester Lounge, something out of place in the little bright racing car. Upon the top of the down the words blew back along the dusty road to meet an ancient Morris rocking and receding in their wake at forty miles an hour, with flapping hood, bent fender and discoloured windscreen.

The words came through the flap, flap, flap of the old hood to the Boy's ears. He sat beside Spicer who drove the car. Brides and bouquets: and he thought of Rose with sullen disgust.[39]

The woman's song, audible in the first car, carries through to the car behind it—to Pinkie and Spicer driving along a dusty road. The sequence illustrates Greene's self-proclaimed 'cinematic' approach. The narration follows the movement of one car, then latches onto the song, and uses the song to transition to the second car and the characters sitting inside it. As such, it presents readers with a textual adaptation of filmic continuity editing, which equally uses sound to manage transitions between locations and to smooth over cuts between scenes.

Beyond such narrative procedures, *Brighton Rock* further spins connections between audio-vision and brutality especially through the character of Pinkie and his attitudes to both sound recording and photography. Here, the novel explicitly ties itself to a broader spectrum of available media forms and shows how audio-vision is not merely a matter confined to sound film. When Pinkie walks on the pier, he hears an orchestra and registers the sound as 'wail[ing] in his guts'.[40] The music 'moaned in his head in the hot electric light, it was the nearest he knew to sorrow'.[41] Music, to Pinkie, is an unpleasant experience that causes a sense of threat and makes him feel hatred and disdain. When he takes Rose out to dance, the live performance of the swing band and the singer make him

stare...at the spotlight: music, love, nightingale, post-men: the words stirred in his brain like poetry: one hand caressed the vitriol bottle in his pocket, the other touched Rose's wrist. The inhuman voice whistled round the gallery...It was he this time who was being warned; life held the vitriol bottle and warned him...*It spoke to him in the music*, and when he protested that he for one would never get mixed up, *the music had its own retort at hand*.[42]

[39] Greene, *Brighton Rock*, p. 108.   [40] Greene, *Brighton Rock*, p. 20.
[41] Greene, *Brighton Rock*, p. 48.
[42] Greene, *Brighton Rock*, pp. 52–53 (my emphasis).

The text combines elements of vision, audition, and haptic sensation to evoke discomfort and threat: as Pinkie stares, listens, and caresses the bottle in his coat pocket, the experience of having taken Rose to dance becomes overwhelming. The singer's voice seems 'inhuman' and sounds like a warning to Pinkie. To his horror, the crooner 'tenderly' embraces the microphone 'as if it were a woman, swinging it gently this way and that, wooing it with his lips while from the loudspeaker under the gallery his whisper reverberated hoarsely over the hall, like a dictator announcing victory'.[43] Pinkie views the crooner as degenerate, inhuman, and dangerous, because the singer mimics the tender speech, looks, and soft touch that Rose may expect, even crave, from Pinkie and that he is utterly unable and unwilling to give.

Crooning was made possible by improvements in microphony in the twentieth century: these new microphones were more sensitive to quieter sounds, and could comfortably pick up a wider frequency range and more subtle voice modulation. These improvements allowed singers to perform in a more intimate style. The sensitive amplification of the microphone allowed the singer to apply less breath to the vocal cords which ultimately achieved a quieter, softer, and more subdued singing style. Although crooning as a style of 'intimate singing' became immensely popular in the 1920s, it had fallen out of fashion by the 1930s. As Allison McCracken writes, male crooners were often portrayed as effeminate and undesirable, lacking in masculinity and strength.[44] Such pushback against crooning was part of 1930s Anglo-American culture and may, at least partly, explain Pinkie's negative response to the singer. The intimacy and tenderness associated with crooning is precisely what he finds 'dangerous': the soft-spoken whisper and the singer's tender embrace of the microphone is both alien and repulsive to Pinkie whose brutal and emotionally controlling treatment of Rose culminates in his own personal encounter with a microphone of a different kind. When walking on the pier, Rose asks for a recording of Pinkie's voice as a souvenir of their wedding day, but Pinkie angrily dismisses her request: 'He didn't like the idea of putting anything on a record: it reminded him of finger-prints.'[45] To Pinkie, the voice recording would come to serve as evidence, leaving a permanent trace of his crimes. Despite his protestations, Rose insists on the recording: 'Perhaps one day you might be away somewhere and I could borrow a gramophone. And you'd speak.'[46] Rose subscribes to a

---

[43] Greene, *Brighton Rock*, p. 52.
[44] On the cultural backlash against crooning see Allison McCracken, *Real Men Don't Sing: Crooning in American Culture* (Duke University Press, 2015), pp. 208–263.
[45] Greene, *Brighton Rock*, p. 193.      [46] Greene, *Brighton Rock*, p. 193.

## 154 LITERATURE AND SOUND FILM IN MID-CENTURY BRITAIN

nostalgic and romantic idea of voice recording, believing that a copy of Pinkie's voice would serve not only as a memento of their wedding day, but also as an affirmation of his affection for her. When she insists on the recording, Pinkie

> went into the box and closed the door. There was a slot for his sixpence: a mouthpiece: an instruction, 'Speak clearly and close to the instrument.' The scientific paraphernalia made him nervous. He looked over his shoulder and there outside she was watching him, without a smile. He saw her as a stranger: a shabby child from Nelson Place, and he was shaken by an appalling resentment. He put in a sixpence, and, speaking in a low voice for fear it might carry beyond the box, he gave his message up to be graven on vulcanite: 'God damn you, you little bitch, why can't you go back home for ever and let me be?' He heard the needle scratch and the record whirr: then a click and silence.[47]

The text stylistically emulates Pinkie's detached and cold manner as his reaction moves from discomfort and nervousness at the 'scientific paraphernalia' to the resentment and hatred expressed by his voice recording. As he stands inside the soundproof recording booth, looking outside at Rose, whilst, in turn, also being observed by her, the silence of the recording booth couples with the experience of viewing her from this enclosed point of view: he sees her as a 'shabby child' and his anger grows exponentially, so that he is 'shaken by appalling resentment'. There is the sound of the needle as it scratches over the vulcanite surface to engrave his voice message, then silence.

As Susanne S. Cammack notes, the recording process itself reflects a form of violence if read as the forceful physical-material engraving of sound waves into a malleable fabric.[48] Sound recording's symbolic and material connotations of violence are underscored by Pinkie's cruel message. Following his death, Rose fetches the recording of Pinkie's voice to listen to it. Unaware of the message awaiting her on the gramophone record, she walks 'towards the worst horror of all'.[49] The recording leaves a permanent

---

[47] Greene, *Brighton Rock*, p. 193.

[48] Susanne S. Cammack, 'The Death of a Gramophone in Elizabeth Bowen's *The Last September*', *Journal of Modern Literature*, 40.2 (2017), 132–146 (pp. 134–135).

[49] Greene, *Brighton Rock*, p. 269. For further discussion of this moment vis-à-vis gender and voice, see Laurel Harris, '"From 'The Worst Horror of All" to "I Love You": Gender and Voice in the Cinematic Soundscapes of *Brighton Rock*', *Literature/Film Quarterly*, 46.1 (2018). Open access online at: https://lfq.salisbury.edu/_issues/46_1/from_the_worst_horror_of_all_to.html.

trace of Pinkie's deceit, violence, and cruelty. Pinkie's deep-seated resistance to sound recording is further paralleled by his resistance to being photographed: 'they came out on to the parade. A pavement photographer saw them coming and lifted the cap from his camera. The Boy put his hands in front of his face and went by.'[50] Pinkie wants to leave neither voice nor image trace behind. This anxiety surrounding photography and sound recording gives expression to what Elliott Malamet describes as *Brighton Rock*'s fundamental tension between 'detection and evasion'.[51] Pinkie seeks to evade being recorded, but the novel ultimately shows the futility of trying to outrun the networks of audio-visual capture that populate Greene's thriller world.

Ambler and Greene's works thus take up the audio-visual cues of the film thriller and translate these for the literary text: silences become means of delay, interrupting the flow of information and creating suspense. They are most deafening when punctured by selective sounds and other sense impressions. Silence is multi-dimensional and multi-medial; it exists as part of a new audio-visual media ecology in which everything seems wired, connected, ready for data capture. Both Greene and Ambler equally write thrillers as fictions of media networks: there are microphones, photographs, light signals, and sound recording technologies, which all, on the one hand, express the thriller's particular interest in tracing data and information whilst characters seek to evade this kind of tracking. On the other hand, they also show how the thriller is deeply embedded into the mid-century's multi-sensory media ecology.

## Wired Minds

So far, this chapter has outlined the ways in which the thriller develops audio-visual conventions for conveying suspense, crisis, and violence. I have further argued that these audio-visual conventions are tied to a wider spectrum of media forms. This final section now zooms out to suggest that the audio-visual networks so commonly found in the thriller also circulate more widely in mid-century literature by discussing some of the audio-visual

---

[50] Greene, *Brighton Rock*, p. 68. Pinkie's anxiety about photography also becomes evident in his interrogation of Rose to find out how much she knows about Hale's death. Pinkie wonders whether she may have seen a 'photograph' of Hale (p. 49).

[51] Elliott Malamet, 'Graham Greene and the Hounds of *Brighton Rock*', *Modern Fiction Studies*, 37.4 (1991), 689–703 (p. 690).

156 LITERATURE AND SOUND FILM IN MID-CENTURY BRITAIN

cues for violence and crisis in the works of Jean Rhys and Patrick Hamilton. In addressing the works of Rhys and Hamilton alongside Greene and Ambler, I do not suggest that Rhys and Hamilton are writers of thrillers in the same way that Greene and Ambler are. However, my contention is that Hamilton and Rhys profoundly engage with the emergent audio-visual conventions for the representation of violence and tap into the thriller's audio-visual networks for their own explorations of characters that can no longer outrun the media ecology of their time. Indeed, as I will show, the consciousness of these characters is becoming fully mediatized and the human psyche and their senses become part of the network.

Jean Rhys's novels of the 1930s chronicle abandonment, failed relationships, as well as emotional and physical abuse, expressing women's traumatic experiences through references to music, multi-lingual voices, and the noises and voices of places and inanimate objects.[52] Indeed, as Anna Snaith comments, Rhys's 'interwar novels, in particular, operate as sonic collages, punctured as they are by street criers and performers, memories of French and English Caribbean folksongs, popular song lyrics from music hall and minstrel shows'.[53] Maya in *Quartet* (1928), Julia in *After Leaving Mr Mackenzie* (1931), Anna in *Voyage in the Dark* (1934), and Sasha in *Good Morning, Midnight* (1939) are characters of the demi-monde, working as chorus girls, actresses, or fashion models, who progressively sink into alcoholism, sex work, and despair. Rhys's texts portray the gradual unwinding of these women's lives and minds by saturating the texts with sound, and yet, in the case of Sasha in *Good Morning, Midnight*, also making characters yearn for 'quiet'.

*Voyage in the Dark*, Rhys's personal favourite, was initially titled *Two Tunes*, which was meant to designate the 'two musics which neither [Rhys] nor Anna [the protagonist] could ever fit together'.[54] Allusions and references to popular music and music recording pervade the text, with popular songs of the late nineteenth and early twentieth centuries seemingly offering a

---

[52] See, for instance, Rhys, *Good Morning*, p. 18: 'Jesus, Help me! Ja, ja, nein, nein, was kostet es, Wien ist eine sehr schöne Stadt, Buda-Pest auch ist sehr schön, ist schön, mein Herr, ich habe meinen [*sic*] Blumen vergessen, aus meinen grossen Schmerzen mach ich die kleinen Lieder, homo homini lupus (I've got that one, anyway), aus meinen grossen Schmerzen homo homini doh ré mi fah so la ti doh ....'

[53] Anna Snaith, 'Jean Rhys and the Politics of Sound', in Delia da Sousa Correa (ed.), *The Edinburgh Companion to Literature and Music* (Edinburgh: Edinburgh University Press, 2020), 570–576 (p. 570).

[54] Carole Angier, 'Introduction', in Jean Rhys, *Voyage in the Dark* (London: Penguin, 2000), p. vii.

conceptual system that helps Anna to make sense of the world and to 'function' within her environment: 'All that evening I did everything to the tune of Camptown Racecourse. "I'se gwine to ride all night, I'se gwine to ride all day...".'[55] The songs referenced by Anna are precariously balanced between resistance to and complicity in reinforcing racial stereotypes and power dynamics.[56] As noted by Snaith, Stephen Foster's 'Camptown Races', which is referenced here, 'perform[s] and rehearse[s] racist caricatures of blackness.... Rhys is clearly evoking the aural atmosphere of pre-war London's nightclubs and restaurants, but also the role of popular song in circulating and trading in racial caricature.'[57] From remembering the tunes sung by her family's Caribbean servant Francine to twentieth-century popular songs that accompany her alcohol-fuelled nights in bars and nightclubs, music acts as an important sensory stimulus for Anna's behaviour, memory, and imagination in the novel. *Voyage in the Dark* is built on networks of musical reference, used to express the protagonist's precarious position, both as a Creole migrant and as a young woman.

When Anna falls pregnant, despair and confusion set her mind racing, but her thoughts largely centre on the songs of her Caribbean childhood: 'I undressed and got into bed. Everything was still heaving up and down. "Connais-tu le pays où fleuret l'oranger?"...Miss Jackson used to sing that in a thin quavering voice.[58] Following an illegal abortion, Anna falls seriously ill and experiences feverish dreams and hallucinations of herself dancing involuntarily to the songs of a man playing a concertina accompanied by a trio of musicians. As she dips in and out of consciousness, the music and dancing become hectic and disjointed, reflecting her fatigue and vertigo as a result of extreme blood loss:

'I'm giddy', I said.

*I'm awfully giddy—but we went on dancing forwards and backwards and forwards whirling round and round The concertina-man was very black—he sat sweating and the concertina went forwards and backwards backwards and forwards one two three one two three pourquoi ne pas aimer Bonheur supreme—the triangle-man kept time on his triangle and with his foot tapping*

---

[55] Jean Rhys, *Voyage in the Dark* (London: Penguin, 2000), p. 132.
[56] Snaith, 'Jean Rhys and the Politics of Sound', pp. 573–575.
[57] Snaith, 'Jean Rhys and the Politics of Sound', p. 574. On *Voyage in the Dark* and its references to ragtime and 'blackface minstrelsy', see Sue Thomas, *Jean Rhys's Modernist Bearings and Experimental Aesthetics* (London: Bloomsbury, 2022), pp. 82–83.
[58] Rhys, *Voyage in the Dark*, p. 139.

## 158   LITERATURE AND SOUND FILM IN MID-CENTURY BRITAIN

*and the little man who played the chak-chak smiled with his eyes fixed...I heard the concertina-music playing behind me all the time and the noise of the people's feet dancing—the street was in a greenish shadow—*[59]

Although music and dance apparently turn into a nightmare, these elements also, as Cynthia Davis notes, signal important moments of resistance in Rhys's work.[60] As a Creole writer born in Dominica, Rhys's fiction of the 1930s frequently borrows and adapts Afro-Caribbean rhetorical and cultural patterns of expression, such as carnival performance, heteroglossia, as well as musical 'call-and-response' structures.[61] On such a view, the novel's explicit framing of its protagonist as a chorus-girl performer who is fully embedded in the networks of contemporary music and the songs of her past (live and recorded, remembered and imagined), also entails an expression of resistance and emerging independence.

*Good Morning, Midnight* explores the life and consciousness of Sophia 'Sasha' Jansen, an impoverished middle-aged woman who returns to Paris after many years in the hope of a 'quiet' holiday. Having been abandoned by her husband Enno following the death of their infant son, Sasha struggles to come to terms with her traumatic past. Like in *Voyage in the Dark*, sound and song take centre stage in *Good Morning, Midnight* during Sasha's lonely wanderings through Paris as inanimate objects gain agency and voice:

'While we live, let us live', say the bottles of wine. When we give, let us give. Besides, it isn't my face, this tortured and tormented mask. I can take it off whenever I like and hang it up on a nail. [...] Singing defiantly 'You don't like me, but I don't like you either. Don't like jam, ham or lamb, and I *don't* like roly-poly....' Singing 'One more river to cross, that's Jordan, Jordan....' I have no pride—no pride, no name, no face, no country. I don't belong anywhere. Too sad, too sad....All this time I am reading the menu over and over again.[62]

Seeking to console herself with drink and men, Sasha wanders the streets of Paris. Her only goal is 'to have a programme, not to leave anything to chance—no gaps. No trailing around aimlessly with cheap gramophone

---

[59] Rhys, *Voyage in the Dark*, pp. 157–158.

[60] Cynthia Davis, 'Jamette Carnival and Afro-Caribbean Influences on the Work of Jean Rhys', *Anthurium: A Caribbean Studies Journal*, 3.2 (2005), Article 9, n.p. doi: 10.33596/anth.53.

[61] Davis, 'Jamette Carnival', n.p.

[62] Jean Rhys, *Good Morning, Midnight* (London: Penguin, 2016), p. 33.

records starting up in your head, no "Here this happened, here that happened".'[63] Sasha is confronted with two worlds—her past and her present, both of which become increasingly difficult to separate. Sasha's past, her memories of 'here this happened, here that happened' are presented as 'gramophone records starting up in [her] head.'[64] Taking up *Brighton Rock*'s idea of recorded sound as the symbolic inscription of violence, *Good Morning, Midnight* revolves constantly around the gramophone record as a convenient metaphor for cycles of traumatic memory that must be avoided at all cost, but which are impossible to evade or switch off. In representing the workings of memory as a disc of recorded music, the novel metaphorically expresses the sheer endless and repetitive nature of Sasha's physical wanderings in Paris as well as the cyclical motion of her thoughts and feelings. She devalues her own memory as a '*cheap* gramophone record', thereby undercutting any possible highbrow connotations.

Following her monotonous programme, Sasha visits the same cafés, restaurants, and cinemas repeatedly to evade her impending psychological breakdown and to reintroduce some sense of stability into her life: 'At four o'clock next afternoon I am in a cinema on the Champs-Elysées, according to the programme. Laughing heartily in the right places. It's a very good show and I see it through twice.'[65] Despite following the schedule she has created for herself, the record of her memory hardly ever stops playing: 'I walk along, remembering this, remembering that, trying to find a cheap place to eat—not so easy round here. The gramophone record is going strong in my head: "Here this happened, here that happened...".'[66] Sasha wants nothing more than for the world to be quiet, telling herself that what she needs is a 'quiet' stay in Paris.[67] 'Quiet', of course, may be read as 'uneventful'— however, Sasha's frequent encounters with sound and music suggest a particular need for silence which she equates with sanity and calm. Seeking out silence, Sasha desperately attempts to extricate herself from the memories and the sonic networks in which she is caught up: 'Now, quiet, quiet...This is going to be a nice sane fortnight. "Quiet, quiet", I say to the clock when I am winding it up, and it makes a noise between a belch and a giggle.'[68]

There is noise everywhere in the Parisian cityscape that Sasha cannot outrun. Acoustic stimuli, particularly music, bring back her painful thoughts and traumatic memories:

---

[63] Rhys, *Good Morning*, p. 8.
[64] Rhys, *Good Morning*, p. 8.
[65] Rhys, *Good Morning*, p. 9.
[66] Rhys, *Good Morning*, p. 10.
[67] Rhys, *Good Morning*, p. 24.
[68] Rhys, *Good Morning*, p. 24.

160  LITERATURE AND SOUND FILM IN MID-CENTURY BRITAIN

Walking to the music of *L'Arlésienne*, remembering the coat I wore then...The orchestra was playing *L'Arlésienne*, I remember so well. I've just got to hear that music now, any time, and I'm back in the Café Buffalo, sitting by that man. And the music going heavily. And he's talking away about a friend who is so rich that he has his photograph on the bands of his cigars. A mad conversation.[69]

Translating a listener's experience of musical variations onto the page, the phrase returns only a few pages later, slightly altered and more ironically self-conscious, when Sasha is 'walking to the music of *L'Arlésienne*...Pull yourself together, dearie. This is late October, 1937, and that old coat had its last outing a long time ago.'[70] Sound and music accompany Sasha's memory walks through the streets of Paris, not least because her husband Enno 'was a chansonnier before he became a journalist'.[71] When first married, Sasha could only think of herself as a musical instrument 'tuned up to top pitch. Everything is smooth, soft and tender. Making love. The colours of the pictures.... Tuned up to top pitch. Everything tender and melancholy—as life is sometimes, just for one moment....'[72] At one point in her happy past, Sasha was able to participate in the networks of music, sound, and colour of the Parisian cityscape. As an instrument 'tuned up to top pitch', she was as much part of the city's soundscape as anyone else. Everything seemed more vivid, more alive, then: the capacity to join in the cacophony of the city also make images ('colours of pictures') more expressive and animated. Now, abandoned by Enno and mourning the death of their baby, Sasha returns to the image of herself as a music-making device. With her circumstances so drastically changed, she cannot help but think of herself as a broken instrument: 'Yes, I am sad, sad as a circus-lioness, sad as an eagle without wings, sad as a violin with only one string and that one broken.'[73] Rehearsing these similes, Sasha settles on the broken instrument, because it most aptly denotes her downward spiral, suggesting that in a world that is filled to the brim with sound, her desperation and trauma can really only find expression in the idea of a broken instrument as something that used to belong to, but is now unable to participate in, the soundscape enveloping it. As a broken instrument, all she can offer is discord or silence.

The narrative style of *Good Morning, Midnight* anchors the novel in its wider media ecology and presents this media environment as preoccupied

---

[69] Rhys, *Good Morning*, pp. 70–71.  [70] Rhys, *Good Morning*, p. 74.
[71] Rhys, *Good Morning*, p. 94.  [72] Rhys, *Good Morning*, p. 96.
[73] Rhys, *Good Morning*, p. 34.

with both audition and vision, especially when Sasha tells readers of her 'film-mind'.[74] Driving in a taxi with a young man, Sasha asks him to 'whistle that tune, will you? The one you said is the march of the Legion'.[75] Only when he obliges, does her mind begin to wander. While she is listening to the tune, she remembers an encounter with another man who was also whistling the same song.[76] As the sound begins again, she thinks of her 'film-mind…("For God's sake watch out for your film-mind…")'.[77] In Rhys's text, image and sound belong together. As Judith Kegan Gardiner notes, 'throughout the novel, Sasha makes us conscious of the tunes and pictures that float through her head. This is her "film-mind"'.[78] Sound and vision are intricately linked and difficult to disentangle; to Sasha, movement through the city entails the incessant encounter with filmic (or film-minded) audio-vision and music recording. Although Sasha is on a mission to find calm and silence, the novel demonstrates their unattainability.

Patrick Hamilton's *Hangover Square* (1941) is equally, intriguingly, concerned with the interplay of sound, image, and silence. In this novel, the metaphor of a film soundtrack breaking down is used consistently to represent the protagonist's experience of mental illness:

> *Click!*…Here it was again! He was walking along the cliff at Hunstanton and it had come again…*Click!*…Or would the word '*snap*' or '*crack*' describe it better? It was a noise inside his head, and yet it was not a noise. It was the sound which a noise makes when it abruptly ceases: it had a temporarily deafening effect.…It was as though a shutter had fallen. It had fallen noiselessly, but the thing had been so quick that he could only think of it as a snap or crack.…A film. Yes, it was like the other sort of film, too—a 'talkie'. It was as though he had been watching a talking film, and all at once the sound-track had failed. The figures on the screen continued to move, to behave more or less logically: but they were figures in a new, silent, indescribably eerie world. Life, in fact, which had been for him a moment ago a 'talkie', had all at once become a silent film. And there was no music.[79]

---

[74] See, for instance, Lisa Stead's *Off to the Pictures: Cinema-going, Women's Writing and Movie Culture in Interwar Britain* (Edinburgh: Edinburgh University Press, 2016), p. 107. Stead devotes an entire chapter to the discussion of Rhys's fiction of the 1930s and its relationship to the visual aspect of cinema.

[75] Rhys, *Good Morning*, p. 145.     [76] Rhys, *Good Morning*, p. 146.

[77] Rhys, *Good Morning*, p. 146.

[78] Judith Kegan Gardiner, '*Good Morning, Midnight*; Good Night, Modernism', *boundary 2*, 11.1/2 (Autumn 1982–Winter 1983), 233–251 (p. 238).

[79] Patrick Hamilton, *Hangover Square: A Story of Darkest Earl's Court* (London: Penguin, 2001), p. 15.

162 LITERATURE AND SOUND FILM IN MID-CENTURY BRITAIN

The novel commences with a sound, the 'click!' experienced by George Harvey Bone on Christmas Day 1938. This sound recurs throughout the text, sometimes in variations, as a 'snap', 'pop', or 'crack'. Each 'click' forms the beginning (and sometimes the end) of George's bouts of schizophrenia.[80] Reminiscent of a Dr Jekyll and Mr Hyde plot, the rather quiet and sensitive George dips in and out of a second personality whose aim it is to kill the cold, calculating, aspiring actress Netta Longdon, with whom George is hopelessly infatuated. Treated cruelly by Netta and her circle of fascist friends, George ultimately kills her and one of her lovers before taking his own life.

Whenever George undergoes one of his schizophrenic episodes, the narrator describes this experience by referring to the breaking down of a film soundtrack. Steeped in the experience of the late 1930s mediascape, life for George is a 'talkie' which suddenly ceases to play with sound. George's experience of schizophrenia turns the world into 'a silent film without music— ....He looked at passing objects and people, but they had no colour, vivacity, meaning—he was mentally deaf to them.'[81] The 'silent film without music' provides a peculiar anchoring point for George's experience of mental illness. Although George can still hear other people and also answer them, the experience is somehow automated, mechanical, and unnatural. There is a sensation of disconnection, isolation, and numbness underlying the way in which George moves through the diegetic world when he undergoes one of his episodes. He can witness other people speaking, but it is 'as though they had not spoken, as though they had moved their lips but remained silent', a comparison which takes its cue directly from George's (and the reader's) experience of silent film.

The novel further pursues the idea of mental illness as an experience of 'mental deafness' for the protagonist. The narration frames and represents the experience as a sudden shift that moves from the realm of everyday noise and conversation into the realm of silence. It is not simply that the world appears as a 'silent film', but as a silent film 'without music'. The absence of music as well as other forms of sound indicates the complete and utter estrangement George experiences. The idea of 'mental deafness' is particularly interesting as it aligns George's condition with his hearing faculties

---

[80] The small noises that introduce George's schizophrenic episodes also recall the white noise and slight acoustic distortion that is produced when a needle is first placed onto a gramophone record.

[81] Hamilton, *Hangover Square*, p. 17.

and his ability to process and understand sound. This idea is perpetuated consistently throughout the novel as George experiences '*inclosure*—a shutting down, a locking in.…A moment before his mind had heard and answered: now he was mentally deaf and dumb.'[82] The sensation of being 'locked in' his body is expressed and felt through the absence of sound–image interaction. George can still see and observe the world around him, but he is unable to listen and to process the soundscapes of his environment. He dubs these intervals his 'dead moods'.[83]

The novel thus establishes a set of connotations for sound and silence. While the intervals of schizophrenia, experienced as a silent film, carry associations of death, mystery, and numbness, George's everyday life, experienced as a sound film, appears 'bright, clear, vivacious, sane':

> He was on Hunstanton station and it had happened again. Click, snap, pop—whatever you like—and it all came flooding back! The sound-track had been resumed with a sudden switch; the grim, dreary, mysterious silent film had vanished utterly away, and all things were bright, clear, vivacious, sane, colourful and logical around him, as he carried his bag, at three o'clock on Boxing Day, along the platform of the little seaside terminus.[84]

Every time the soundtrack resumes in George's life, he becomes hyperaware of the sounds and sights of his surroundings and enjoys the experience of audio-vision, of being able to see and hear again. Everything is as if 'heard by him for the first time.'[85] By reintegrating George back into the flow of everyday life, hearing and seeing become markers of sanity and well-being. Indeed, George feels happy and elated whenever he is able to fully participate in the world surrounding him: 'what a noise that engine made! And yet it exhilarated him. He always had these few moments of exhilaration after his brain had "blinked" and he found himself hearing and understanding sounds and sights once again.'[86] While the novel predominantly centres on this dichotomy between the experience of sound film and the experience of silent film to map George's mental illness, sound and sound technology's potential for expressing or mediating emotion and cognition is exploited

---

[82] Hamilton, *Hangover Square*, p. 165.  [83] Hamilton, *Hangover Square*, p. 16.
[84] Hamilton, *Hangover Square*, p. 20.  [85] Hamilton, *Hangover Square*, p. 21.
[86] Hamilton, *Hangover Square*, p. 21.

164　LITERATURE AND SOUND FILM IN MID-CENTURY BRITAIN

further by the text in other contexts, too. Remembering how he fell in love with Netta, George reminisces:

> She was telling him about herself, the small part she was playing in the film. Then it happened. At one moment she was just something he was talking to and looking at; at the next she was something of which he was physically sensible by some means other than that of sight or sound: she was sending out a ray, a wave, from herself, which seemed to affect his whole being, to go all through him like a faint vibration. It was as though she were a small amateur wireless station, and he alone was tuned in to her and listening.[87]

Falling in love with Netta, to George, felt like he was 'listening in' as if the recipient of a radio broadcast. Expressing his devotion and attentiveness towards Netta, George describes his affection as a kind of attunement to her whole being. The only way he can grasp the sensation of falling in love with her is to think about himself as the receiving end of her invisible sound waves, a 'faint vibration'. It is sound waves and sound technology such as radio which become suitable metaphors for George's falling in love. The novel makes a point of presenting George not as a talker, but as a sensitive listener who enjoys hearing others and the world surrounding him. A character entirely of his time, George is fully emerged in the media ecology of the interwar years, where sound and sound–image interaction are everyday features, while his bouts of schizophrenia are described as an oddity, as silent film without music, which serves to express the disturbing nature of his condition.

Compounded by the unfeeling treatment he receives from Netta and some of her acquaintances, George's schizophrenic episodes become progressively worse: 'Crack!...It made him reel. It was as though he had been hit by something....this time his brain had almost burst in two: it had practically knocked him off his feet.'[88] The sound of the 'crack!' takes on a more sinister nature as George experiences its physical, violent impact. George is not so much bothered by the length of time that he has been experiencing schizophrenic intervals, but by the volume and violence of the sound in his head which, as he notes, is getting louder and more painful throughout the course of the novel. A little 'click' or 'pop' is suddenly transformed into a loud and forceful 'crack' which emphasizes the severity of George's condition.

---

[87] Hamilton, *Hangover Square*, p. 50.　　[88] Hamilton, *Hangover Square*, p. 170.

NETWORKS OF AUDIO-VISION   165

Finally, George experiences his last transition from everyday life into a schizophrenic break that will ultimately lead him to kill Netta and her lover Peter before taking his own life:

CLICK!...

...It was an extraordinary sensation, but he was used to it. It was as though a shutter had rolled down on his brain, and clicked tight. It was as though the sound-track in a talkie had broken down and the still-proceeding picture on the screen of existence had an utterly different character, mysterious, silent, indescribably eerie.[89]

The severity and finality of this last transition is expressed through capital letters, a feature used frequently by Hamilton to lend additional emphasis to a word. The metaphor for George's mental illness consistently remains the same from beginning to end of this novel. The text embeds itself into a multi-media network and explores how media experience may be mobilized to give expression to George's mental illness by framing it in terms of cinematic audio-vision and its involuntary breakdown. Although by its very nature as a prose text the novel is dealing in words, its inventory of language comprehensively draws on extra-textual media experience.

*Hangover Square* frames silence as isolation, numbness, even danger, thereby recalling the sophisticated use of silence in *The 39 Steps* and *Gaslight* as well as the oppressive silences of Greene's and Ambler's thriller worlds, which express the menacing, isolating, and threatening connotations of silence in a world wired for sound. The 'silent film' in which George finds himself during his schizophrenic episodes is a grim and sinister world, and the recurring switch from sound to silence becomes a means of expressing George's sense of increasing displacement. In this way, *Hangover Square* uses the familiarity with both silent and sound film of its contemporary readers to create new associative and imaginative networks for mediating and presenting the gradual unravelling of a character's mind. Hamilton's novel embeds itself into a new representational ontology through its rendition of character psychology: the character George Harvey Bone has fully embraced the omnipresence of audio-vision in modern culture, which, in turn, also leads to the perception of complete silence as sordid and sinister. Patricia Waugh rightly observes of *Hangover Square* that 'everything feels mediated':

---

[89] Hamilton, *Hangover Square*, p. 265.

## 166 LITERATURE AND SOUND FILM IN MID-CENTURY BRITAIN

technology is the vehicle for the distribution of mood thought of as 'wired'. Lives are lived through wires, phones, reproduction of talk. Images of the 'net' and the mediated and distributed network of modern communications, wireless waves, magnetic resonances, phone lines string themselves across the locked-in, the screened, distant and celluloid, the cinematic performance....[90]

Waugh's comments return *Hangover Square* to the networked orbit of the thriller and to the idea that audio-visual conventions come to designate violence, suspense, and crisis. Media representation and media networks in *Hangover Square* are all-encompassing, to the point where George Harvey Bone himself becomes part of the network. Media experience in *Hangover Square* encodes violence and crisis, but it also firmly embeds the novel in a media ecology, in which the missing alignment (or misalignment) of vision and audition might spell disaster.

*Literature and Sound Film in Mid-Century Britain.* Lara Ehrenfried, Oxford University Press.
© Lara Ehrenfried 2025. DOI: 10.1093/9780198950790.003.0006

---

[90] Patricia Waugh, 'Precarious Voices: Moderns, Moods, and Moving Epochs', in David Bradshaw, Laura Marcus, and Rebecca Roach (eds), *Moving Modernisms: Motion, Technology, and Modernity* (Oxford: Oxford University Press, 2016), 191–216, (p. 201).

# 6

# The Senses at War

This chapter turns its focus to the context of the Second World War and to another popular type of commercial film: the costume melodrama. I argue that audio-vision and synchronicity cease to act as markers or facilitators of linear temporality, comprehensibility, and causality in the costume melodrama of Second World War Britain. Instead, sound and vision compete with each other; they vie for attention and thereby also act against the grain of narrative continuity and causality. As the Second World War threw into question the understanding of self and history in terms of linear time, the loss of narrative control and the sense of existing 'out-of-time' or of being 'out of sync' became a phenomenon widely reflected in the literature and culture of the Home Front.[1] In the short stories of Elizabeth Bowen and the Blitz novels of Bowen, Henry Green, and James Hanley, readers encounter forms of stylistic and temporal complexity that call into question the possibility of any kind of linear understanding of time, space, and experience. Specifically, both the literary fiction of the Blitz and the Home Front, as well as the costume melodrama, engage in the production of textual, visual, and sonic excess and complicated, non-linear temporalities. These works pursue what I call an 'aesthetics of excess' to deconstruct notions of narrative and temporal control.[2]

One motivation for this particular aesthetic is a reaction to the totalizing vision of a 'wartime culture, with its big propaganda machines, its fabricated communal feelings and military regimentation, aimed at transforming private imagination into public spirit.'[3] The turn to the mode of melodrama (in commercial film), alongside the self-conscious performativity and artifice of, for instance, Green and Hanley's literary fiction of the Blitz, can be read as direct responses to what Bowen described as the '*desiccation,*

---

[1] Beryl Pong, *British Literature and Culture in Second World Wartime: For the Duration* (Oxford: Oxford University Press, 2020), pp. 1–25.

[2] Peter Brooks defined the melodramatic mode specifically by its 'aesthetics of excess'. See Peter Brooks, *The Melodramatic Imagination* (New Haven, CT: Yale University Press, 1995).

[3] Adam Piette, *Imagination at War: British Fiction and Poetry, 1939–1945* (London: Papermac, 1995), p. 2.

# 168  LITERATURE AND SOUND FILM IN MID-CENTURY BRITAIN

by war, of our day-to-day lives', a state of 'parched' 'senses', 'nerves', and thoughts.[4] In answer to these conditions outlined by Bowen, the British B-movie studio Gainsborough Pictures drew on a wartime strategy of producing and promoting 'cinematic excess'. Coining the term, Kristin Thompson differentiates between film 'style' on the one hand and filmic 'excess' on the other.[5] While style is 'the use of repeated techniques which become characteristic of the work', excess pushes beyond style. Thompson suggests that 'excess arises from the conflict between the materiality of a film and the unifying structures within it'.[6] Cinematic excess is therefore 'counternarrative and counter-unity'; it consists of a surplus of stylistic and sensual elements that draw attention to themselves, but that appear unmotivated, even random, thereby causing 'gaps' in motivation and 'lags' in viewer perception and attention.[7]

Kent Puckett has shown the productivity of applying Thompson's differentiation between cinematic style and excess in *War Pictures* (2017): he argues for the 'stylistic eccentricity' of some British Second World War films that negotiate fundamental issues at the heart of the British experience of war, such as the coming-to-terms with the idea that a war against fascism may in itself entail 'a commitment to totalitarianism'.[8] In response to this problem, Puckett observes a stylistic turn towards particularity, a 'formal rejection of the idea of totality' through 'impacted moments of stylistic excess or eccentricity' in selected works of British cinema.[9] While Puckett convincingly argues for a tactical 'cinematic eccentricity' that can be found in selected British films of the Second World War, I am here specifically interested in the idea of cinematic excess in the genre of costume melodrama and in reading the melodramatic production of excess alongside Home Front fiction by Bowen, Hanley, and Green.

## Writing the Home Front

Henry Green's *Caught* (1943), his novel of the interwoven lives of two auxiliary fire service (AFS) volunteers during the Blitz, enacts the loss of

---

[4] See Elizabeth Bowen, Postscript to *The Demon Lover* (US edn), in Hermione Lee (ed.), *The Mulberry Tree: Writings of Elizabeth Bowen* (London: Vintage, 1999), 94–99 (p. 96), and Elizabeth Bowen, *The Heat of the Day* (New York: Anchor, 2002), p. 4.

[5] Kristin Thompson, 'The Concept of Cinematic Excess', *Ciné-Tracts*, 1.2 (Summer 1977), 54–63.

[6] Thompson, 'Cinematic Excess', p. 55.      [7] Thompson, 'Cinematic Excess', pp. 56–57.

[8] Kent Puckett, *War Pictures* (New York: Fordham University Press, 2017), p. 2.

[9] Puckett, *War Pictures*, p. 11.

THE SENSES AT WAR    169

narrative control through its temporal (dis)organization, stylistic indeterminacy, and synaesthetic narration. It is, as Mark Rawlinson notes, a work that consistently evokes 'sensuous…disorientation'.[10] The novel opens with the upper-class Richard Roe who visits his family on their country estate when on leave from his AFS duties in London. Roe's son Christopher, the novel discloses, had been abducted in London by the mentally ill sister of Richard's AFS supervisor Pye prior to the beginning of the war. By alluding to the abduction and its consequences within the first few pages, the reader begins to expect that the novel may slowly, over time, disclose the circumstances of Christopher's abduction: 'Yet he had to admit that he could, at the time, feel nothing stronger than irritation when, some months earlier, as will appear, Christopher had really been lost in London.'[11] The sentence is difficult, simultaneously pulling readers into the past by analepsis ('some months earlier') and also presenting the narrator's proleptic announcement of circumstances which will become clearer over the course of the novel ('as will appear'). There is a tension, not merely between story time and discourse time, but also a tension in the narrator's simultaneous account of past and future. This strategy recurs throughout the novel, especially towards the end, when Roe tries to describe his experiences of working as an AFS volunteer during the Blitz.

> Even when, twelve months later, he had begun to forget raids, and when, in the substation, they went over their experiences from an unconscious wish to recreate, night after night in the wet canteen, even then he found he could not go back to his old daydreams about this place. It had come to seem out of date. '…but when at last we drove through the Dock', he continued, taken up by this urge to explain, 'there was not one officer to report to, no one to give orders, we simply drove on up a road towards what seemed to be our blaze'.[12]

Here, too, the narrator pulls the reader forward in a proleptic announcement ('twelve months later') before re-entering the present moment of Roe's narration that is concerned with the experience of a few months before ('…but when at last'). Roe's life of the past has 'come to seem out of

---

[10] Mark Rawlinson, 'The Second World War: British Writing', in Kate McLoughlin (ed.), *The Cambridge Companion to War Writing* (Cambridge: Cambridge University Press, 2009), 197–211 (p. 202).
[11] Henry Green, *Caught*, in *Caught, Back, Concluding* (London: Vintage, 2016), p. 9.
[12] Green, *Caught*, pp. 187–188.

# 170 LITERATURE AND SOUND FILM IN MID-CENTURY BRITAIN

date'—there is a pervasive sense of being misaligned, of being 'out of sync', with the life that was lived previously, but has now become irretrievable.

The tension between Roe's recollection of time and events and the narrator's heterodiegetic accounting and revisiting of time and events also becomes clear in the frequent use of parentheses: '(The moment they were outside, in the dull light of autumn...he began to question his surroundings.) (In the bus, whenever she caught a woman's eye, she smiled.) (He sat, holding the bag on his knee, gradually losing what he held....).'[13] Christopher's abduction is presented by the narrator by using Christopher as the main focalizer in multiple sets of parentheses, one following the other.[14] Meanwhile, Roe's recollections of the same event are purely based on his imagination and assumptions since 'he did not know what Christopher had been through...when the boy had been returned by the police, holding his boat tight, Roe was not in the house to put the questions expected'.[15]

*Caught* contains continuous references to time and duration, sometimes referring to the same day at different points throughout the narrative, accompanied by a shift in focus: twice, for instance, the day of 'three days before the outbreak of war' is mentioned—but different events on this same day, both involving Roe, are recounted in each instance.[16] Returns to a point in (story) time are marked by repetition in the discourse, too; the narrator tends to digress only to return to a previous point by repeating a sentence, a phrase, or an expression: 'He remembered how, from curiosity, he had been to look at the store out of which Christopher had been abducted' recurs one page later as 'when, from curiosity, he went to see for himself the store out of which Christopher had been abducted'.[17]

*Caught* avoids narrative resolution. In Roe's final conversation with Dy, for instance, he circles repeatedly around the death of one of his fellow AFS volunteers, Shiner, who, upon saving Roe's life, was killed in the aftermath of an air raid. Asserting that he will 'get to it in a minute', he does not, after all, disclose the details of how Shiner saved him, only reporting to Dy that 'of course, Shiner was killed later on' and making assumptions about how he must have found his end.[18] The parentheses also play an important role here, because they function as apparent corrective commentary to Roe's report:

> 'The first night', he said, 'we were ordered to the docks. As we came over Westminster Bridge it was fantastic, the whole of the left side of London seemed to be alight.'

---

[13] Green, *Caught*, p. 14.     [14] Green, *Caught*, pp. 12–16.     [15] Green, *Caught*, p. 16.
[16] Green, *Caught*, pp. 28, 37.     [17] Green, *Caught*, pp. 10–11.
[18] Green, *Caught*, pp. 201, 202, 204.

THE SENSES AT WAR  171

(It had not been like that at all. As they went, not hurrying, but steadily towards the river, the sky in that quarter, which happened to be the east, beginning at the bottom of streets until it spread over the nearest houses, was flooded in a second sunset, orange and rose, turning the pavements pink. Civilians hastened by twos or threes, hushed below the stupendous pall of defeat until, in the business quarter, the streets were deserted.)[19]

On several occasions, the parentheses are seemingly inserted to verify or disprove characters' statements—but the reliability of such parenthetical commentary is thrown into question itself, by changes in focalization (sometimes, the point of view given in the parentheses seem to be Christopher's, sometimes Roe's, sometimes the narrator's). Some of the parenthetical commentary uses free indirect discourse and can therefore hardly count as a reliable source of information or as a corrective to Roe's report.[20]

In its account of the Blitz, *Caught* is fundamentally anchored in audio-visual framing and synaesthetic description. Rex Ferguson argues that within the novel's representation of the Blitz, 'color is produced in place of sounds'.[21] Indeed, Ferguson goes further to make the intriguing and convincing case for Roe's partial deafness (mirroring Green's own). Consequently, the novel's focus at first seems to lie on articulating Roe's experience of the Blitz in primarily visual terms, especially with reference to colour, whereby the colours themselves are stimulated by the Blitz's soundscape and cannot be fully apprehended by Roe otherwise.[22] Yet, the novel supplements these moments of synaesthetic narration with moments of audio-visual framing; for instance when Roe remembers one of his earliest encounters with his wife and is subsequently pulled out of this memory by the arrival of Pye's mistress Prudence:

Richard, after his fresh tide of longing for Dy had ebbed, found he was increasingly absorbed by what was left to him of the sights and sounds, and by the feeling, as he had it now, of that early summer they had first met, the year he got to know her.... He turned to her and she seemed his in her white clothes, with a cry the blackbird had flown and in her eyes as,

---

[19] Green, *Caught*, p. 185.
[20] On this point, see Patrick Deer, *Culture in Camouflage: War, Empire, and Modern British Literature* (Oxford: Oxford University Press, 2009), p. 129.
[21] Rex Ferguson, 'Blind Noise and Deaf Visions: Henry Green's *Caught*, Synaesthesia and the Blitz', *Journal of Modern Literature*, 33.1 (2009), 102–116 (p. 103).
[22] Ferguson, 'Blind Noise', pp. 107–114.

172  LITERATURE AND SOUND FILM IN MID-CENTURY BRITAIN

speechless, she turned, still a stranger, to look into him, he thought he saw
the hot, lazy, luxuriance of a rose, the heavy, weightless, luxuriance of a
rose.... Roses had come above her bare knees under the fluted skirt she
wore, and the swallows flying so low made her, in his recollection, much
taller than she had ever been.

Back in his present, he heard a tap of high heels. Looking up, he saw
Prudence, dressed in green as of dark olives like to the colour of that cod's
head. She smiled, but did not stop. Still under the influence of his memories, he thought how sharp she appeared against the black wall with
AMBULANCE painted in grey letters three foot high, knife sharp compared to the opulence his darling had carried about in her skin, sheathed
for display to his senses, in the exuberance of his mother's garden.[23]

Roe's recollection of this moment in his family estate's garden contains an
interplay of vision and audition; the blackbird's cry is part of the scene as
much as the vision of the young woman framed by roses. Roe, and the
reader, are then taken out of this reminiscence by the approach of diegetic
sound in the present: 'he heard a tap of high heels' before he looks up to see
Prudence. There is a marked contrast between the luscious Technicolor
assemblage of reds, whites, greens, and yellow, accompanied by the sound
of birds, in Roe's memory and the present-day encounter with Prudence,
who is dressed in dark olive and 'sharply' appearing in focus against a
wall of black and grey while accompanied by the tapping sounds of her
heeled shoes.

Lighting, colour, and contrast are key to framing *Caught*: as Lara Feigel
notes, 'now that the city has become the set for a film, Green experiments with
other lighting effects', including moonlight, stained-glass windows, and
artificial light.[24] There is such an abundance of colour and light throughout
this text that it is taken to a point of 'oversaturation'. Stylistic excess, including
the narrative insistence on repetition, for instance, discloses a kind of
obsessive-compulsive reiteration of the same thought (or the same memory)
over and over again: 'The roses, when they came to the rose garden, were
full out...on each bush and tree of roses, rose after rose after rose of every
shade.'[25] This kind of semantic 'oversaturation' gives expression to what

[23] Green, *Caught*, pp. 66–67.
[24] Lara Feigel, *Literature, Cinema and Politics 1930–1945: Reading Between the Frames*
(Edinburgh: Edinburgh University Press, 2010), pp. 196–197.
[25] Green, *Caught*, p. 66. For further discussion, see chapter 3, 'Bombs and Roses: The
Writing of Anxiety in Henry Green's *Caught*' by Lyndsey Stonebridge, in *The Writing of*

THE SENSES AT WAR    173

Lyndsey Stonebridge calls the 'anxious historicity' of *Caught*: 'memories are not just cushions of existential support; in shock we awaken memories from yesterday so that we can die with them tomorrow. The past runs into the unthinkable future.'[26]

This same principle can also be found in James Hanley's *No Directions* (1943), which, as Gerard Barrett notes, is equally concerned with the colours of the bombed cityscape.[27] The short novel follows a group of people who share the same tenement house in Chelsea one night during the Blitz: there is the painter Clem and his wife Lena, Mr Frazer and his wife Emily, Gwen and Richard, Mr Johns (a drunk sailor who, by chance, finds shelter in the house), and Celia (who used to be an artist's model for Clem). These characters are thrown together, suspended in a state of tension as they await, and ultimately experience, an air raid. When, in the final chapter, aerial bombardment partially destroys the tenement house, the painter Clem hastens to leave the building. Now,

> every level of air hurling as he ran, and wherever he ran he saw that great shuddering sailor, dark against the river of light, against a reeling wall, looming up as from some great hole in the earth…. He stopped dead, looked up, light was scattering light, a steeple careered crazily through space, under his feet a river in tumult, flowing wild. Great engines roaring past, and faces, faces, faces. He ran up some steps, he reached a roof, he leaned against the iron railings and he watched, he felt tremble under him, the city rocked with outrageous power. A life lived to see this…. Not what you felt, you couldn't even think, mind's door closed up. It was what you saw. He stared entranced at the blazing sky. All that light, a sea, an ocean of light, from what vast reservoir had it flooded up, this drenching light, blazing red, and suddenly to his left a falling green, cataracts of light, red, and yellow and green, this riot of colour shouted at you.[28]

Joining this vivid play of colours are 'hollow sounds', the 'grinding of brakes', 'hissing noises', and, ultimately, everything merges into 'an orgy of movement'.[29]

---

*Anxiety: Imagining Wartime in Mid-Century British Culture* (Basingstoke: Palgrave Macmillan, 2007), pp. 55–74.

[26] Stonebridge, *The Writing of Anxiety*, p. 58.

[27] Gerard Barrett, 'James Hanley and the Colours of War', in Marina MacKay and Lyndsey Stonebridge (eds), *British Fiction after Modernism: The Novel at Mid-Century* (Basingstoke: Palgrave Macmillan, 2007), pp. 77–87.

[28] James Hanley, *No Directions* (London: André Deutsch, 1990), p. 135.

[29] Hanley, *No Directions*, p. 136.

174 LITERATURE AND SOUND FILM IN MID-CENTURY BRITAIN

Clem's eye is taking in the burning cityscape as 'river', 'sea', and, finally, as 'an ocean of floating trash'.[30] Barrett observes that 'the sheer predominance of marine imagery in this fiery setting' forms perhaps 'the novel's major distortion'.[31] The elements of fire, water, earth, and air are not merely joined, but conflated in the audio-visual perception of Clem, who can no longer distinguish between the real and the surreal as the 'mind's door [has been] closed up'. Instead of thought or cognition, there is only sensory impression—vision ('it was what you saw'), audition, and motion ('orgy of movement')—unfolding: these 'powerful descriptions focalized through a painter's eye' are coupled with 'auditory cues'.[32] Patrick Deer here aligns *No Directions* closely with Hanley's experience of working for the BBC on radio drama, but the combination of moments of vision and audition in the novel might equally bear close resemblance to the audio-visual combinations of sound film. Indeed, as the city's bombardment becomes 'uncomfortably aestheticized' in the narrative representation and interlinking of colour, sound, and movement, the Blitz attains a strange status of spectacle and performance that has to be witnessed.[33]

The idea of the overtly performative nature, both of *No Directions* specifically but also of Second World War literature more broadly, has been explored by Adam Piette and Marina MacKay.[34] In Hanley's novel, as implied by the title, there is a marked 'lack of direction' with characters behaving as if they were in a play without any instructions on how to act.[35] Like Green's *Caught*, this lack of direction shows clearly in the narrative enactment of disorientation.[36] One might consider, for instance, the beginning of the novel:

[30] Hanley, *No Directions*, p. 136.
[31] Barrett, 'James Hanley and the Colours of War', p. 81.
[32] Deer, *Culture in Camouflage*, p. 145.       [33] Deer, *Culture in Camouflage*, p. 149.
[34] See Piette, *Imagination at War*, pp. 2–4 on the theatrical nature of the Home Front and pp. 44–45 on *No Directions*. See also Marina MacKay, *Modernism, War, and Violence* (London: Bloomsbury, 2017), pp. 116–119. MacKay discusses Green's *Caught* and Bowen's *The Heat of the Day* with reference to processes of self-dramatization. Piette, MacKay, and Patrick Deer draw on Michael North's seminal observation of the 'disconcerting tendency toward instant fictionalization of overwhelming experiences' in Blitz and Home Front fiction. See Michael North, *Henry Green and the Writing of his Generation* (Charlottesville: University of Virginia Press, 1984), p. 117.
[35] Deer, *Culture in Camouflage*, p. 145, and Piette, *Imagination at War*, pp. 2–4.
[36] Jean-Christophe Murat, 'City of Wars: The Representation of Wartime London in Two Novels of the 1940s: James Hanley's *No Directions* and Patrick Hamilton's *The Slaves of Solitude*', *Caliban*, 25 (2009): para. 6. Open access online at: https://doi.org/10.4000/caliban.1652 (accessed 5 December 2022).

After the deluge of sound ceased, after the wind passed, the sailor fell, was sick. They were in a desert of air. 'Goddam! Get me out of this', the sailor shouted. 'Stand up', the little man said; he began to pull. Crunching sounds came up. 'It's ice', the sailor said. 'Get me out of this.' Falling again, hands became feelers, pawed about. 'I know ice', he said, 'always something moving under ice, I know.' 'Glass, you crazy bastard', the little man said, the cheap raincoat dripped water, his tin helmet kept falling over his forehead.[37]

*No Directions* begins with indeterminacy: a 'deluge of sound', a 'desert of air', the character of the sailor identifies his surroundings as the most treacherous kind of 'ice', namely a sheet of ice on water ('always something moving under ice'). The next sentence introduces a different kind of interpretive possibility ('Glass, you crazy bastard'), which only through situational context (the raincoat, the tin helmet), can finally be identified as the more likely interpretation. However, the sailor, in his drunken state, continues to struggle with adjusting to the other man's explanations. Even as the other man 'picked up a large sheet of glass, held it to the sailor's face, said, "*Now*! Now you have to believe me"', the sailor 'still dragged his way over ice-fields, saw glassy, transparent seas, watched bergs float by, heard great boulders falling'.[38] These widely divergent perceptions and interpretations of the same event enact confusion; they illustrate the failure of aligning (or synchronizing) perception and interpretation. Literary fiction of the 1940s, as Leo Mellor notes, tends to reflect how 'the teleology of experience in the war was fragmentary, partial, splintered, and the unknown ending was the condition for life as lived'.[39] Here, the novel's beginning gestures towards this fragmentary and 'splintered' nature of lived experience, alongside its marked emphasis on sensory disorientation and indeterminacy.

The novel's temporal complexities further indicate that the text deals with issues of synchronicity. In the moment of Clem's witnessing of the burning cityscape cited above, for instance, enumeration, parataxis, and ellipsis construct a fast-paced textual movement that draws the reader's eye forward, supported by the use of commas. Yet, simultaneously, these textual features oriented towards fast-paced narrative progression form a stark

---

[37] Hanley, *No Directions*, p. 9.     [38] Hanley, *No Directions*, p. 11.
[39] Leo Mellor, *Reading the Ruins: Modernism, Bombsites and British Culture* (Cambridge: Cambridge University Press, 2011), p. 50.

## 176 LITERATURE AND SOUND FILM IN MID-CENTURY BRITAIN

contrast to the representation of time, which noticeably stretches and elongates as the narrator is providing extensive—even repetitive—descriptions to convey Clem's view, thereby also prolonging the moment of witnessing the sounds and sights of the burning city.

As in *Caught*, there is a simultaneous pulling-forward and a standstill; a double-bind of fast-paced narrative progression and suspension that reflects competing and contradictory notions of time in the context of war and aerial bombardment.[40] *Caught* and *No Directions* work towards the disintegration of narrative temporality and implode with fragmented accounts of vision, colour, and sound that push against the unifying structures of the text. Both novels cause 'gaps' or 'lags' in the reader's understanding and interpretation of the text and emphasize artifice and self-conscious, even performative narration and behaviour of their characters. As such, they approximate closely—in textual form—the idea of 'cinematic excess' as something that might be both 'counternarrative and counter-unity'.[41]

Shaped by 'disorderly temporalities, alternating narratives, [and] ghostly returns', Elizabeth Bowen's short stories of the war years similarly confront readers with stylistic excess and indeterminacy.[42] 'The Demon Lover', one of Bowen's most widely known stories, draws on gothic tropes and deconstructs narrative continuity, causality, and control. There is gothic suspense and discomfort from the start as the middle-aged Mrs Drover walks through London's blitzed streets. The narrator records 'unoccupied houses' and 'broken parapets'.[43] Having arrived at her boarded-up house, 'no human eye watched Mrs. Drover's return' while 'dead air came out to meet her as she went in'.[44] Inside the house, 'the piano, having gone away to be stored, had left what looked like claw-marks on its part of the parquet'.[45] This beginning already signals the story's rather excessive use of gothic tropes: there is a combination of destruction and dereliction in the description of empty streets and bombed buildings. These impressions are bound to a supernatural (or, at the very least, non-human) cause as signalled by the semantic chain of 'no human eye', 'dead air', and 'claw marks'. A moment of 'crisis' then

---

[40] Pong, *Second World Wartime*, p. 85. With reference to the temporal dimension of photography, Pong remarks that 'suspension' might also be 'constitutive of temporal flux or flow'.

[41] Thompson, 'Cinematic Excess', p. 55.

[42] Thomas S. Davis, 'Elizabeth Bowen's War Gothic', *Textual Practice*, 27.1 (2013), 29–47 (p. 33).

[43] Elizabeth Bowen, 'The Demon Lover', *The Collected Stories of Elizabeth Bowen* (London: Vintage, 1999), 743–749 (p. 743).

[44] Bowen, 'Demon Lover', p. 743.     [45] Bowen, 'Demon Lover', p. 743.

ensues when Mrs Drover finds a mysterious letter waiting for her inside the house. This letter seems to have been written by her former fiancé, a soldier who went missing in action during the First World War and was presumed to have died in 1916. The letter now announces his return to meet her: 'You will not have forgotten that today is our anniversary, and the day we said. The years have gone by at once slowly and fast. In view of the fact that nothing has changed, I shall rely upon you to keep your promise....You may expect me, therefore, at the hour arranged.'[46] A flashback to Mrs Drover's past follows: as a young girl, she says her goodbye to the soldier whose deployment to France is imminent. His ghostly promise echoes in Mrs Drover's memories: 'I shall be with you...sooner or later. You won't forget that. You need do nothing but wait.'[47] In the emptiness of the house, the ominous threat of the letter triggers anxiety and fear. As Mrs Drover opens the bedroom door to check whether someone else (the letter writer?) may have entered the house, 'she heard nothing—but while she was hearing nothing the *passé* air of the staircase was disturbed by a draught that travelled up to her face. It emanated from the basement: down there a door or window was being opened by someone who chose this moment to leave.'[48] 'The Demon Lover' constructs an anachronic, temporally unstable narrative alongside its gothic tropes and mixes this with different narrative techniques and narrative situations, including free indirect discourse as well as omniscient and first-person narration, as noted by Sarah Dillon.[49]

'The Happy Autumn Fields' (1944), which is one of Bowen's most enigmatic stories, equally draws on disorderly temporality and stylistic excess. The story moves back and forth between two female characters, Sarah and Mary, who seem to be connected across time by supernatural means. Mary, who lives in a bombed house in 'blitzed' London, dreams of Sarah and believes herself to be a reincarnation or descendant of Sarah, who is the daughter of an Edwardian or Victorian landowning family. Mary's dreams show Sarah's interactions with her family and her suitor Eugene on a sunny, autumnal day in the past. The story begins with a seemingly ordered description of a 'family walking party'. The external, descriptive view provided by the narrator does not, initially, suggest anything strange or dreamlike: 'Papa, who carried his Alpine stick, led, flanked by Constance

---

[46] Bowen, 'Demon Lover', p. 744.    [47] Bowen, 'Demon Lover', p. 746.
[48] Bowen, 'Demon Lover', p. 748.
[49] Sarah Dillon, 'Elizabeth Bowen: "The Demon Lover" and "Mysterious Kôr"', in Cheryl Alexander Malcolm and David Malcolm (eds), *A Companion to the British and Irish Short Story* (London: Wiley, 2008), 236–243 (p. 239).

# 178 LITERATURE AND SOUND FILM IN MID-CENTURY BRITAIN

and little Arthur. Robert and Cousin Theodore, locked in studious talk, had Emily attached but not quite abreast.'[50] Yet, as the narrative begins to centre more firmly on Sarah and on Sarah's experience of the walk, the text slides into patterns of strangeness, verbal complexity, and linguistic excess:

> It was Sarah who saw the others ahead on the blond stubble, who knew them, knew what they were to each other, knew their names and knew her own. It was she who felt the stubble under her feet, and who heard it give beneath the tread of the others a continuous different more distant soft stiff scrunch. The field and all these outlying fields in view knew as Sarah knew that they were Papa's....Arthur, whose hand Papa was holding, took an anxious hop, a skip and a jump to every stride of the great man's. As for Constance—Sarah could often see the flash of her hat-feather as she turned her head, the curve of her close bodice as she turned her torso. Constance gave Papa her attention but not her thoughts, for she had already been sought in marriage.[51]

The repetition of 'knew' is notable for the story's subsequent unfolding of a mystery that cannot be known or explained as the precise nature of the connection between Sarah and Mary across time remains unresolved for the reader and for the two women themselves. There is repetition and doubling ('stubble', 'field', 'turn') as well as some alliterative composition ('soft stiff scrunch'). The climactic enumeration 'hop, a skip and a jump' equally draws attention to a language that is rich in visual and acoustic connotation. This poetic complexity continues with a frequent use of double negatives throughout: 'Robert, it could be felt, was not unwilling to return to his books.'[52]

The emotional bond between Sarah and her sister Henrietta is developed throughout the story and demonstrates the text's extreme oscillation between the happy matter of a family outing and a sunny autumnal day and the sad, ominous foreboding of death and catastrophe: 'She must never have to wake in the early morning except to the birdlike stirrings of Henrietta...Rather than they should cease to lie in the same bed she prayed they might lie in the same grave.'[53] Sarah's reflections are especially pertinent in the context

---

[50] Elizabeth Bowen, 'The Happy Autumn Fields', *The Collected Stories of Elizabeth Bowen* (London: Vintage, 1999), 755–771 (p. 755).

[51] Bowen, 'Happy Autumn Fields', p. 755.

[52] Bowen, 'Happy Autumn Fields', p. 756.      [53] Bowen, 'Happy Autumn Fields', p. 756.

THE SENSES AT WAR    179

of the story's three temporal layers of the contemporary present of Second World War London, the intense emotional connection between the two sisters in the imagined or dreamed past, and the anticipation of the sisters' future which, as the story discloses at the end, will lead to their unexplained, untimely death following the deadly riding accident of Sarah's suitor Eugene.

The text encircles temporal, linguistic, and psychological meaning and, yet, evades precision on all three counts in its poetic structures and narrative procedures. There is strangeness in the mechanics of narrative delay and in the changing narrative perspective, too. Towards the end of this first dream-like vision of Sarah and Henrietta walking with their family, there is a sudden shift to the first person: 'We surmount the skyline: the family come into our view, we into theirs...Stop oh stop Henrietta's heart-breaking singing! Embrace her close again! Speak the only possible word! Say—oh, say what? Oh the word is lost!'[54] Immediately following this reflection, the reader suddenly finds a further shift in tone and perspective as the narrative turns to Mary, awaking from her dream in her bombed house. Her bedroom, in the present of Second World War London, however, strikes Mary as substantially more unreal than her dreams of Sarah and Henrietta.[55] As Trevor, Mary's partner, anxiously tries to coax her from the house that is already partly ruined, Mary resists, unable and unwilling to leave:

'How are we to live without natures? We only know inconvenience now, not sorrow. Everything pulverizes so easily because it is rot-dry; one can only wonder that it makes so much noise. The source, the sap must have dried up, or the pulse must have stopped, before you and I were conceived. So much flowed through people; so little flows through us. All we can do is imitate love or sorrow.'[56]

Rod Mengham notes that 'The Happy Autumn Fields', 'locates the center of shared experience during the Blitz in the intensity of dreams, fantasies, hallucinations; in an imaginative surplus that cannot be housed satisfactorily in a realist aesthetic, and that is motivated by a compulsion to see beyond the temporal hiatus of the present'.[57] Bowen's imaginative landscape expresses the 'psychological strain involved in trying to sustain the possibility of

---

[54] Bowen, 'Happy Autumn Fields', p. 760.    [55] Bowen, 'Happy Autumn Fields', p. 762.
[56] Bowen, 'Happy Autumn Fields', p. 770.
[57] Rod Mengham, 'British Fiction of the War', in Marina MacKay (ed.), *The Cambridge Companion to the Literature of World War II* Cambridge: Cambridge University Press, 2009), 26–42 (p. 28).

# 180  LITERATURE AND SOUND FILM IN MID-CENTURY BRITAIN

integrating past and present selves'.[58] Not only does this apply to the curious and unexplained connection between Mary and Sarah, between a character of the present and a character of an unknown past, but it also applies to the way in which the two sisters, Sarah and Henrietta, conceive of their own existence in time: 'we know this is only something happening again. It happened last year, and it will happen next', suggesting a circular, non-linear temporality that is at once comforting and disquieting.[59] Bowen's short stories thus deconstruct linear temporality and, in their recursive use of dreams, fantasies, and sensory excess, as well as their complexity of style and form, they emphasize artifice and performativity alongside interpretive indeterminacy.

These issues culminate in Bowen's *The Heat of the Day*, which she had begun writing in 1944. Even though she did not publish the novel until 1948, it is now viewed as a seminal text of Home Front writing. In the novel, the protagonist Stella repeatedly reflects on her life as cinematic and as a fictional story. There is a pervasive 'theatricality' and artifice at the heart of Stella's existence and relationships—confronted with the possibility of her lover's secret allegiance to Nazi Germany as a spy, Stella begins to examine her life as if it were a story.[60] She reflects very early on that she has 'melodramatic fears'; that she is the kind of character 'with whom the unspecified threat would work'.[61] The narrator discloses in this very first conversation between Stella and Harrison, which forms the starting point for the entire plot of the novel, that the reader may be dealing with characters and a storyline taken straight from melodrama, whose generic features already point to the idea that the story which lies ahead is one of artifice and stylistic excess.

Film-going and the language of cinema are never far from Stella's mind: when she joins Robert on a visit to his family's country house, the shadows thrown by the intense light of the sun inside the sitting room appear to Stella with the 'glossy thinness of celluloid'.[62] Similarly, Robert himself, when she manages to '[bring] the scene back again into focus', looks to her 'like a young man in Technicolour'.[63] Stella's first view of Holme Dene, Robert's family estate, is presented as if the house had appeared straight out of a costume film set:

---

[58] Mengham, 'British Fiction of the War', p. 28.
[59] Bowen, 'Happy Autumn Fields', p. 756.
[60] Piette, *Imagination at War*, pp. 166–167.    [61] Bowen, *Heat of the Day*, p. 30.
[62] Bowen, *Heat of the Day*, p. 124.    [63] Bowen, *Heat of the Day*, p. 125.

THE SENSES AT WAR 181

A break in the evergreens of the drive allowed the first view of Holme Dene, across paddock and lawns. The house, which must have been built about 1900, was of the size of a considerable manor, rose with gables to the height of three ample stories, and combined half-timbering with bow and french windows and two or three balconies. The façade was partially draped with virginia creeper, now blood red. In the fancy-shaped flower-beds under the windows and round the sweep the eye instinctively sought begonias—one or two beds, it was true, still showed late roses; in the others, vegetables of the politer kind packed the curves of crescents and points of stars.... A backdrop of trees threw into relief a tennis pavilion, a pergola, a sundial, a rock garden, a dovecote, some gnomes, a seesaw, a grouping of rusticated seats and a bird-bath. Stella, who could not stop looking, could think of nothing to say.[64]

Holme Dene's idyllic yet eclectic outward appearance contains too many signs for Stella to read: while she cannot 'stop looking', she also 'could think of nothing to say'. The display invites visual appraisal, even admiration, but it does not lend itself to rational, cognitive interpretation. This, as Peter Brooks writes, is a fundamental element of melodramatic representation: individual scenes in melodrama function as a 'play of signs' containing a 'high emotional and ethical charge'. Indeed, as Brooks continues, 'all these signs...have a depth of symbolic meaning. We are not, however, asked to meditate upon their connotations, to plumb their depths. On the stage they are used virtually as pure signifiers, in that it is their spectacular, their visual, interaction that counts.'[65] In its visual and architectural make-up, Holme Dene is little more than a film set that can house Stella's 'melo-dramatic fears' and suppositions about Robert.

*The Heat of the Day* further displays a complexity of style 'almost to the point of unintelligibility'.[66] As Anna Teekell notes, Bowen's writing delights in 'inversions, ellipses, subjunctives, and double or even triple negatives'.[67] The effect, Susan Osborn writes, is the sustained production of a 'disorien-tation of sense'.[68] Teekell observes that *The Heat of the Day* constructs a language that reflects instability and immanent collapse through its gothic

---

[64] Bowen, *Heat of the Day*, p. 115.
[65] Brooks, *The Melodramatic Imagination*, p. 28.
[66] Anna Teekell, 'Elizabeth Bowen and Language at War', *New Hibernia Review*, 15.3 (2011), 61–79 (p. 61).
[67] Teekell, 'Language at War', p. 61.
[68] Susan Osborn, 'Reconsidering Elizabeth Bowen', *Modern Fiction Studies*, 52.1 (2006), 187–197 (p. 192).

182   LITERATURE AND SOUND FILM IN MID-CENTURY BRITAIN

spy-thriller epistemology and its real-world wartime context: the novel consistently 'encodes distrust' in its structure and semantics.[69] The temporal structures are part of the text's refusal to offer clarity and continuity:

> She returned to Robert—both having caught a breath, they fixed their eyes expectantly on each other's lips. Both waited, both spoke at once, unheard. Overhead, an enemy plane had been dragging, drumming slowly round in the pool of night, drawing up bursts of gunfire—nosing, pausing, turning, fascinated by the point for its intent. The barrage banged, coughed, retched; in here the lights in the mirrors rocked. Now down a shaft of anticipating silence the bomb swung whistling. With the shock of detonation, still to be heard, four walls of in here yawped in then bellied out; bottles danced on glass; a distortion ran through the view. The detonation dulled off into the cataracting roar of a split building: direct hit, somewhere else. It was the demolition of an entire moment: he and she stood at attention till the glissade stopped. What they *had* both been saying, or been on the point of saying, neither of them ever now were to know. Most first words have the nature of being trifling; theirs from having been lost began to have the significance of a lost clue.[70]

The 'demolition' of the moment here manifests itself as a disjuncture between the levels of story and discourse, a split caused by the bomb. The narrative constructs a web of sensory and chronological disorientation which is not merely narrated, but enacted, by the text: both Stella and Robert have been speaking ('What they *had* both been saying'). Yet, as the bomb detonates, their first words to each other are lost and 'neither of them ever now were to know'. While this occurs on the story level, the discourse reverts to an ellipsis in the narration of time, refusing to return to an account of what had been spoken and implying that the characters' words, rendered 'unheard' by the event of bombing, must also be lost to the reader. Not only does the text explore how human interaction falls victim to the impact of bombing, it actually enacts disorientation and loss for the reader by erasing a crucial moment of its own narrative progression. This becomes evident by attending further to the narration of time: 'both *waited*, both *spoke* at once, unheard. Overhead an enemy plane *had been dragging*....' The momentary reversal in grammatical time also rewinds the chronology of events. While the bomb's detonation forms the end of the order of events

---

[69]   Teekell, 'Language at War', p. 63.    [70]   Bowen, *Heat of the Day*, p. 104.

THE SENSES AT WAR    183

in the story's chronology, it is taken as the starting point of discourse in this passage. The novel's 'radical disruption of a classical, linear temporality' works at this small-scale level of individual paragraphs and scenes as well as on a larger scale vis-à-vis the novel's entire chronology.[71] Beryl Pong observes how the novel repeatedly asks the reader to enact Robert's final directive to Stella to 're-read me backwards, figure me out': the novel's 'reversals in chronology', followed at least twice by 're-continuing the narrative chronology', force the reader to attempt a reconstruction of timelines through the act of re-reading.[72] To complicate matters of time and chronology further, *The Heat of the Day*, as Claire Seiler has shown, is also fundamentally concerned with the act of waiting, which 'perpetuate[s] the temporality of suspension' that may be reflective of experiencing wartime temporality itself.[73] In Bowen's novel, these different and contradictory conceptions of time intersect and pull the reader, alongside Stella, into different temporal directions, even suspending temporality, and thereby creating a sense of asynchronicity.[74]

## The Gainsborough Melodrama

Following the initial government directive to close all cinemas at the outbreak of war, *Kinematograph Weekly* had campaigned for a quick reopening, arguing that film fundamentally supplied 'a relief from the very ugly world in which we are living today'.[75] As cinemas were permitted to open again about a week following the initial closure in September 1939, cinema attendance at the Home Front rose steadily throughout the war years.[76] At the same time, the British film industry decreased in size. Clive Coultass notes that by 1943, 'only nine studios were still in operation'.[77] The industry's

---

[71] Andrew Bennett and Nicholas Royle, *Elizabeth Bowen and the Dissolution of the Novel: Still Lives* (New York: St. Martin's Press, 1995), p. 91.
[72] Beryl Pong, 'Space and Time in the Bombed City: Graham Greene's *The Ministry of Fear* and Elizabeth Bowen's *The Heat of the Day*', *Literary London*, 7.1 (2009). Open access online at: www.literarylondon.org/london-journal/march2009/pong.html (accessed 10 June 2023).
[73] Claire Seiler, *Midcentury Suspension: Literature and Feeling in the Wake of World War II* (New York: Columbia University Press, 2020), p. 150.
[74] This failure of the synchronization of time is also expressed by Stella and Robert's watches 'never perfectly synchronizing'. Bowen, *Heat of the Day*, p. 107.
[75] 'Reopen the Cinemas', *Kinematograph Weekly*, 7 September 1939, p. 2.
[76] Robert Murphy, *British Cinema and the Second World War* (London: Continuum, 2000), pp. 2–3.
[77] Clive Coultass, 'British Feature Films and the Second World War', *Journal of Contemporary History*, 19.1 (1984), 7–22 (p. 10).

184   LITERATURE AND SOUND FILM IN MID-CENTURY BRITAIN

wartime output initially centred on productions with a realist aesthetic that addressed wartime subjects directly, including military attack and defence, cross-class camaraderie, and espionage. Popular films included Alexander Korda's *The Lion has Wings* (1939), Michael Powell and Emeric Pressburger's *49th Parallel* (1941), and Michael Balcon's *Went the Day Well?* (1942). Meanwhile, the Crown Film Unit (CFU) worked on a number of successful 'story documentaries' on the war effort, including *Target for Tonight* (1941), *Coastal Command* (1942), *Close Quarters* (1943), and *Western Approaches* (1944). The Army Film and Photographic Unit (AFPU), in cooperation with the US Office of War Information, also released their own feature-length films documenting the Allied cause, including *Desert Victory* (1943) and *The True Glory* (1945).[78] In addition to these films with wartime subjects and a realist aesthetic, it became clear that more escapist entertainment was needed in the shape of comedies, romances, and costume films.[79] Gainsborough Pictures, a B-movie sister company to Gaumont-British, produced some of the most surprising crowd pleasers of the later war years: a cycle of costume melodrama films released between 1943 and 1947, including *The Man in Grey* (1943), *Fanny by Gaslight* (1944), *Madonna of the Seven Moons* (1944), and *The Wicked Lady* (1945). Although these films were largely viewed as escapist entertainments by most (male) film critics, their consistent box office success throughout the war years makes them important milestones in the history of British cinema of the Second World War. *The Wicked Lady*, for instance, attracted approximately 18.4 million viewers in Britain upon its release in 1945.[80]

The Gainsborough melodrama cycle was actively addressing female audiences in Second World War Britain: these films centre on female protagonists, their lives and desires.[81] In all cases, the female characters find themselves struggling against (and sometimes actively undermining) the social and sexual constraints under which they are placed. The Gainsborough melodrama films construct historically specific visions of

---

[78] *The True Glory* won an Academy Award for 'Best Documentary Feature' in 1946.

[79] Coultass, 'British Feature Films and the Second World War', p. 10. On a change in taste and the move towards comedy, costume film, melodrama, and romance, see Murphy, *British Cinema and the Second World War*, pp. 4–6.

[80] Sarah Barrow and John White (eds), 'The Wicked Lady (1945)', *Fifty Key British Films* (London: Routledge, 2008), 60–64 (p. 60).

[81] Laura Mulvey and Pam Cook have noted that melodrama can highlight women's perspectives and uses female desire as a catalyst for devising plots and characters. See Laura Mulvey 'Visual Pleasure and Narrative Cinema', *Screen*, 16.3 (1975), 6–18, and Pam Cook, *Screening the Past: Memory and Nostalgia in Cinema* (London: Routledge, 2005), p. 75.

THE SENSES AT WAR   185

femininity tailored towards a British middle-class audience.[82] The films launched the careers of James Mason and Stewart Granger, as well as those of Margaret Lockwood, Patricia Roc, and Phyllis Calvert. While Mason and Granger were positioned as objects of female desire, Lockwood, Roc, and Calvert acted in roles that invited (at least in part) women's identification with their characters. 'The "packaging" of Lockwood', Sue Harper writes, 'was clearly extremely successful. There is evidence to suggest that female adolescents sympathised with her to such an extent as to affect their memory of a film's characters.'[83] In all cases bar one, the films were based on middlebrow women's writing, including Lady Eleanor Smith's *The Man in Grey* (1941), Margery Lawrence's *The Madonna of the Seven Moons* (1931), and Magdalen King-Hall's *The Life and Death of the Wicked Lady Skelton* (1944). These texts were historical novels, or rather, middlebrow historical romances, that were deemed especially suited to being adapted as film melodrama by the Gainsborough writer and producer R. J. Minney.[84] 'Middlebrow fiction', as Lisa Stead convincingly argues, 'interrogate[s] a gendered middle-class identity, depicting characters who negotiated...class-inflected expectations regarding issues such as marriage, work, independence and physical appearance'.[85] Similarly, Nicola Humble notes of the middlebrow novel that it negotiates the 'desires' and 'self-images' of its readers, participating actively in the construction of women's middle-class identities.[86] In the Gainsborough melodrama, audiences might discover a similar mechanism at work: these film romances could, in lavish costume and framed by beautiful settings, negotiate the challenges women faced in navigating their private and public lives.

In creating these fantasies of the past, Gainsborough also offered an important alternative to the widespread realist aesthetic and propaganda angle of films produced during the war years in Britain. Maurice Ostrer, head of production at Gainsborough, famously stated in *Kinematograph Weekly* in January 1943 that the studio refused to 'bow to the prevailing

---

[82]   Cook, *Screening the Past*, pp. 85–88.

[83]   Sue Harper, 'Historical Pleasures: Gainsborough Costume Melodrama', in Marcia Landy (ed.), *The Historical Film: History and Memory in Media* (New Brunswick: Rutgers University Press, 2001), 98–122 (p. 115).

[84]   Sue Harper, 'Historical Pleasures', p. 101.

[85]   Lisa Stead, *Off to the Pictures: Cinemagoing, Women's Writing and Movie Culture in Interwar Britain* (Edinburgh: Edinburgh University Press, 2016), p. 10.

[86]   Nicola Humble, *The Feminine Middlebrow Novel, 1920s to 1950s: Class, Domesticity and Bohemianism* (Oxford: Oxford University Press, 2001), pp. 3–5.

186  LITERATURE AND SOUND FILM IN MID-CENTURY BRITAIN

tendency to concentrate on war subjects'.[87] While Ostrer's view was, by some, considered 'aggressively anti-realist', his push for costume melodrama was also a prescient move that earned Gainsborough significant commercial success and recognition in the 1940s.[88] Minney equally 'insisted that documentary realism would not fulfil the emotional needs of a mass audience'.[89] It was also likely Minney who suggested to Gainsborough executives to try their hand at their first melodrama, *The Man in Grey*, because the original novel (a Regency romance) 'had been a bestseller'.[90] Gainsborough thus came to be aligned with a stance against the realist propaganda aesthetic of, for instance, CFU and AFPU productions. The Gainsborough melodramas of the 1940s thus 'represent a rich tradition of visceral, garish, flamboyant popular cinema'.[91]

When Gainsborough released *The Man in Grey* (1943) featuring James Mason and Margaret Lockwood, the film had a largely positive reception. However, there were some apprehensive voices: one critic in *Sunday Graphic* judged that 'to enjoy it, you need to have a mind that throbs to every sob of the novelette and a heart that throbs to every exposure of Stewart Granger's torso'.[92] In defiance of such criticism, Ostrer maintained that Gainsborough catered to the public need for entertainment: the films offered 'an escape from the drabness of this present-day world'.[93] The choice of melodrama was also key to Ostrer's agenda of creating lavish entertainment for a (female) mass audience. As I will show, the Gainsborough productions mobilize audio-vision to produce cinematic excess: visual composition, framing, lighting, set design, costumes, sound effects, and music are combined to create a complex interplay of visual and acoustic signs.

As cinema's audio-visual dimensions provide ample opportunity for sensory immersion, the experience of melodramatic excess may be read as an experience of overwhelming sensory stimulation in which not everything can be accounted for or made sense of. There might be too much music, too

---

[87] Pam Cook, *Gainsborough Pictures* (London: Cassell, 1997), p. 143.

[88] Murphy, *British Cinema and the Second World War*, p. 13.

[89] Harper, 'Historical Pleasures', p. 101.

[90] Robert Murphy, 'Gainsborough after Balcon', in Pam Cook (ed.), *Gainsborough Pictures* (London: Cassell, 1997), 137–154 (p. 142).

[91] Robert Murphy, *Realism and Tinsel: Cinema and Society in Britain 1939–1948* (London: Routledge, 1989), p. 56.

[92] Review of 'The Wicked Lady', *Sunday Graphic*, 14 April 1946, quoted by Harper in 'Historical Pleasures', p. 99.

[93] Maurice Ostrer quoted by Garrett A. Sullivan in *Shakespeare and British World War Two Film* (Cambridge: Cambridge University Press, 2022), p. 100.

THE SENSES AT WAR    187

many clashing sound effects, or too many visual cues and framing devices, all of which might trigger a psychological and even a physical response. Ben Singer rightly notes that 'excess' in melodrama substantially pertains to a bodily and emotional response:

> Melodrama…activates various kinds of excess in the spectator's visceral responses. A good Hollywood melodrama is one that makes you cry, or one that arouses strong sentiment, particularly powerful feelings of pathos. Melodramatic excess is a question of the body, of physical responses. The term *tearjerker* underscores the idea that powerful sentiment is in fact a physical sensation, an overwhelming feeling.[94]

The intensity of sensory experience and its concomitant emotional, affective responses are key to understanding melodramatic design. As the viewer's body in the cinema is in one place, the mind and the senses can engage in a world of lavish costumes and locations, expressive music, and emotionally charged storytelling. C. A. Lejeune captured precisely this escapist and sensory-physical appeal of the Gainsborough productions in 'A Filmgoers War Diary', when she wrote that 'we were ready for a good cry over something that was far removed from the war….We wallowed in the tragedy of *Fanny by Gaslight*, *Love Story*, and *Madonna of the Seven Moons*.'[95] Indeed, Gainsborough's *The Man in Grey*, Lejeune wrote, 'proved to be the surprise hit of the autumn' in 1943.[96] *The Man in Grey* had been a 'a kind of escapist trial balloon' for Gainsborough: 'even though Hollywood provided plenty of escapism, the film certainly showed that there was a big market for home-grown escapism too.'[97] Margaret Lockwood, the film's main star, also noted the movie's escapist appeal: 'its Regency settings are away from the war. It has plenty of emotional, dramatic quality.'[98]

With Lockwood's star power, lavish set and costume designs, and a '(discreet) exploitation of sex and sadism', the film became one of the top

[94] Ben Singer, *Melodrama and Modernity* (New York: Columbia University Press, 2001), pp. 39–40.

[95] C. A. Lejeune, 'A Filmgoer's War Diary', in Guy Morgan, *Red Roses Every Night: London Cinemas under Fire* (London: Quality Press, 1948), 67–77 (p. 72).

[96] Lejeune, 'A Filmgoer's War Diary', p. 71.

[97] William K. Everson, 'The Man in Grey', reprinted in 'William K. Everson and the British Cinema: Program Notes for the New School for Social Research', *Film History*, 15.3 (2003), 279–375 (pp. 327–328).

[98] Ann Matheson, 'Margaret is on her Mettle', *The Australian Women's Weekly*, 31 October 1942, p. 11.

188 LITERATURE AND SOUND FILM IN MID-CENTURY BRITAIN

ten box office hits of 1943.[99] Based on the successful novel by Eleanor Smith, the film introduces audiences to what would become Gainsborough's signature style. The Regency costume drama centres on the unhappy relationship of the wealthy, dutiful, and beautiful Clarissa (Phyllis Calvert) and the impoverished, ambitious, and headstrong Hesther (Margaret Lockwood). Hesther elopes with a young military officer and Clarissa marries Lord Rohan (James Mason), the titular 'Man in Grey'. The women lose touch and Clarissa is treated coldly by Rohan. To distract herself from her unhappy marriage, Clarissa attends a theatre performance of *Othello*, in which Hesther performs as Desdemona and Othello is played by a handsome young actor called Rokeby (Stewart Granger). Clarissa wants to help Hesther out of her financially precarious circumstances and employs her as a companion. Hesther thus meets Lord Rohan, becomes his mistress, and schemes to get rid of Clarissa. When Clarissa falls in love with Rokeby, Hesther attempts to facilitate Clarissa's elopement with the actor, but Hesther's plan fails when Rohan refuses to let his wife go. In a final attempt to get her way, Hesther causes Clarissa's death. When Rohan finds out, he beats Hesther to death with a cane. This story is embedded in a frame narrative of 1940s London: the Rohan estate is auctioned, including a portrait of Rohan and a box of trinkets that once belonged to Clarissa. At this auction, a man and a woman (it is implied that they are descendants of Rokeby and Clarissa) meet and become romantically involved.

The film works with visual coding methods, chiefly through costume design. One of Clarissa and Hesther's earliest conversations, for instance, begins when the two young women stay at their finishing school whilst all other students have left on an excursion. As Clarissa and Hesther begin talking to each other, the camera shows their upper bodies and employs overt visual coding methods through costumes that present the young women as inverted mirror images of each other. The triangular shape of Clarissa's dark corset top is mirrored invertedly by a white shawl worn by Hesther around her shoulders, which is also tied in a triangular shape. While Clarissa's dress is light with dark accessories, Hesther's dress is dark with lighter accessories. The light and dark contrast is further enhanced through Calvert's light hair and Lockwood's dark curls. The upper body shot enhances the visual impact of the women's contrasting costumes and their body movement and positioning in relation to the camera and to each

---

[99] Everson, 'The Man in Grey', pp. 327–328. On the film's box office performance, see Murphy, *Realism and Tinsel*, p. 203.

THE SENSES AT WAR   189

other (blocking) further serves to highlight their contrasting appearances and the idea of inversion. The women stand close to each other, yet face in the direction of the camera, thus allowing for a complete and immediate view of their costumes, hair, and accessories. The film's costumes thus code the women as contrasting, inverted mirror images of each other.

*The Man in Grey* further visually pursues the idea of contrast and inversion through the repeated use of actual mirrors as framing devices that reflect and reinforce camera work. As Rohan proposes to Clarissa, she sits on a chair and he stands slightly diagonally away from her, with his back to the audience, and towering over Clarissa's seated form. The camera provides a low angle view of Clarissa and a slightly tilted over-the shoulder view of Rohan. While the camera here seemingly focusses on Clarissa's facial response to his proposal, the central element of the scene is actually formed by a mirror showing Rohan's nonchalant and domineering posture. Rohan and his mirror image oppose Clarissa's seated upper body, thereby producing the visual impression of cornering or encircling her from two sides.

The film also uses window panes, paintings of Clarissa and Rohan, as well as reflective surfaces to enhance the visual impression of constant framing of the action. The film thereby self-consciously presents itself as performance—from the narrative structure that entails frame narrative and embedded narrative, to the frequent use of mirrors and reflective surfaces in its visual composition. Issues of contrast and reflection also become central to the film through the contradictory relationship between dialogue and visual action as these two elements are constantly opposing each other and appear to work against a causally motivated development of the plot. When Clarissa and Hesther converse at finishing school, Clarissa is warned by a fortune teller never to befriend a woman as this would be fatal for her. As soon as she has received this warning, Clarissa sets out to make friends with Hesther. Similarly, Rohan declares at a ball that he will never court Clarissa, appearing wholly disinterested and dismissive, only to appear in her sitting room to propose marriage about two minutes later. A causal narrative development of action is abandoned in favour of the extensive *mise-en-scène* of lavish sequences that are loosely tied together. Hesther's initial elopement with a young officer is another case in point: her relationship is unmotivated, the man unknown. The elopement is simply introduced by a letter instructing her to leave the finishing school. Prior to this letter, audiences had no indication of her carrying on a clandestine affair.

*The Man in Grey* lays the foundation for Gainsborough's approach to its melodrama cycle: *everything* that is shown is made expressive and aesthetic,

190 LITERATURE AND SOUND FILM IN MID-CENTURY BRITAIN

and yet there is hardly a coherent development of a causally motivated story. The film does not aim to produce historical accuracy or intricate narrative, but sensory and stylistic excess and a conscious, luscious performativity to feed a 'parched' imagination. Melodrama, as Sue Harper writes, is characterized by such 'stylistic flamboyance and emotional excess', which Gainsborough's costume films display and foster in their 'rich visual texture'.[100] *The Man in Grey*, specifically, shows a 'series of intense sensual moments which constitute the past'.[101] The film's 'art direction' presents 'history as a source of sensual pleasures' that can be mobilized to offer a special kind of cinematic experience in the years of wartime economy and deprivation.[102] The film constructs its melodramatic Regency world by relying on techniques of sensory excess: the visual design of the film, especially, produces an effect of mirroring, doubling, and layering. This form of sensual excess certainly catered to the gender dynamic of its intended audiences. Sue Harper notes that the 'Gainsborough publicists confidently implied that the films would usher the female audience in to an "unspeakable" realm of sexual pleasure'.[103] Women's cinema-going habits and female fan culture provided a clear anchoring point for the Gainsborough productions and their publicity decisions.

*The Man in Grey* was followed by *Madonna of the Seven Moons* (1944) and *The Wicked Lady* (1945). *Madonna of the Seven Moons*, William K. Everson noted, 'is both absurd and yet wonderfully overblown in its own way, given such pictorial gloss (by a director who was formerly a cameraman) and such totally artificial art direction that there's never any need to take it seriously'.[104] Based on a novel by Margery Lawrence, *Madonna of the Seven Moons* is especially notable for its overt emphasis on one particular piece of music: the film's *Rosanna* theme, composed by Hans May.[105] The film itself is a take on the familiar Jekyll/Hyde trope and follows the life of the dutiful sensitive Italian housewife Maddalena, who (unbeknownst to herself) leads a double-life as the passionate Rosanna (both roles played by Phyllis

---

[100] Harper, 'Historical Pleasures', p. 98.     [101] Harper, 'Historical Pleasures', p. 104.
[102] Harper, 'Historical Pleasures', p. 108.     [103] Harper, 'Historical Pleasures', p. 101.
[104] William K. Everson, 'Madonna of the Seven Moons', reprinted in 'William K. Everson and the British Cinema: Program Notes for the New School for Social Research', *Film History*, 15.3 (2003), 279–375 (p. 327).
[105] K. J. Donnelly, *British Film Music and Film Musicals* (Basingstoke: Palgrave Macmillan, 2007), p. 48: '*Madonna of the Seven Moons* (1944) has a striking underscore provided by Austrian émigré Hans May, who, like Levy, had been a silent film pioneer. He had worked on Giuseppe Becce's *Kinothek* of 1919, a groundbreaking library of printed music for silent films that gained widespread use. May had worked as a film composer in Germany until the Nazi accession to power in 1933.'

THE SENSES AT WAR   191

Calvert). As Maddalena, the woman cares for her husband and young adult daughter in a strictly conservative, Catholic family setting in Rome. As Rosanna, she spends periods of time at the Inn of the Seven Moons with her lover, the criminal gang leader Nino (Stewart Granger). The film strongly suggests that Maddalena's initial transformation into Rosanna was first triggered by a traumatic experience of sexual abuse, which led to the split in Maddalena/Rosanna's personality.

As K. J. Donnelly argues, Maddalena's transformation into Rosanna, which occurs several times over the course of the film, is put into motion by music. This music, which consists of variations on May's *Rosanna* theme, jumps back and forth between diegetic world and non-diegetic frame.[106] One sequence of the film, for instance, follows Maddalena's transformation into Rosanna and her return to the Inn of the Seven Moons. During this ten-minute sequence, the *Rosanna* theme recurs multiple times, changing from non-diegetic to diegetic music and back again: first, as non-diegetic string and harp arrangements, and then, diegetically, in the shape of a musical box playing in Rosanna and Nino's bedroom at the Inn. The tune is then also whistled by Nino as he approaches the Inn where Rosanna impatiently awaits his return. The lovers' passionate reunion following this movement of diegetic and non-diegetic music is suggestive, even quite explicit in its portrayal of passion and sexual abandon. The relationship between Nino and Rosanna, as Harper writes, recalls the iconic silent film romances of Rudolph Valentino.[107] The music 'lead[s] to a musical overload that breaks the rule of narrative integration.'[108] As Donnelly states, the Gainsborough melodrama cycle arranges music that is 'regularly encroaching on the action and fracturing the diegesis.'[109] The music refuses to be subsumed into a larger signifying system (or 'style') for the film overall. Instead, the music draws attention to itself and moves between narrative levels, thereby repeatedly transgressing norms of continuity and classical film style.

*Madonna of the Seven Moons* couples this musical transgressiveness of the *Rosanna* theme with a visual style that frames the double life of Maddalena/Rosanna as a struggle between freedom and constraint. There is, for instance, a freedom of movement expressed through hair and costume design, as well as jewellery, whenever Maddalena turns into Rosanna. Harper perceptively observes that Maddalena's transformation into Rosanna is visually coded through costume change: as Rosanna, the character wears

---

[106]  Donnelly, *British Film Music*, p. 49.   [107]  Harper, 'Historical Pleasures', p. 114.
[108]  Donnelly, *British Film Music*, p. 46.   [109]  Donnelly, *British Film Music*, p. 46.

192 LITERATURE AND SOUND FILM IN MID-CENTURY BRITAIN

free-flowing skirts that allow for greater range of movement in comparison to her more constricting and conservative dress as a wealthy housewife.[110] In addition, Rosanna wears more noticeable, large items of jewellery (such as earrings) and more noticeable make-up.[111] As Maddalena, her hair is either braided or in an updo, always carefully coiffed and controlled. As Rosanna, her hair is free-flowing and wavy. *Madonna of the Seven Moons* pairs music, costume and hair design, as well as accessories to express Rosanna's passionate, vivacious nature and her deliberate pursuit of adventure and love in contrast to Maddalena's carefully controlled demeanour as housewife and mother.

Based on the bestselling historical novel *Life and Death of the Wicked Lady Skelton* (1944) by Magdalen King-Hall, the Gainsborough production *The Wicked Lady* (1945) takes up again the theme of a woman's secret double life: in this film, which was produced during the final year of the Second World War and released in the UK in November 1945, Margaret Lockwood plays Barbara, a Caroline noblewoman who stops at nothing in her search for pleasure, adventure, and fulfilment of personal ambition. After marrying her best friend's love interest for his status and title, Lady Barbara quickly becomes disillusioned with married life and bored by her landowning husband, the local magistrate Sir Ralph Skelton (Griffith Jones). Chasing excitement and adventure, Barbara disguises as a highwayman at night and commits several robberies. In her disguise, she meets the notorious criminal Captain Jerry Jackson (James Mason) and begins a passionate affair with him whilst also pursuing another extramarital romance with a friend of her husband's, the architect Kit Locksby (Michael Rennie). In the end, Barbara's double life is discovered when she is fatally wounded during one of her nightly robberies. Dying, she confesses her deeds to Kit who, disapproving of her behaviour, distances himself from her.

Directed by Leslie Arliss, the film was Gainsborough's most successful costume melodrama despite its critical reception: Simon Harcourt-Smith, writing for the *Tribune* in 1945, reviewed *The Wicked Lady* by stating that the film 'arouses in me a nausea out of proportion to the subject'. He further criticized the film's 'complete misunderstanding of Restoration England'.[112] Like *The Man in Grey* and *Madonna of the Seven Moons*, *The Wicked Lady*

---

[110] Harper, 'Historical Pleasures', pp. 110–111.
[111] Harper, 'Historical Pleasures', pp. 110–111.
[112] Simon Harcourt-Smith, 'Review of *The Wicked Lady*', *Tribune*, 23 November 1945, n.p.

THE SENSES AT WAR    193

does not aim for historical accuracy. Instead, it combines camera work, set and costume design, and music to produce aesthetic excess and sensory pleasure. The film puts at its centre Lady Barbara's character, her ambition, and her desire for independence and adventure. Despite her role as protagonist of the story, the film does not show her as a transparent character. Although Barbara's ruthless actions appear to find moral sanction in her death, she ultimately leads a life of adventure and sexual freedom until her death, thereby also finding a sense of liberation and self-determination. The set designs of the film are key to the film's combination of aesthetic excess and interpretive ambiguity. Harper observes that the film's set designs

> are highly eclectic in their construction. Each object is reproduced in an historically accurate way, but it relates to the other objects in an unpredictable way spatially. Generally, the surfaces on which they are placed— bland, unmarked, and plain—throw them into heightened relief. The avoidance of tapestry, carpets, and serried paintings is not historically accurate and cannot be accounted for by wartime shortages or lack of expertise, and it must therefore be 'read' as a deliberate aesthetic strategy. A Jacobean door, a Baroque candle-holder, an Elizabethan canopied bed, a Puritan bible, a medieval fire basket are combined to form an unpredictable and dense visual texture. The past is signified not as a casual, linear structure, but as a chaotic amalgam....[113]

The sets create an eclectic sense of being 'out of time'. The assemblage of objects avoids, rather than supports, proper or cohesive historicization or contextualization, but, instead, offers competing signs as 'deliberate aesthetic strategy'. What may appear incoherent and 'out of place' or 'out of time', then, is a visualization of indeterminacy and ambiguity that ought to be displayed and celebrated.

The ambiguity achieved through an excessive display of staged, anachronistic objects is further supported through costume design: Elizabeth Haffenden, the costume designer, cleverly exploits the period dresses' capacity for ambiguous visual coding in *The Wicked Lady*.[114] Like *The Man in Grey*,

---

[113]  Harper, 'Historical Pleasures', p. 109.
[114]  Harper outlines how Haffenden's designs for the Gainsborough melodrama cycle were heavily influenced by her previous work in theatre design, which had not been very well received. Haffenden's work for the stage in the 1930s was viewed as 'expressionist' and

194 LITERATURE AND SOUND FILM IN MID-CENTURY BRITAIN

*The Wicked Lady* uses costume to express contrasts and connections. It is especially Barbara's entanglement in a number of different relationships that is shown repeatedly—either through parallel design or inverted costume design. At her wedding celebration, Barbara wears a wedding dress that initially signals her connection to her new husband Sir Ralph. However, at the wedding reception, she also meets the architect Kit, who is one of the wedding guests. Barbara's immediate attraction to Kit, and the romantic connection between these two characters that will ensue, is established by their costumes, facial expression, and posture. As the camera captures their movements and physical response to each other in upper body shots and shot-reverse shot dialogue sequences, their clothing visually codes attraction and belonging through parallel design. The vertical lines created by the folds of Barbara's dress sleeves are mirrored by the vertical lines of Kit's coat sleeves. The voluminous dress sleeves that enhance Barbara's shoulder line are reflected in several prominent, white tassels placed on the shoulders of Kit's dark jacket. In profile, it becomes even more evident how these two characters are seemingly 'made' (designed) for each other as their hair styles (dark brunette with draped curls framing the neck) look almost identical. As a wedding dress, Barbara's outfit is set to express her legal connection to her husband—yet, simultaneously, the gown and hairstyle place her in a direct visual relationship with Kit. Costume establishes a non-verbal, visual channel of communication and immediately codes attraction and belonging.

The same principle applies to inverted designs by Haffenden: as Barbara turns to disguising herself as a highwayman, she meets the charismatic criminal Jackson and the two begin their affair. From the moment of their first meeting, the characters are visually presented as simultaneously complementing and contrasting each other. In a shot-reverse shot sequence followed by a medium shot showing both characters in profile on horseback, the audience witnesses Barbara's first encounter with Jackson while robbing a party travelling by carriage. Both Barbara and Jackson wear dark, widebrimmed hats decorated with large feathers and both carry pistols. However, their accessories also point to their competing relationship. While the lower half of Barbara's face is covered by a black scarf, Jackson's disguise consists of a mask worn over the top half of his face, notably his eyes. Costume

therefore 'pro-German'. In this context, it is perhaps surprising that Haffenden's designs for Gainsborough in the 1940s were so successful. Yet, they clearly set the Gainsborough productions apart from other wartime films in Britain and allowed the studio to take a clear visual stand against wartime economy and realist design in favour of creating elaborate escapist fantasies through costume. See Harper, 'Historical Pleasures', pp. 112–113.

here establishes visual connections that accumulate information—either as parallel design or inverted design.

Their affair is simultaneously passionate and destructive: Barbara has no qualms betraying Jackson's confidence to save her own reputation and later bears responsibility for his arrest and apparent execution by hanging. However, Jackson manages to escape the noose at the last moment and seeks out Barbara to take revenge. When he reappears at night in her bedroom, he is intent on killing her. The film builds layers of visual, musical, and textual registers to express Jackson's attempted strangling of Barbara. The camera follows his movements in an over-the-shoulder shot, keeping focus on his face and his gloved hands as they close around her neck. The image uses slight rack focus, meaning that Jackson's hands and face remain sharp and clear, Barbara's face moves out of focus and blurs slightly. As the image track is thus underlining Barbara's struggle for breath, Jackson simultaneously narrates his fantasy of killing her in the same way in which he remembers the experience of his own hanging, of the noose tightening around his neck (see Figure 6.1):

**Figure 6.1** Jackson attempts to strangle Barbara; frame grab from *The Wicked Lady* (Gainsborough Pictures, 1945), directed by Leslie Arliss.

'You don't know what it feels like to be strangled, do you? Milady, it's an experience we ought to share. You feel the rope crushing your wind pipe, choking the life out of you. The whole world goes black with spots of vivid colour flashing against the awful darkness, you feel as if your head is going to burst. You kick and struggle and squirm.'

His speech is accompanied by low, non-diegetic orchestral music, starting with strings and, as the strangling intensifies, wind instruments give musical expression to Barbara's struggle for air. Jackson's narration, the intermittent close-ups of Barbara's face and neck, and the choice of wind instruments are combined to drive home the message of running out of breath. The film visually and sonically encodes a moment of violence that is startling in its explicitness. In this sequence, the layers of music, speech, and film image create excess: a redundancy of information that complicates any distinction between message and noise. Everything (and simultaneously nothing) seems to be charged with meaning. The sequence's visual composition also gestures to other scenes of violence committed against female characters in other Gainsborough productions, such as *The Man in Grey*. The moment of attempted murder in *The Wicked Lady* notably cross-references Rohan's killing of Hesther in *The Man in Grey*, which also features Lockwood and Mason in the constellation of victim and perpetrator respectively. Excess is thus not simply produced through the interaction of acoustic and visual signs, but also through extradiegetic, intermedial references to other films of the melodrama cycle.

In the post-war years, the popularity of the Gainsborough melodrama waned. *The Magic Bow* (1946), for instance, failed at the box office and there was a sense that the heyday of costume melodrama had passed. While it is certainly possible that audiences simply lost interest after they had been presented with Gainsborough's formulaic designs for a number of years, it remains an intriguing historical fact that the costume melodrama lost its power over (female) audiences after the end of the war. Nonetheless, during the war years, these films had offered small means to combat what Bowen termed the 'desiccation of day-to-day lives by war'. The Gainsborough melodrama, as Pam Cook notes, contained 'anti-consensual aspects' and consciously 'flouted demands for realism and authenticity'.[115]

---

[115] Pam Cook, 'Neither Here nor There: National Identity in Gainsborough Costume Drama', in Andrew Higson (ed.), *Dissolving Views: Key Writings on British Cinema* (London: Bloomsbury, 1997), 51–65 (p. 52).

THE SENSES AT WAR    197

The key to this rejection of realism and authenticity lies in these films' use of audio-vision to create sensory excess; as in the writing of Hanley, Bowen, and Green, there is a self-conscious performativity and artifice at the heart of the Gainsborough melodrama that works consistently against the grain of war culture's totalizing vision. As Jonathan Goldberg has shown, melodrama is an inherently transgressive mode that pursues an 'aesthetics of impossibility'.[116] Melodrama expresses and celebrates states of ambiguity and indeterminacy as forms of imaginative liberation.[117] In the Gainsborough melodrama cycle, filmic audio-vision culminates in excessive pleasure which no longer attends to the demands of causality, continuity, or narrative control. In fact, moving beyond the mechanisms of narrative control and linear temporality is a crucial feature: these films 'are an uncomfortable reminder that history is always masquerade'; 'they eschew the very idea of authentic, stable identities'.[118] While the Gainsborough melodrama's excess of visual and acoustic signs may be viewed as inauthentic, hyperbolic, and flamboyant, it also gave expression to the processes of 'self-dramatization', 'artificial dreams', and 'fabricated emotions' of Home Front culture, with which Hanley, Green, and Bowen are equally strongly preoccupied in their writings.[119]

If read in the cultural context of the Gainsborough melodrama, Bowen, Hanley, and Green's stylistic and temporal difficulties, as well as the apparent artifice and self-conscious performativity of their Home Front literary works, become more fully legible as the deliberate deconstruction of any notion of narrative or temporal control. The Gainsborough costume melodrama, in its own way, similarly pursued stylistic excess and performative artifice, showing audiences beautifully constructed set designs and lavish costumes, repetitive coding through music and dialogue, and a surplus of audio-visual information that was not causally motivated by plot and

---

[116] Jonathan Goldberg, *Melodrama: An Aesthetics of Impossibility* (Durham: Duke University Press, 2016).

[117] On this point, see for instance Goldberg's exemplary analysis of *Fidelio* (1814): 'Melodrama offers more than such an either/or in which disguise, opacity, and impasse must be exchanged for identity, knowledge, and action....We can see this formally if instead of understanding the Melodram as a violation of the rule of the opera's separations of speech and song that needs to be repaired, we view it as a moment dense with musical invention, filled with experiments in the relationship between speech and music. These various states of hesitation, musical irresolution, cross-purpose, key change, suspension, and half-voicing are themselves kinds of knowledge. They point in fact to something that exceeds the rule that keeps music and speech separate. In its plotting, too, the Melodram continues the opera's exploration of states of possibility' (Goldberg, *Melodrama*, pp. 8–9).

[118] Cook, 'Neither Here nor There', p. 57.

[119] MacKay, *Modernism, War, and Violence*, p. 116, and Piette, *Imagination at War*, p. 4.

sometimes appeared to juxtapose sonic and visual *mise-en-scène*. This apparent lack of alignment of vision and audition, as well as the assemblages of objects that are arranged 'out of time' and 'out of place', construct indeterminacy; they create forms of asynchronicity that refuse to submit to the totalizing vision of an official wartime culture.

*Literature and Sound Film in Mid-Century Britain*. Lara Ehrenfried, Oxford University Press.
© Lara Ehrenfried 2025. DOI: 10.1093/9780198950790.003.0007

# Coda

On Thursday, 6 February 1947, Evelyn and Laura Waugh arrived at the Bel Air Hotel in Los Angeles. At check-in, they found that the spacious suite originally intended for them had been let to a man 'suffering from rheumatic fever'. To Waugh's dismay, they were given a 'pretty but inadequate' attic bedroom instead.[1] At six o'clock that evening, they were called on by Leon Gordon, a screenwriter and director, and James McGuinness, an executive producer. Both were working for Metro-Goldwyn-Mayer. Over the course of the following days, Waugh was chauffeured several times to the MGM offices at Culver City to negotiate a film adaptation of *Brideshead Revisited* and taken to lunch in MGM's staff canteen. (There was no wine at lunch—a bad omen if ever there was one.)[2] MGM's adaptation of *Brideshead* never got off the ground: Waugh was not inclined to give his permission, but kept the writers and producers on their toes for as long as he could.[3] Although the film was not made, Waugh had ample opportunity over a stay of six weeks to rub shoulders with studio executives, global film stars such as Anna May Wong and Merle Oberon, as well as the chance to 'pay homage to the two artists of the place': Charlie Chaplin and Walt Disney.[4] Upon his return to England, Waugh published magazine articles on his experiences in Los Angeles and began work on his novella *The Loved One: An Anglo-American Tragedy*.

Although *The Loved One* is usually read as Waugh's acerbic critique of Hollywood, largely based on his experiences with MGM, it would be misleading to assume that Waugh only targets Hollywood's post-war mass culture from his assumed view of British cultural superiority.[5] Published in

---

[1] Evelyn Waugh, 'Thursday 6 February 1947', in Michael Davie (ed.), *The Diaries of Evelyn Waugh* (Harmondsworth: Penguin, 1979), p. 672.

[2] Waugh, 'Friday 7 February 1947', *Diaries*, pp. 672–673.

[3] Waugh, *Diaries*, p. 672. Waugh makes a point of stating that 'I keep it in Gordon's mind that I have agreed to nothing.'

[4] Waugh, 'Easter Monday 7 April 1947', *Diaries*, pp. 674–675.

[5] For detailed critical discussions of Waugh's novella, see Ian Scott Todd, 'Editing Corpses in Evelyn Waugh's Hollywood', *Twentieth Century Literature*, 59.3 (2013), 414–440, and Naomi Milthorpe '"Death is at the Elbow": *The Loved One* and *Love Among the Ruins*', *Renascence*, 62.3 (2010), 201–17.

## 200 LITERATURE AND SOUND FILM IN MID-CENTURY BRITAIN

1948, *The Loved One* traces the path of Dennis Barlow, a British expat poet living in California who, after having lost his contract as a scriptwriter at Megalopolitan film studios, now works as a pet mortician for a funeral business called 'The Happier Hunting Ground'. Like Orwell's Gordon Comstock, Dennis Barlow does not make a lot of money in his line of work, but the job allows him to read, to work on his poetry, and, crucially, to extricate himself from the claws of mass culture (here the Hollywood studio system). Readers learn that, during the Second World War, Barlow had earned some moderate literary success as a war poet and was therefore subsequently invited to Hollywood to 'help write the life of Shelley for the films'. But, 'in the Megalopolitan studios he found reproduced, and enhanced by the nervous agitation endemic to the place, all the gross futility of service life'. Now, having 'fled' the studio, 'he was content; adept in a worthy trade'.[6]

While the novella criticizes Hollywood's film industry as a chief source and proponent of Anglo-American mass culture, Waugh's text also heavily targets a community of British expats who have made themselves 'mindlessly' available to this particular industry.[7] Even Dennis Barlow's friend and mentor, the elderly Sir Francis Hinsley, has given himself fully to the lure of Hollywood.[8] When his scriptwriting services at Megalopolitan Pictures are no longer needed, he hangs himself. Upon Sir Francis's death, the British expat community is shaken—not with grief, but with concern as to how Francis's death and Barlow's recent employment as pet mortician will reflect negatively on the expat community's employability and future success with the film studios.[9] The novella is a satirical comment on the problem of the writer's alleged complicity in the commercial film industry and contemplates, in typically Wavian style, the means by which a British writer and poet (like Barlow) might extricate himself from this nasty Hollywood business.

And yet, formally, Waugh's novella is also tightly constructed, textually enacting the principles of audio-vision, synchronicity, and mediatized

---

[6] Evelyn Waugh, *The Loved One: An Anglo-American Tragedy* (London: Penguin, 2000), pp. 22–23.

[7] On this point, see also 'Unsigned Review, *Time*', of 12 July 1948, in Martin Stannard (ed.), *Evelyn Waugh: The Critical Heritage* (London: Routledge, 1984), 301–302 (p. 302): 'The story of the patriotic pretensions and fussy snobbishness of the British film colony is grade A Waugh.'

[8] Waugh, *The Loved One*, p. 15. Sir Francis declares to be 'in deep thrall to the Dragon King' (he means the film industry) and states further 'Hollywood is my life'.

[9] Waugh, *The Loved One*, pp. 29–32.

textuality. Indeed, when composing *The Loved One*, Waugh wrote in his diary that he was trying out a new approach to his writing:

> I have decided to try a new method of work. When I began writing I worked straight on into the void, curious to see what would happen to my characters, with no preconceived plan for them, and few technical corrections. Now I waste hours going back and over my work. I intend trying in *The Loved One* to push straight ahead with a rough draft, have it typed and then work over it once, with the conclusion firmly in my mind when I come to give definite form to the beginning. Eve of Corpus Christi. I decided my new method of work left me with an itch to get things into shape. Accordingly I shall begin rewriting at once what I hastily jotted down.[10]

Waugh's 'method' in *The Loved One* reads more like the composition of a film script: with the 'conclusion firmly in mind', 'definite form' can be given to the rest; the process of revision is optimized by creating one full draft which is consequently rewritten with a fully 'preconceived plan' in mind. The novella, not structured into chapters, employs section breaks that remind the reader of discrete scenes. Lighting, sound, and the predominant use of external focalization first introduce the reader to Sir Francis and Dennis Barlow:

> [A breeze] shook the rusty fingers of palm-leaf and swelled the dry sounds of summer, the frog-voices, the grating cicadas, and the ever present pulse of music from the neighbouring native huts. In that kindly light the stained and blistered paint of the bungalow and the plot of weeds between the veranda and the dry water-hole lost their extreme shabbiness, and the two Englishmen, each in his rocking-chair, each with his whisky and soda and his outdated magazine, the counterparts of numberless fellow-countrymen exiled in the barbarous regions of the world, shared in the brief illusory rehabilitation.
>
> 'Ambrose Abercrombie will be here shortly', said the elder. 'I don't know why. He left a message he would come. Find another glass, Dennis, if you can.'[11]

---

[10] Waugh, 'Monday 2 June 1947', *Diaries*, p. 680.    [11] Waugh, *The Loved One*, p. 7.

# 202 LITERATURE AND SOUND FILM IN MID-CENTURY BRITAIN

This beginning reflects the mechanics of a classic, audio-visual establishing shot in narrative cinema: the setting, location, outward appearance of the veranda (bathed in 'kindly light') is coupled with accompanying diegetic sound effects (frog-voices, cicadas) and some faint, diegetic music to set the mood. The external (camera-eye) view of the two characters, whom readers have not met yet, is transferred into the text by referring to Sir Francis as 'the elder', whose speech establishes that the other man's name is 'Dennis' and that they are expecting a visitor.

Ambrose Abercrombie arrives as announced and the men reminisce about the past. Waugh uses this moment to also translate flashback techniques of narrative cinema into the text by letting the narrator repeat a line of Ambrose's speech: 'Where was it I used to live? Just across the street, wasn't it?' asks Ambrose. The narrator then follows up:

> Just across the street, twenty years or more ago, when this neglected district was the centre of fashion; Sir Francis, in prime middle-age, was then the only knight in Hollywood, the doyen of English society, chief scriptwriter in Megalopolitan Pictures and President of the Cricket Club. Then the young, or youngish Ambrose Abercrombie used to bounce about the lots in his famous series of fatiguing roles, acrobatic heroic historic, and come almost nightly to Sir Francis for refreshment.[12]

The narrator's repetition of the character's spoken line is used as a means of transitioning into a brief account of the past, a way of introducing the flashback that clearly connects the present and the past of the diegetic world, thereby synchronizing timelines and creating a chronology of events. Similarly, the novella uses textual equivalents of fade-outs at the end of discrete sequences. When the expat community gathers to discuss how to proceed in light of Francis's death and Barlow's questionable employment, Ambrose speech appears to 'fade out' as the sun sets: '"In any case I don't think the studios will keep away if they know we are solid..." As he spoke the sun sank below the bushy western hillside. The sky was still bright but a shadow crept over the tough and ragged grass of the cricket field, bringing with it a sharp chill.'[13] The ellipsis here indicates a continuation of speech while the narrator moves outward to give an account of the sunset that also carries the stereotypical imagery of foreboding (a creeping shadow, a sharp chill).

---

[12] Waugh, *The Loved One*, p. 9.   [13] Waugh, *The Loved One*, p. 32.

CODA    203

Waugh's novella, while satirizing the (British) writer's complicity in the Hollywood dream factory, also proves its playful, tongue-in-cheek capacity to appear more like a film script itself. Having been to Hollywood and back, it's not all doom and gloom—neither for Waugh nor for Dennis Barlow:

> On the last evening in Los Angeles Dennis knew he was a favourite of Fortune. Others, better men than he, had foundered here and perished.... He was leaving it not only unravished but enriched. He was adding his bit to the wreckage, something that long irked him, his young heart, and was carrying back instead the artist's load, a great, shapeless chunk of experience; bearing it home to his ancient and comfortless shore; to work on it hard and long, for God knew how long.[14]

Barlow, like Waugh, takes home impressions that can be converted into writing. Indeed, the ending of the novella suggests that Barlow's experiences perfectly lend themselves to the writer. Barlow composes poems—and will continue to do so once back in England. It is the 'artist's load' to bring into shape the 'chunk of experience' gathered over the course of his stay in Hollywood. Meanwhile, Waugh was equally able to put into words and to monetize his LA vacation in various ways: the short essay 'Why Hollywood is a Term of Disparagement' for the *Daily Telegraph*, for instance, brought him £200 while *The Loved One* appeared in Cyril Connolly's *Horizon* in February 1948 to great success: the magazine 'sold out in a week'.[15] Indeed, Connolly's introduction to the first printing of *The Loved One* in *Horizon* has all the trappings of a Hollywood premiere announcement: 'we let our readers in for a treat—a sneak pre-view! Why have they been chosen to receive this smooth, all-star performance?'[16] Connolly continues by comparing Waugh to canonical names of Anglophone literature—Donne and Swift.[17] Waugh is offering a literary 'all-star performance' that is both 'serious' literature and satirical entertainment. Thus, in considering *The Loved One*, readers may get the sense that the Waugh of 1930 (with his fierce defence of the novel over sound film in *Vile Bodies*) is, and simultaneously is not, the Waugh of 1948. The formal manoeuvres of *The Loved One* might indicate that there was no longer the frantic sense of

---

[14]  Waugh, *The Loved One*, p. 127.

[15]  'Unsigned Review, *Time*', in Stannard (ed.), *The Critical Heritage*, p. 302.

[16]  Cyril Connolly, 'Introduction to *Horizon*' (February 1948), in Martin Stannard (ed.), *Evelyn Waugh: The Critical Heritage* (London: Routledge, 1984), 299–300 (p. 299).

[17]  Connolly, '*Horizon*', in Stannard (ed.), *The Critical Heritage*, p. 300.

competition between cinema and literature that Waugh had initially targeted in 1930, but, rather, a sense of one being able to inspire and draw on the other (even if it turns out to be satire). Over the space of about two decades, the possibility of conceiving of literature cinematically and—vice versa—of reading film in literary terms had been fully realized.

The coming of synchronized sound to film, which had so substantially changed the phenomenological and cultural experience of cinema itself, had also brought a change to literature, and to literature's relationship with film. The experience of audio-vision expanded and challenged the narrative and aesthetic possibilities for film and literature. The new media environment of sound film, as this book has shown, was fundamentally constituted by sound and image acting together in time. The twin phenomena of audio-vision and synchronicity significantly contributed to a process of alignment between film and literary fiction that had already been on its way in the wake of modernism's teens and twenties.[18] Now, at mid-century, film and literature were more in synch than ever before.

*Literature and Sound Film in Mid-Century Britain.* Lara Ehrenfried, Oxford University Press.
© Lara Ehrenfried 2025. DOI: 10.1093/9780198950790.003.0008

---

[18] On this point, consider, for instance, the works of James Joyce and the discussion of Joyce in David Trotter's *Cinema and Modernism*.

# Films Cited

*Blackmail*, directed by Alfred Hitchcock, performances by Anny Ondra and John Longden (British International Pictures, 1929).

*Coal Face*, directed by Alberto Cavalcanti (GPO Film Unit, 1935).

*The Desert Song*, directed by Roy del Ruth, performances by John Boles and Myrna Loy (Warner Bros., 1929).

*The Divorce of Lady X*, directed by Tim Whelan, performances by Merle Oberon and Laurence Olivier (London Films, 1938).

*Elstree Calling*, directed by Adrian Brunel and Alfred Hitchcock, performances by Tommy Handley and Cicely Courtneidge (British International Pictures, 1930).

*Enough to Eat? The Nutrition Film*, directed by Edgar Anstey, sponsored by the Gas, Light and Coke Company (GPO Film Unit, 1936).

*Gaslight*, directed by Thorold Dickinson, performances by Anton Walbrook and Diana Wynyard (British National Films, 1940).

*Housing Problems,* directed by Arthur Elton and Edgar Anstey, produced for the British Commercial Gas Association (GPO Film Unit, 1935).

*Madonna of the Seven Moons*, directed by Arthur Crabtree, performances by Phyllis Calvert and Stewart Granger (Gainsborough Pictures, 1945).

*The Man in Grey*, directed by Leslie Arliss, performances by Margaret Lockwood and James Mason (Gainsborough Pictures, 1943).

*Night Mail*, directed by Harry Watt and Basil Wright (GPO Film Unit, 1936).

*Pett and Pott: A Fairy Story of the Suburbs*, directed by Alberto Cavalcanti (GPO Film Unit, 1934).

*Rebecca*, directed by Alfred Hitchcock, performances by Joan Fontaine and Laurence Olivier (Selznick International Pictures, 1940).

*The Song of Ceylon*, directed by Basil Wright (GPO Film Unit, 1934).

*The 39 Steps*, directed by Alfred Hitchcock, performances by Robert Donat and Madeleine Carroll (Gaumont-British, 1935).

*Suspicion*, directed by Alfred Hitchcock, performances by Joan Fontaine and Cary Grant (RKO Pictures, 1941).

*The Wicked Lady*, directed by Leslie Arliss, performances by Margaret Lockwood and James Mason (Gainsborough Pictures, 1945).

# Select Bibliography

'1929–1930', *Kinematograph Weekly*, 2 January 1930, 113.

Abel, Richard and Rick Altman (eds), *The Sounds of Early Cinema* (Bloomington: Indiana University Press, 2001).

Afra, Kia, '"Vertical Montage" and Synaesthesia: Movement, Inner Synchronicity, and Music–Image Correlation in *Alexander Nevsky* (1938)', *Music, Sound, and the Moving Image*, 9.1 (2015), 33–61.

Aitken, Ian (ed.), 'Ceylon Tea Propaganda Board', *Encyclopedia of the Documentary Film*, Vol. 1 (New York: Routledge, 2006), 194–195.

Aitken, Ian (ed.), 'Introduction', *The Documentary Film Movement: An Anthology* (Edinburgh: Edinburgh University Press, 2008), 1–68.

Altman, Rick, 'Introduction', *Yale French Studies*, 60 (1980), 3–15.

Altman, Rick, 'The Evolution of Sound Technology', in Elisabeth Weis and John Belton (eds), *Film Sound: Theory and Practice* (New York: Columbia University Press, 1985), 44–53.

Altman, Rick, *Silent Film Sound* (New York: Columbia University Press, 2004).

Altman, Rick (ed.), *Sound Theory, Sound Practice* (New York: Routledge, 1992).

Altman, Rick and Richard Abel (eds), 'Introduction', *Film History*, 11.4 (1999), 395–399.

Ambler, Eric, *Epitaph for a Spy* (New York: Vintage, 2002).

Ambler, Eric, *Uncommon Danger* (London: Penguin, 2009).

Ambler, Eric, *The Mask of Dimitrios* (London: Penguin, 2009).

Anon., 'The Censor Relents', *Daily Telegraph*, 26 March 1932, 6.

Anon., 'The London Revue', *The Times*, 3 September 1925, 8.

Anon., 'The Wicked Lady', *Sunday Graphic*, No. 1619, 14 April 1946, n. p.

Appignanesi, Lisa, *Cabaret: The First Hundred Years* (London: Methuen, 1984).

Auden, W. H., *The Age of Anxiety: A Baroque Eclogue* (London: Faber & Faber 1948).

Auden, W. H., *The English Auden: Poems, Essays and Dramatic Writings 1927–1939*, ed. Edward Mendelson (London: Faber & Faber, 1977).

Balázs, Béla, 'Theory of the Film: Sound', in Elisabeth Weis and John Belton (eds), *Film Sound: Theory and Practice*, (New York: Columbia University Press, 1985), 116–125.

Balázs, Béla, *Bela Balázs: Early Film Theory: 'Visible Man' and 'The Spirit of Film'*, ed. Erica Carter, trans. Rodney Livingstone (New York: Berghahn Books, 2010).

Barnouw, Erik, *Documentary: A History of the Non-Fiction Film* (New York: Oxford University Press, 1974).

Barrett, Gerard, 'James Hanley and the Colours of War', in Marina MacKay and Lyndsey Stonebridge (eds), *British Fiction after Modernism: The Novel at Mid-Century* (Basingstoke: Palgrave Macmillan, 2007), 77–87.

Barrios, Richard, *A Song in the Dark: The Birth of the Musical Film* (New York: Oxford University Press, 2010).

Barrow, Sarah and John White (eds), *Fifty Key British Films* (London: Routledge, 2008).

Barsam, Richard M., *Non-Fiction Film: A Criticial History* (Bloomington, IN: Indiana University Press, 1992).

208  SELECT BIBLIOGRAPHY

Baxendale, John and Christopher Pawling, *Narrating the Thirties* (Basingstoke: Macmillan, 1996).

Beaty, Frederick L., *The Ironic World of Evelyn Waugh: A Study in Eight Novels* (DeKalb, IL: Northern Illinois University Press, 1992).

Belton, John, 'Awkward Transitions: Hitchcock's "Blackmail" and the Dynamics of Early Film Sound', *Musical Quarterly*, 83.2 (1999), 227–246.

Belton, John and Elisabeth Weis (eds), *Film Sound: Theory and Practice* (New York: Columbia University Press, 1985).

Bennett, Andrew and Nicholas Royle, *Elizabeth Bowen and the Dissolution of the Novel: Still Lives* (New York: St. Martin's Press, 1995).

'Best Talk-Film Yet', *The Daily Mail*, 24 June 1929.

Berensmeyer, Ingo, 'Henry Green, *Party Going* (1939)', in Christoph Reinfandt (ed.), *Handbook of the English Novel of the Twentieth and Twenty-First Centuries* (Berlin: de Gruyter, 2017), 232–251.

Betts, Ernest, *Heraclitus or The Future of Films* (London: Kegan Paul, 1928).

Betts, Ernest, 'Why "Talkies" are Unsound', in James Donald, Anne Friedberg, and Laura Marcus (eds), *Close Up 1927–1933: Cinema and Modernism* (London: Cassell, 1998), 89–90.

Blondel, Nathalie, 'Patrick Hamilton', *Oxford Dictionary of National Biography* (2004), https://doi.org/10.1093/ref:odnb/38308, accessed 3 June 2024.

Bloom, Emily C., *The Wireless Past: Anglo-Irish Writers and the BBC, 1931–1968* (Oxford: Oxford University Press, 2016).

Bluemel, Kristin, 'Beyond Englishness: The Regional and Rural Novel in the 1930s', in Benjamin Kohlmann and Matthew Taunton (eds), *A History of 1930s British Literature* (Cambridge: Cambridge University Press, 2019), 17–30.

Bold, Valentina (ed.), *Smeddum: A Lewis Grassic Gibbon Anthology* (Edinburgh: Canongate, 2001).

Bordwell, David, 'The Introduction of Sound', in David Bordwell, Janet Staiger, and Kristin Thompson (eds), *The Classical Hollywood Cinema: Film Style & Mode of Production to 1960* (London: Routledge, 2002), 298–308.

Bowen, Elizabeth, 'Why I Go to the Cinema', in Charles Davy (ed.), *Footnotes to the Film*, Reader's Union Edition (New York: Arno Press & *The New York Times*, 1970), 205–220.

Bowen, Elizabeth, 'Dead Mabelle', *The Collected Stories of Elizabeth Bowen* (London: Vintage, 1999), 302–312.

Bowen, Elizabeth, 'Oh, Madam…', *The Collected Stories of Elizabeth Bowen* (London: Vintage, 1999), 647–652.

Bowen, Elizabeth, 'Songs My Father Sang Me', *The Collected Stories of Elizabeth Bowen* (London: Vintage, 1999), 730–742.

Bowen, Elizabeth, 'The Demon Lover', *The Collected Stories of Elizabeth Bowen* (London: Vintage, 1999), 743–749.

Bowen, Elizabeth, 'The Happy Autumn Fields', *The Collected Stories of Elizabeth Bowen* (London: Vintage, 1999), 755–771.

Bowen, Elizabeth, 'Notes on Writing a Novel', in Hermione Lee (ed.), *The Mulberry Tree: Writings of Elizabeth Bowen* (London: Vintage, 1999), 35–48.

Bowen, Elizabeth, 'Parents and Children by Ivy Compton-Burnett', in Hermione Lee (ed.), *The Mulberry Tree: Writings of Elizabeth Bowen* (London: Vintage, 1999), 160–163.

Bowen, Elizabeth, Postscript to *The Demon Lover* (US edn), in Hermione Lee (ed.), *The Mulberry Tree: Writings of Elizabeth Bowen* (London: Vintage, 1999), 94–99.

Bowen, Elizabeth, *The Heat of the Day* (New York: Anchor, 2002).

## SELECT BIBLIOGRAPHY 209

Bowen, Elizabeth, 'A Matter of Inspiration', in Allan Hepburn (ed.), *People, Places, Things: Essays by Elizabeth Bowen* (Edinburgh: Edinburgh University Press, 2008), 263–268.

Bowen, Elizabeth, *Listening In: Broadcasts, Speeches, and Interviews by Elizabeth Bowen*, ed. Allan Hepburn (Edinburgh: Edinburgh University Press, 2010).

Bowen, John, 'An Interview with Ivy Compton-Burnett' (BBC Home Programme, 17 September 1960), *Twentieth Century Literature*, 25.2 (Summer 1979), 165–172.

Bradshaw, David, Laura Marcus, and Rebecca Roach (eds), *Moving Modernisms: Motion, Technology, and Modernity* (Oxford: Oxford University Press, 2016).

Brecht, Bertolt, 'Notes on the Folk Play', *Brecht on Theatre: The Development of an Aesthetic*, trans. John Willett (London: Bloomsbury, 2013), 153–157.

Briggs, Julia, 'Commentary on *Paris*', in Sandeep Parmar (ed.), Hope Mirrlees, *Collected Poems* (Manchester: Carcanet, 2011), 254–283.

Britten, Benjamin, Diary Entry for 'Wednesday 15 January 1936', in John Evans (ed.), *Journeying Boy: The Diaries of the Young Benjamin Britten 1928–1938* (London: Faber & Faber, 2009), 326–327.

Brooks, Peter, *The Melodramatic Imagination* (New Haven, CT: Yale University Press, 1995).

Brown, Geoff, 'When Britannia Ruled the Sound Waves: Britain's Transition to Sound in its European Context', *Music, Sound, and the Moving Image*, 12.2 (2018), 93–119.

Brown, Royal S., *Overtones and Undertones: Reading Film Music* (Berkeley, CA: University of California Press, 1994).

Brown, Spencer Curtis, 'Foreword', in Elizabeth Bowen, *Pictures and Conversations* (London: Allen Lane, 1975), vii–xlii.

Brownrigg, Mark, *Film Music and Film Genre*, Doctoral Dissertation (University of Stirling, 2003).

Bryant, Marsha, *Auden and Documentary in the 1930s* (Charlottesville: University Press of Virginia, 1997).

Buchanan, Judith, *Shakespeare on Silent Film* (Cambridge: Cambridge University Press, 2009).

Buhler, James, *Theories of the Soundtrack* (Oxford: Oxford University Press, 2018).

Burgess, Anthony, *Little Wilson and Big God* (London: Penguin, 1988).

Burkhart, Charles (ed.), 'I. Compton-Burnett and M. Jourdain: A Conversation', in *The Art of I. Compton-Burnett: A Collection of Critical Essays* (London: Gollancz, 1972), 21–31.

Calder, Angus and Dorothy Sheridan (eds), *Speak for Yourself: A Mass-Observation Anthology, 1937–1949* (London: Jonathan Cape, 1984).

Cameron, Ken, *Sound in the Documentary Film* (London: Pitman, 1947).

Cammack, Susanne S., 'The Death of a Gramophone in Elizabeth Bowen's *The Last September*', *Journal of Modern Literature*, 40.2 (2017), 132–146.

Carruthers, A. J., *Notational Experiments in North American Long Poems, 1961–2011* (Cham: Palgrave Macmillan, 2017).

Carter, Ian, 'Lewis Grassic Gibbon, *A Scot's Quair*, and the Peasantry', *History Workshop Journal*, 6 (1978), 169–185.

Cavalcanti, Alberto, 'Sound in Films', in Elisabeth Weis and John Belton (eds), *Film Sound: Theory and Practice* (New York: Columbia University Press, 1985), 98–111.

Chaplin, Charlie, 'Why I Prefer Silent Films', *Daily Mail*, 7 February 1931, 10.

Chapman, James, 'Celluloid Shockers', in Jeffrey Richards (ed.), *The Unknown 1930s: An Alternative History of the British Cinema, 1929–1939* (London: Tauris, 2000), 75–98.

Chapman, James, *A New History of British Documentary* (Basingstoke: Palgrave Macmillan, 2015).

210 SELECT BIBLIOGRAPHY

Chion, Michel, *Audio-Vision: Sound on Screen*, trans. Claudia Gorbman (New York: Columbia University Press, 1994).

Chion, Michel, *The Voice in Cinema*, trans. Claudia Gorbman (New York: Columbia University Press, 1999).

Clarke, Ben, '"Beer and Cigarettes and a Girl to Flirt with": Orwell, Drinking and the Everyday', *English Studies*, 96.5 (2015), 541–561.

Coetzee, J. M., 'Introduction', in Graham Greene, *Brighton Rock* (London: Vintage, 2004), vii–xv.

Cohen, Debra Rae, 'Wireless Imaginations', in Anna Snaith (ed.), *Sound and Literature* (Cambridge: Cambridge University Press, 2020), 334–350.

Compton-Burnett, Ivy, 'A Conversation between I. Compton-Burnett and Margaret Jourdain', in Charles Burkhart (ed.), *The Art of I. Compton-Burnett: A Collection of Critical Essays* (London: Gollancz, 1972), 21–31.

Compton-Burnett, Ivy, *A House and Its Head* (New York: New York Review of Books, 2001).

Compton-Burnett, Ivy, *Manservant and Maidservant* (New York: New York Review of Books, 2001).

Connor, Steven, 'The Modern Auditory I', in Roy Porter (ed.), *Rewriting the Self: Histories from the Renaissance to the Present* (London: Routledge, 1997), 203–223.

Connor, Steven, 'Making an Issue of Cultural Phenomenology', *Critical Quarterly*, 42.1 (2000), 2–6.

Cook, Pam, 'Neither Here nor There: National Identity in Gainsborough Costume Drama', in Andrew Higson (ed.), *Dissolving Views: Key Writings on British Cinema* (London: Bloomsbury, 1997), 51–65.

Cook, Pam, *Screening the Past: Memory and Nostalgia in Cinema* (London: Routledge, 2005).

Cook, Pam (ed.), *Gainsborough Pictures* (London: Cassell, 1997).

Corcoran, Neil, *Elizabeth Bowen: The Enforced Return* (Oxford: Oxford University Press, 2004).

Cording, Alastair, 'Adapting Sunset Song for the Stage: Notes by Alastair Cording', in *Lewis Grassic Gibbon's Sunset Song*, dramatized by Alastair Cording (London: Nick Hern, 2004), xiii–xxi.

Coultass, Clive, 'British Feature Films and the Second World War', *Journal of Contemporary History*, 19.1 (1984), 7–22.

Crafton, Donald, *The Talkies: American Cinema's Transition to Sound, 1926–1931* (New York: Scribner, 1997).

Craig, Cairns, 'Twentieth Century Scottish Literature: An Introduction', in Cairns Craig (ed.), *The History of Scottish Literature, Vol. 4: Twentieth Century* (Aberdeen: Aberdeen University Press, 1987), 1–9.

Crook, Tim, 'George Orwell and the Radio Imagination', in Richard Lance Keeble (ed.), *George Orwell Now!* (New York: Peter Lang, 2015), 193–208.

Cunningham, Valentine, *British Writers of the Thirties* (Oxford: Oxford University Press, 1988).

Davies, Peter, 'Note on the Text', in George Orwell, *A Clergyman's Daughter* (London: Penguin, 2000), v–viii.

Davis, Cynthia, 'Jamette Carnival and Afro-Caribbean Influences on the Work of Jean Rhys', *Anthurium: A Caribbean Studies Journal* 3.2 (2005), Article 9. doi: 10.33596/anth.53.

Davis, Robert Murray, *Evelyn Waugh and the Forms of his Time* (Washington: Catholic University of America Press, 1989).

Davis, Thomas S., 'Elizabeth Bowen's War Gothic', *Textual Practice*, 27.1 (2013), 29–47.

SELECT BIBLIOGRAPHY    211

Davison, Peter, *George Orwell: A Literary Life* (Basingstoke: Palgrave Macmillan, 1996).
DeCoste, Damon Marcel, '"(AND YOU GET FAR TOO MUCH PUBLICITY ALREADY WHOEVER YOU ARE)": Gossip, Celebrity, and Modernist Authorship in Evelyn Waugh's *Vile Bodies*', *Papers on Language and Literature*, 49.1 (Winter 2013), 3–36.
Deer, Patrick, *Culture in Camouflage: War, Empire, and Modern British Literature* (Oxford: Oxford University Press, 2009).
Denning, Michael, *Cover Stories: Narrative and Ideology in the British Spy Thriller* (Abingdon: Routledge, 2014).
DiBattista, Maria, *Fast-Talking Dames* (Yale: Yale University Press, 2001).
DiBattista, Maria, 'This Is Not a Movie: *Ulysses* and Cinema', *Modernism/Modernity*, 13.2 (2006), 219–235.
Diemert, Brian, *Graham Greene's Thrillers and the 1930s* (Montreal: McGill-Queens University Press, 1996).
Dillon, Sarah, 'Elizabeth Bowen: "The Demon Lover" and "Mysterious Kôr"', in Cheryl Alexander Malcolm and David Malcolm (eds), *A Companion to the British and Irish Short Story* (London: Wiley, 2008), 236–243.
Dinsman, Melissa, *Modernism at the Microphone: Radio, Propaganda, and Literary Aesthetics During World War II* (London: Bloomsbury, 2017).
Doane, Mary Ann 'The Voice in the Cinema: The Articulation of Body and Space', *Yale French Studies*, 60 (1980), 33–50.
Donald, James, 'Introduction', in James Donald, Anne Friedberg, and Laura Marcus (eds), *Close Up 1927–1933: Cinema and Modernism* (London: Cassell, 1998), 79–82.
Donald, James, Anne Friedberg, and Laura Marcus (eds), *Close Up 1927–1933: Cinema and Modernism* (Princeton: Princeton University Press, 1998).
Donnelly, K. J., *British Film Music and Film Musicals* (Basingstoke: Palgrave Macmillan, 2007).
Donnelly, K. J., *Occult Aesthetics: Synchronization in Sound Film* (Oxford: Oxford University Press, 2014).
Dwan, David, *Liberty, Equality, and Humbug: Orwell's Political Ideals* (Oxford: Oxford University Press, 2018).
Eisenstein, Sergei, *The Film Sense*, trans. Jay Leda (New York: Meridian, 1957).
Eisenstein, Sergei, 'The Dialectical Approach to Film Form', in Richard Taylor (ed.), *The Eisenstein Reader* (London: BFI, 1998), 93–110.
Eisenstein, Sergei, W. I. Pudovkin, and G. V. Alexandrov, 'Statement on Sound', in Richard Taylor (ed.), *The Eisenstein Reader* (London: BFI, 1998), 80–81.
Elleström, Lars, 'Adaptation and Intermediality', in Thomas Leitch (ed.), *The Oxford Handbook of Adaptation Studies* (Oxford: Oxford University Press, 2017), 509–526 (p. 511).
Ellis, Steve, *British Writers and the Approach of World War II* (Cambridge: Cambridge University Press, 2015).
'Elstree Calling', *The Times*, 10 February 1930, p. 10.
Enemark, Nina, 'Antiquarian Magic: Jane Harrison's Ritual Theory and Hope Mirrlees's Antiquarianism in *Paris*', in Elizabeth Anderson et al. (eds), *Modernist Women Writers and Spirituality* (London: Palgrave Macmillan, 2006), 115–33.
Everson, William K., 'The Man in Grey', in 'William K. Everson and the British Cinema: Program Notes for the New School for Social Research', *Film History*, 15.3 (2003), 279–375.
Everson, William K., 'Madonna of the Seven Moons', in 'William K. Everson and the British Cinema: Program Notes for the New School for Social Research', *Film History*, 15.3 (2003), 279–375.

212    SELECT BIBLIOGRAPHY

Feigel, Lara, *Literature, Cinema and Politics 1930-1945: Reading between the Frames* (Edinburgh: Edinburgh University Press, 2010).

Ferguson, Rex, 'Blind Noise and Deaf Visions: Henry Green's *Caught*, Synaesthesia and the Blitz', *Journal of Modern Literature*, 33.1 (2009), 102–116.

Ferrall, Charles, 'From Wells to John Berger: The Social Democratic Era of the Novel', in Robert L. Caserio and Clement Hawes (eds), *The Cambridge History of the English Novel* (Cambridge: Cambridge University Press, 2012), 807–822.

Fielding, Raymond (ed.), *A Technological History of Motion Pictures and Television: An Anthology from the Pages of the Journal of the Society of Motion Picture and Television Engineers* (Berkeley, CA: University of California Press, 1967).

Flinn, Carol, 'The Most Romantic Art of All: Music in the Classical Hollywood Cinema', *Cinema Journal*, 29.4 (1990), 35–50.

Foltz, Jonathan, *The Novel after Film: Modernism and the Decline of Autonomy* (New York: Oxford University Press, 2018).

Forster, E. M., 'The 1939 State', *The New Statesman and Nation*, 10 June 1939, pp. 888–889.

Fowler, Roger, *The Language of George Orwell* (Basingstoke: Macmillan, 1995).

Frattarola, Angela, *Modernist Soundscapes: Auditory Technology and the Novel* (Gainesville, FL: University Press of Florida, 2018).

Frick, Robert, 'Style and Structure in the Early Novels of Evelyn Waugh', *Papers on Language and Literature*, 28.4 (1992), 417–441.

Frost, Laura, *The Problem with Pleasure: Modernism and its Discontents* (New York: Columbia University Press, 2013).

Gallagher, Shaun and Dan Zahavi, *The Phenomenological Mind* (New York: Routledge, 2012).

Gellen, Kata, *Kafka and Noise: The Discovery of Cinematic Sound in Literary Modernism* (Evanston, IL: Northwestern University Press, 2019).

Gitelman, Lisa, *Always Already New: Media, History, and the Data of Culture* (Cambridge, MA: MIT, 2008).

Goldberg, Jonathan, *Melodrama: An Aesthetics of Impossibility* (Durham: Duke University Press, 2016).

Good, Graham, 'Orwell and Eliot: Politics, Poetry, Prose', in Peter Buitenhuis and Ira B. Nadel (eds), *George Orwell: A Reassessment* (London: Macmillan, 1988), 139–156.

Gorbman, Claudia, *Unheard Melodies: Narrative Film Music* (London: BFI Publishing, 1987).

Grassic Gibbon, Lewis, 'A Novelist Looks at the Cinema', *Cinema Quarterly*, 3.2 (1935), 81–85.

Grassic Gibbon, Lewis, *Sunset Song* (Edinburgh: Canongate, 2020).

Green, Henry, *Pack my Bag: A Self-Portrait* (London: Hogarth, 1979).

Green, Henry, 'A Novelist to His Readers', in Matthew Yorke (ed.), Henry Green, *Surviving: The Uncollected Writings of Henry Green* (London: Harvill, 1993), 136–142.

Green, Henry, 'The Art of Fiction', Interview by Terry Southern, in Matthew Yorke (ed.), Henry Green, *Surviving: The Uncollected Writings of Henry Green* (London: Harvill, 1993), 234–250.

Green, Henry, 'The Spoken Word as Written', in Matthew Yorke (ed.), Henry Green, *Surviving: The Uncollected Writings of Henry Green* (London: Harvill, 1993), 170–173.

Green, Henry, *Living, Loving, Party Going* (London: Vintage, 2005).

Green, Henry, *Caught, Back, Concluding* (London: Vintage, 2016).

Greene, Graham, 'Subjects and Stories', in Charles Davy (ed.), *Footnotes to the Film*, Reader's Union Edition (New York: Arno Press & *The New York Times*, 1970), 57–70.

## SELECT BIBLIOGRAPHY 213

Greene, Graham, 'Song of Ceylon', in John Russell Taylor (ed.), Graham Greene, *The Pleasure Dome: The Collected Film Criticism, 1935–40* (Oxford: Oxford University Press, 1980), 25–26.

Greene, Graham, *The Ministry of Fear* (London: Vintage, 2001).

Greene, Graham, *Brighton Rock* (London: Vintage, 2004).

Greene, Graham, 'A Film Principle', in David Parkinson (ed.), Graham Greene, *Mornings in the Dark: The Graham Greene Film Reader* (Manchester: Carcanet, 2007), 392–394.

Greene, Graham, 'Dood Wasser, Me and Marlborough, The Barretts of Wimpole Street', in David Parkinson (ed.), Graham Greene, *Mornings in the Dark: The Graham Greene Film Reader* (Manchester: Carcanet, 2007), 24–25.

Greene, Graham, 'Jazz Comedy, Two for Tonight', in David Parkinson (ed.), Graham Greene, *Mornings in the Dark: The Graham Greene Film Reader* (Manchester: Carcanet, 2007), 30–32.

Greene, Graham, 'The Novelist and the Cinema: A Personal Experience', in David Parkinson (ed.), Graham Greene, *Mornings in the Dark: The Graham Greene Film Reader* (Manchester: Carcanet, 2007), 441–445.

Greene, Graham, *Stamboul Train* (London: Vintage, 2010).

Grierson, John, 'The GPO Gets Sound', *Cinema Quarterly*, 2.4 (Summer 1934), 215–221.

Grierson, John, 'Creative Use of Sound', in Forsyth Hardy (ed.), *Grierson on Documentary* (New York: Harcourt, Brace & Co., 1947), 112–118.

Groth, Helen, 'Literary Soundscapes', in Anna Snaith (ed.), *Sound and Literature* (Cambridge: Cambridge University Press, 2020), 135–153.

Gunning, Tom, 'Doing for the Eye What the Phonograph Does for the Ear', in Richard Abel and Rick Altman (eds), *The Sounds of Early Cinema* (Bloomington: Indiana University Press, 2001), 13–31.

Guy, Stephen, 'Calling All Stars: Musical Films in a Musical Decade', in Jeffrey Richards (ed.), *The Unknown 1930s: An Alternative History of the British Cinema, 1929–1939* (London: Tauris, 2000), 99–118.

Guynn, William, 'The Art of National Projection: Basil Wright's *Song of Ceylon*', in Barry Keith Grant and Jeannette Sloniowski (eds), *Documenting the Documentary: Close Readings of Documentary Film and Video* (Detroit: Wayne State University Press, 2013), 64–80.

Hamilton, Bruce, *The Light Went Out: The Life of Patrick Hamilton by His Brother Bruce Hamilton* (London: Constable, 1972).

Hamilton, Patrick, *Hangover Square: A Story of Darkest Earl's Court* (London: Penguin, 2001).

Hanley, James, *No Directions* (London: André Deutsch, 1990).

Hanson, Helen, *Hollywood Soundscapes: Film Sound Style, Craft and Production in the Classical Era* (London: BFI, 2017).

Harcourt-Smith, Simon, 'Review of *The Wicked Lady*', *Tribune*, 23 November 1945.

Harper, Sue, 'Historical Pleasures: Gainsborough Costume Melodrama', in Marcia Landy (ed.), *The Historical Film: History and Memory in Media* (New Brunswick: Rutgers University Press, 2001), 98–122.

Harris, Laurel, 'Hearing Cinematic Modernism in the 1930s: The Audiovisual in British Documentary Cinema and Virginia Woolf's *Between the Acts*', *Literature & History*, 21.1 (2012), 61–75.

Harris, Laurel, 'From "The Worst Horror of All" to "I Love You": Gender and Voice in the Cinematic Soundscapes of *Brighton Rock*', *Literature/Film Quarterly*, 46.1 (2018).

Heidegger, Martin, *Being and Time*, trans. John Macquarrie and Edward Robinson (New York: Harper & Row, 2008).

214  SELECT BIBLIOGRAPHY

Hepburn, Allan, 'Thrillers', in Robert L. Caserio (ed.), *The Cambridge History of the English Novel* (Cambridge: Cambridge University Press, 2012), 693–708.

Hepburn, Allan, *A Grain of Faith: Religion in Mid-Century British Literature* (Oxford: Oxford University Press, 2018).

Hepburn, Allan, 'The Heroic Today: Elizabeth Bowen and the Technique of the Novel', *Irish University Review*, 51.1 (2021), 57–71.

Hepburn, Allan (ed.), 'Introduction', *People, Places, Things: Essays by Elizabeth Bowen* (Edinburgh: Edinburgh University Press, 2008), 1–23.

Hepburn, Allan (ed.), 'Introduction', *Listening In: Broadcasts, Speeches, and Interviews by Elizabeth Bowen* (Edinburgh: Edinburgh University Press, 2010), 1–23.

Higham, Charles and Roy Moseley, *Princess Merle: The Romantic Life of Merle Oberon* (New York: Pocket Books, 1952).

Highmore, Ben, *Everyday Life and Cultural Theory* (London: Routledge, 2002).

Higson, Andrew, 'The British Film Industry and its Genres in the Mid-1930s', in Andrew Higson (ed.), *Waving the Flag: Constructing a National Cinema in Britain* (Oxford: Clarendon, 1997), 105–112.

Hitchcock, Alfred, 'Direction', in Charles Davy (ed.), *Footnotes to the Film*, Reader's Union Edition (New York: Arno Press & *The New York Times*, 1970), 3–15.

Hoare, Jon. 'Song of Ceylon: Analysis', *Colonial Film: Moving Images of the British Empire*, 2010. Open access online at http://www.colonialfilm.org.uk/node/486.

Hood, Stuart, 'John Grierson and the Documentary Film Movement', in James Curran and Vincent Porter (eds), *British Cinema History* (London: Weidenfeld & Nicholson, 1983).

Hopkins, Joel, 'An Interview with Eric Ambler', *Journal of Popular Culture*, 9.2 (1975), 285–93.

Hubble, Nick, *Mass-Observation and Everyday Life* (Basingstoke: Palgrave Macmillan, 2006).

Humble, Nicola, *The Feminine Middlebrow Novel, 1920s to 1950s: Class, Domesticity and Bohemianism* (Oxford: Oxford University Press, 2001).

Inchley, Maggie, *Voice and New Writing, 1997–2007* (London: Palgrave Macmillan, 2015).

Isherwood, Christopher, *The Berlin Novels* (London: Vintage, 1999).

Isherwood, Christopher, *Conversations with Christopher Isherwood*, ed. James J. Berg and Chris Freeman (Jackson: University Press of Mississippi, 2001).

Isherwood, Christopher, *Isherwood on Writing*, ed. James J. Berg (Minneapolis: University of Minnesota Press, 2007).

Isherwood, Christopher, *Christopher and His Kind* (London: Vintage, 2012).

Isherwood, Christopher, *Prater Violet* (London: Vintage, 2012).

Jacobs, Lea, *Film Rhythm after Sound: Technology, Music, and Performance* (Oakland, CA: University of California Press, 2015).

Jacobs, Richard, 'Introduction', in Evelyn Waugh, *Vile Bodies* (London: Penguin, 2000), ix–xxxiv.

Jenkins, Henry, *What Made Pistachio Nuts? Early Sound Comedy and the Vaudeville Aesthetic* (New York: Columbia University Press, 1992).

Jennings, Richard, 'The Theatre', *The Spectator*, 17 October 1931, 12.

Jones, Nigel, *Through a Glass Darkly: The Life of Patrick Hamilton* (London: Scribners, 1991).

Jung, C. G., *Synchronicity: An Acausal Connecting Principle*, trans. R. F. C. Hull (Princeton, NJ: Princeton University Press, 1973).

Kalinak, Kathryn, *Settling the Score: Music and the Classical Hollywood Film* (Madison, WI: University of Wisconsin Press, 1992).

SELECT BIBLIOGRAPHY    215

Kegan Gardiner, Judith, '*Good Morning, Midnight*; Good Night, Modernism', *boundary 2*, 11.1/2 (Autumn 1982–Winter 1983), 233–251.

Kember, Joe, *Marketing Modernity: Victorian Popular Shows and Early Cinema* (Exeter: University of Exeter Press, 2009).

Kennedy, Dennis, 'British Theatre 1895–1946: Art, Entertainment, Audiences', in Baz Kershaw (ed.), *The Cambridge History of British Theatre*, Vol. 3 (Cambridge: Cambridge University Press, 2004), 1–33.

Kerr, Laura, K., 'Synchronicity', in Thomas Teo (ed.), *Encyclopedia of Critical Psychology* (New York: Springer, 2014), 1905–1908.

Kerzoncuf, Alain and Charles Barr, *Hitchcock Lost and Found: The Forgotten Films* (Lexington, KY: University Press of Kentucky, 2015).

Kittler, Friedrich A., *Gramophone, Film, Typewriter*, trans. Geoffrey Winthrop-Young and Michael Wutz (Stanford, CA: Stanford University Press, 1999).

Knowles, Sebastian D. G., 'Death by Gramophone', *Journal of Modern Literature*, 27.1 (2003), 1–13.

Knox, Ronald, 'The Reader Suspended', *Month*, 8.4 (October 1952), 236–238.

Kohlmann, Benjamin, *Committed Styles: Modernism, Politics, and Left-wing Literature in the 1930s* (Oxford: Oxford University Press, 2014).

Kozloff, Sarah, *Overhearing Film Dialogue* (Berkeley, CA: University of California Press, 2000).

Kracauer, Siegfried, 'The Mass Ornament', in Siegfried Kracauer, *The Mass Ornament: Weimar Essays*, trans. and ed. Thomas Y. Levin (Cambridge, MA: Harvard University Press, 1995), 75–86.

Kracauer, Siegfried, *Theory of Film: The Redemption of Physical Reality* (Princeton, NJ: Princeton University Press, 1997).

Lasser, Michael, 'The Glorifier: Florenz Ziegfeld and the Creation of the American Showgirl', *American Scholar*, 63.3 (1994), 441–448.

Lassner, Phyllis, *Espionage and Exile: Fascism and Anti-Fascism in British Spy Fiction and Film* (Edinburgh: Edinburgh University Press, 2016).

Lastra, James, *Sound Technology and the American Cinema* (New York: Columbia University Press, 2000).

Lawrence, Amy, *Echo and Narcissus: Women's Voices in Classical Hollywood Cinema* (Berkeley, CA: University of California Press, 1991).

Leavis, Q. D., 'The Literary Life Respectable: Reviews of Edwin Muir and George Orwell', in G. Singh (ed.), Q. D. Leavis, *Collected Essays. Vol. 3: The Novel of Religious Controversy* (Cambridge: Cambridge University Press, 1989), 283–289.

Leigh, Walter, 'The Musician and the Film', *Cinema Quarterly*, 3.2 (1935), 70–74.

Lejeune, C. A., 'A Filmgoer's War Diary', in Guy Morgan (ed.), *Red Roses Every Night: London Cinemas under Fire* (London: Quality Press, 1948), 67–77.

Levenson, Michael, 'The Fictional Realist: Novels of the 1930s', in John Rodden (ed.), *The Cambridge Companion to George Orwell* (Cambridge: Cambridge University Press, 2007), 59–75.

Lewis, Peter M., '"A Claim to Be Heard": Voices of Ordinary People in BBC Radio Features', *Revue Française de Civilisation Britannique*, 26.1 (2021), 1–13.

Light, Alison, *Forever England: Femininity, Literature, and Conservatism between the Wars* (Abingdon: Routledge, 2001).

Lindsay, Vachel, *The Art of the Moving Picture* (New York: Modern Library Paperback, 2000).

Linton, David, 'English West End Revue: The First World War and After', in Robert Gordon and Olaf Jubin (eds), *The Oxford Handbook of the British Musical* (Oxford: Oxford University Press, 2016), 143–169.

216  SELECT BIBLIOGRAPHY

Lodge, David, 'Dialogue in the Modern Novel', *After Bakhtin: Essays on Fiction and Criticism* (London: Routledge, 1990), 75–86.

Low, Rachael, *The History of the British Film, 1929–1939: Film Making in 1930s Britain* (London: Allen & Unwin, 1985).

Lyall, Scott, '"That Ancient Self": Scottish Modernism's Counter-Renaissance', *European Journal of English Studies*, 18.1 (2014), 73–85.

Macaulay, Rose, 'Evelyn Waugh', in Martin Stannard (ed.), *Evelyn Waugh: The Critical Heritage* (London: Routledge & Kegan Paul, 1984), 109–112.

MacCabe, Colin, 'On Impurity: The Dialectics of Cinema and Literature', in Julian Murphet and Lydia Rainford (eds), *Literature and Visual Technologies: Writing after Cinema* (Basingstoke: Palgrave Macmillan, 2003), 15–28.

MacDonald, Matthew, 'Hitchcock's *Blackmail* and the Threat of Recorded Sound', *Music and the Moving Image*, 8.3 (2015), 40–51.

MacKay, Marina, *Modernism, War, and Violence* (London: Bloomsbury, 2017).

MacKay, Marina, 'Total War', in Benjamin Kohlmann and Matthew Taunton (eds), *A History of 1930s British Literature* (Cambridge: Cambridge University Press, 2019), 362–375.

Madge, Charles and Humphrey Jennings, 'They Speak for Themselves: Mass-Observation and Social Narrative', *Life and Letters Today*, 17 (Autumn 1937), 37–42.

Magot, Céline, '"Careless Talk": Word Shortage in Elizabeth Bowen's Wartime Writing', *Miranda*, 2 (2010). Open access online at: http://journals.openedition.org/miranda/1189.

Malamet, Elliott, 'Graham Greene and the Hounds of *Brighton Rock*', *Modern Fiction Studies*, 37.4 (1991), 689–703.

Malcolm, William K., 'The Exportation of Lewis Grassic Gibbon', *Scottish Literary Review*, 8.1 (2016), 93–109.

Malcolm, William R., *A Blasphemer & Reformer. A Study of James Leslie Mitchell/Lewis Grassic Gibbon* (Aberdeen: Aberdeen University Press, 1984).

Mander, Raymond, and Joe Mitchenson, *Revue: A Story in Pictures* (London: Peter Davies, 1971).

Mansell, James G., 'Rhythm, Modernity and the Politics of Sound', in Scott Anthony and James G. Mansell (eds), *The Projection of Britain: A History of the GPO Film Unit* (London: BFI, 2011), 161–167.

Mansell, James G., *The Age of Noise in Britain: Hearing Modernity* (Urbana, IL: University of Illinois Press, 2017).

Marcus, Laura, *The Tenth Muse: Writing about Cinema in the Modernist Period* (Oxford: Oxford University Press, 2007).

Marcus, Laura, '"The Creative Treatment of Actuality": John Grierson, Documentary Cinema and "Fact" in the 1930s', in Kristin Bluemel (ed.), *Intermodernism* (Edinburgh: Edinburgh University Press, 2011), 189–207.

Marcus, Laura, 'Talking Films' in Benjamin Kohlmann and Matthew Taunton (eds), *A History of 1930s British Literature* (Cambridge: Cambridge University Press, 2019), 177–193.

Matheson, Ann, 'Margaret Is On Her Mettle', *The Australian Women's Weekly*, 31 October 1942, 11.

McCabe, Susan, *Cinematic Modernism: Modernist Poetry and Film* (Cambridge: Cambridge University Press, 2005).

McCartney, George, *Evelyn Waugh and the Modernist Tradition* (New Brunswick, NJ: Transaction, 2004).

McCracken, Allison, *Real Men Don't Sing: Crooning in American Culture* (Duke University Press, 2015).

McEnaney, Tom, *Acoustic Properties Radio, Narrative, and the New Neighborhood of the Americas* (Evanston, IL: Northwestern University Press, 2017).

McFarlane, Brian, 'Reading Film and Literature', in Deborah Cartmell and Imelda Whelehan (eds), *The Cambridge Companion to Literature on Screen* (Cambridge: Cambridge University Press, 2007), 15–28.

McWilliam, Rohan, 'Elsa Lanchester and Bohemian London in the Early Twentieth Century', *Women's History Review*, 23.2 (2014), 171–187.

Mellor, Leo, *Reading the Ruins: Modernism, Bombsites and British Culture* (Cambridge: Cambridge University Press, 2011).

Mellor, Leo, 'The 1930s, the Second World War, and Late Modernism', in Vincent Sherry (ed.), *The Cambridge History of Modernism* (Cambridge: Cambridge University Press, 2016), 142–159.

Mellor, Leo, 'The Documentary Impulse', in Benjamin Kohlmann and Matthew Taunton (eds), *A History of 1930s British Literature* (Cambridge: Cambridge University Press, 2019), 257–270.

Mengham, Rod, 'British Fiction of the War', in Marina MacKay (ed.), *The Cambridge Companion to the Literature of World War II* (Cambridge: Cambridge University Press, 2009), 26–42.

Menke, Richard, 'Literature and Telecommunication', in James Purdon (ed.), *British Literature in Transition, 1900–1920: A New Age?* (Cambridge: Cambridge University Press, 2021), 192–208.

Mepham, John, 'Varieties of Modernism, Varieties of Incomprehension: Patrick Hamilton and Elizabeth Bowen', in Marina MacKay and Lyndsey Stonebridge (eds), *British Fiction after Modernism: The Novel at Mid-Century* (Basingstoke: Palgrave Macmillan, 2007), 59–76.

Merleau-Ponty, Maurice, *The Phenomenology of Perception*, trans. Colin Smith (London: Routledge, 2010).

Meyers, Jeffrey, *Orwell: Life and Art* (Urbana, IL: University of Illinois Press, 2010).

Milthorpe, Naomi, '"Death is at the Elbow": *The Loved One* and *Love Among the Ruins*', *Renascence*, 62.3 (2010), 201–17.

Milthorpe, Naomi, *Evelyn Waugh's Satire: Texts and Contexts* (Madison, NJ: Fairleigh Dickinson University Press, 2016).

Mirrlees, Hope, *Paris: A Poem* (London: Faber & Faber, 2020).

Moore, James Ross, 'Girl Crazy: Musicals and Revue between the Wars', in Clive Barker and Maggie B. Gale (eds), *British Theatre between the Wars, 1918–1939* (Cambridge: Cambridge University Press, 2000), 88–112.

Mulvey, Laura, 'Visual Pleasure and Narrative Cinema', *Screen*, 16.3 (1975), 6–18.

Munro, Ian S., *Leslie Mitchell: Lewis Grassic Gibbon* (Edinburgh: Oliver & Boyd, 1966).

Münsterberg, Hugo, *The Photoplay: A Psychological Study and Other Writings*, ed. Allan Langdale (London: Routledge, 2002).

Murat, Jean-Christophe, 'City of Wars: The Representation of Wartime London in Two Novels of the 1940s: James Hanley's *No Directions* and Patrick Hamilton's *The Slaves of Solitude*', *Caliban*, 25 (2009). Open access online at: https://doi.org/10.4000/caliban.1652.

Murphet, Julian, *Multimedia Modernism* (Cambridge: Cambridge University Press, 2009).

Murphet, Julian, and Lydia Rainford (eds), *Literature and Visual Technologies: Writing after Cinema* (Basingstoke: Palgrave Macmillan, 2003).

Murphy, Robert, 'Coming of Sound to the Cinema in Britain', *Historical Journal of Film, Radio and Television*, 4.2 (1984), 143–160.

## 218 SELECT BIBLIOGRAPHY

Murphy, Robert, *Realism and Tinsel: Cinema and Society in Britain 1939–1948* (London: Routledge, 1989).

Murphy, Robert, 'Gainsborough after Balcon', in Pam Cook (ed.), *Gainsborough Pictures* (London: Cassell, 1997), 137–154.

Murphy, Robert, *British Cinema and the Second World War* (London: Continuum, 2000).

Ness, Richard, R., ' "A Lotta Night Music": The Sound of Film Noir', *Cinema Journal*, 47.2 (Winter 2008), 52–73.

Nicoll, Allardyce, *English Drama, 1900–1930: The Beginnings of the Modern Period*, Part 1 (Cambridge: Cambridge University Press, 2009).

North, Michael, *Henry Green and the Writing of His Generation* (Charlottesville: University of Virginia Press, 1984).

North, Michael, 'International Media, International Modernism, and the Struggle with Sound', in Julian Murphet and Lydia Rainford (eds), *Literature and Visual Technologies: Writing after Cinema* (Basingstoke: Palgrave Macmillan, 2003), 49–66.

North, Michael, *Camera Works: Photography and the Twentieth-Century Word* (Oxford: Oxford University Press, 2005).

O'Brien, Charles, *Cinema's Conversion to Sound: Technology and Film Style in France and the U.S.* (Bloomington, IN: Indiana University Press, 2005).

Orwell, George, 'Hop-Picking', *New Statesman and Nation*, 17 October 1931.

Orwell, George, *A Clergyman's Daughter* (London: Penguin, 2000).

Orwell, George, *Essays* (London: Penguin, 2000).

Orwell, George, *Keep the Aspidistra Flying* (London: Penguin, 2000).

Orwell, George, *The Road to Wigan Pier* (London: Penguin, 2001).

Orwell, George, *Diaries*, ed. Peter Davison (London: Harvill Secker, 2009).

Orwell, George, *George Orwell: A Life in Letters*, selected by Peter Davison (New York: Liveright, 2013).

Osborn, Susan, 'Reconsidering Elizabeth Bowen', *Modern Fiction Studies*, 52.1 (2006), 187–197.

Page, Norman, *Speech in the English Novel* (Basingstoke: Macmillan, 1988).

Parker, David (ed.), 'Introduction', in Graham Greene, *Mornings in the Dark: The Graham Greene Film Reader* (Manchester: Carcanet, 2007), xi–xxxvii.

Permiakova, Sofia, '*Paris: A Poem* by Hope Mirrlees: The Liminal World of Paris in 1919', *Journal of European Studies*, 51.3/4 (2021), 192–203.

'Phono-Films Weekly', *The Film Daily*, 7 April 1923, 1.

Piette, Adam, *Imagination at War: British Fiction and Poetry, 1939–1945* (London: Papermac, 1995).

Platt, Len, *Musical Comedy on the West End Stage, 1890–1939* (Basingstoke: Palgrave Macmillan, 2004).

Pong, Beryl, 'Space and Time in the Bombed City: Graham Greene's *The Ministry of Fear* and Elizabeth Bowen's *The Heat of the Day*', *Literary London*, 7.1 (2009). Open access online at: www.literarylondon.org/london-journal/march2009/pong.html.

Pong, Beryl, *British Literature and Culture in Second World Wartime: For the Duration* (Oxford: Oxford University Press, 2020).

Porter, Laraine, 'The Talkies Come to Britain: British Silent Cinema and the Transition to Sound, 1928–30', in Ian Hunter, Laraine Porter, and Justin Smith (eds), *The Routledge Companion to British Cinema History* (Abingdon: Routledge, 2017), 87–98.

Potter, Simon J., *Broadcasting Empire* (Oxford: Oxford University Press, 2012).

Potter, Simon J., *This Is the BBC: Entertaining the Nation, Speaking for Britain? 1922–2022* (Oxford: Oxford University Press, 2022).

Puckett, Kent, *War Pictures* (New York: Fordham University Press, 2017).

Pudovkin, Vsevolod, *Film Technique and Film Acting: The Cinema Writings of V. I. Pudovkin*, trans. Ivor Montagu (New York: Bonanza, 1949).

Purdon, James, *Modernist Informatics* (Oxford: Oxford University Press, 2016).

Purdon, James, 'Telemediations', in Benjamin Kohlmann and Matthew Taunton (eds), *A History of 1930s British Literature* (Cambridge: Cambridge University Press, 2019), 194–207.

Rae, Patricia, 'Mr. Charrington's Junk Shop: T. S. Eliot and Modernist Poetics in *Nineteen Eighty-Four*', *Twentieth-Century Literature*, 43.2 (1997), 196–220.

Rawlinson, Mark, 'The Second World War: British Writing', in Kate McLoughlin (ed.), *The Cambridge Companion to War Writing* (Cambridge: Cambridge University Press, 2009), 197–211.

Read, Herbert, 'Experiments in Counterpoint', *Cinema Quarterly*, 3.1 (1934), 17–21.

'Regal Theatre: "Blackmail": A British International Picture', *The Times*, 24 June 1929, 12.

Reilly, Kara, 'The Tiller Girls: Mass Ornament and Modern Girl', in Kara Reilly (ed.), *Theatre, Performance and Analogue Technology: Historical Interfaces and Intermedialities* (Basingstoke: Palgrave Macmillan, 2013), 117–132.

'Reopen the Cinemas', *Kinematograph Weekly*, 7 September 1939, 2.

'Reviews of the Week', *Kinematograph Weekly*, 2 January 1930, 83.

Richards, Jeffrey, *The Age of the Dream Palace: Cinema and Society in 1930s Britain*. revd edn (London: Tauris, 2009).

Rhys, Jean, *Smile Please: An Unfinished Autobiography* (Harmondsworth: Penguin, 1984).

Rhys, Jean, *Voyage in the Dark* (London: Penguin, 2000).

Rhys, Jean, *Good Morning, Midnight* (London: Penguin, 2016).

Robinson, Gregory, 'Writing on the Silent Screen', in Deborah Cartmell (ed.), *A Companion to Literature, Film, and Adaptation* (Chichester: Blackwell, 2012).

Rodden, John and John Rossi, *The Cambridge Introduction to George Orwell* (Cambridge: Cambridge University Press, 2012).

Rotha, Paul, *The Documentary Film* (London: Faber, 1936).

Rotha, Paul, *The Film till Now: A Survey of World Cinema* (London: Vision, 1949).

Rotha, Paul, *Documentary Diary: An Informal History of the British Documentary Film, 1928–1939* (London: Secker & Warburg, 1973).

Salt, Barry, 'Film Style and Technology in the Thirties: Sound', in John Belton and Elisabeth Weis (eds), *Film Sound: Theory and Practice* (New York: Columbia University Press, 1985), 37–43.

Salt, Barry, *Film Style and Technology: History and Analysis* (London: Starword, 2009).

Salton-Cox, Glyn, *Queer Communism and The Ministry of Love: Sexual Revolution in British Writing of the 1930s* (Edinburgh: Edinburgh University Press, 2021).

Sass, Louis, *Madness and Modernism: Insanity in the Light of Modern Art, Literature, and Thought* (Oxford: Oxford University Press, 2017).

Saunders, Lorraine, *The Unsung Artistry of George Orwell: The Novels from Burmese Days to Nineteen Eighty-Four* (London: Taylor & Francis, 2016).

Schafer, R. Murray, *The Soundscape: Our Sonic Environment and the Tuning of the World* (Rochester, VT: Destiny, 1994).

Schaller, Karen, '"I Know it to be Synthetic but It Affects Me Strongly": "Dead Mabelle" and Bowen's Emotion Pictures', *Textual Practice*, 27.1 (2013), 163–185.

Sedgwick, John, 'Cinema-Going Preferences in Britain in the 1930s', in Jeffrey Richards (ed.), *The Unknown 1930s: An Alternative History of the British Cinema, 1929–1939* (London: Tauris, 2000), 1–35.

Seiler, Claire, *Midcentury Suspension: Literature and Feeling in the Wake of World War II* (New York: Columbia University Press, 2020).

## 220   SELECT BIBLIOGRAPHY

Shail, Andrew, *The Cinema and the Origins of Literary Modernism* (Abingdon: Routledge, 2012).

Shanks, Edward, Review of *Vile Bodies*, in Martin Stannard (ed.), *Evelyn Waugh: The Critical Heritage* (London: Routledge & Kegan Paul, 1984), 100–101.

Shiach, Morag, "'A Scot's Quair" and the Times of Labour', *Critical Survey*, 15.2 (2003), 39–48.

Shiach, Morag, 'Lewis Grassic Gibbon and Modernism', in Scott Lyall (ed.), *The International Companion to Lewis Grassic Gibbon* (Glasgow: Association for Scottish Literary Studies, 2015), 9–21.

Sheffield, M. L., 'What Do You Think?', *The Picturegoer*, 21.122 (February 1931), 54.

Silverman, Kaja, *The Acoustic Mirror: The Female Voice in Psychoanalysis and Cinema* (Bloomington, IN: Indiana University Press, 1988).

Simpson, Celia, 'The Cinema: Star-Gazing', *The Spectator*, 2 November 1929, 623.

Singer, Ben, *Melodrama and Modernity* (New York: Columbia University Press, 2001).

Sinha, Babli, 'A "Strangely Un-English Actress": Race, Legibility, and the Films of Merle Oberon', *Journal of Popular Film and Television*, 44.4 (2016), 220–226.

Snaith, Anna, 'Jean Rhys and the Politics of Sound', in Delia da Sousa Correa (ed.), *The Edinburgh Companion to Literature and Music* (Edinburgh: Edinburgh University Press, 2020), 570–576.

Snaith, Anna (ed.), *Sound and Literature* (Cambridge: Cambridge University Press, 2020).

Snyder, Robert Lance, 'Eric Ambler's Revisionist Thrillers: *Epitaph for a Spy*, *A Coffin for Dimitrios*, and *The Intercom Conspiracy*', *Papers on Language and Literature*, 45.3 (2009), 227–260.

Spender, Stephen, 'Life Wasn't a Cabaret', *The New York Times*, 30 October 1977, 198.

Stannard, Martin, *Evelyn Waugh: The Early Years 1903–1939* (London: Dent & Sons, 1986).

Stannard, Martin (ed.), *Evelyn Waugh: The Critical Heritage* (London: Routledge, 1984).

Stead, Lisa, *Off to the Pictures: Cinema-going, Women's Writing and Movie Culture in Interwar Britain* (Edinburgh: Edinburgh University Press, 2016).

Sterne, Jonathan, *The Audible Past: Cultural Origins of Sound Reproduction* (Durham, NC: Duke University Press, 2003).

Stonebridge, Lyndsey, *The Writing of Anxiety: Imagining Wartime in Mid-Century British Culture* (Basingstoke: Palgrave Macmillan, 2007).

Stonebridge, Lyndsey and Marina MacKay (eds), 'Introduction: British Fiction after Modernism', *British Fiction after Modernism: The Novel at Mid-Century* (Basingstoke: Palgrave Macmillan, 2007), 1–16.

Straus, Ralph, 'Vile Bodies', in Martin Stannard (ed.), *Evelyn Waugh: The Critical Heritage*, (London: Routledge & Kegan Paul, 1984), 95–96.

Street, Sarah, "'Got to Dance My Way to Heaven": Jessie Matthews, Art Deco and the British Musical of the 1930s', *Studies in European Cinema*, 2.1 (2005), 19–30.

Street, Sarah, *Colour Films in Britain: The Negotiation of Innovation, 1900–1955* (London: Bloomsbury, 2019).

Suárez, Juan A., *Pop Modernism: Noise and the Reinvention of the Everyday* (Urbana, IL: University of Illinois Press, 2007).

Sullivan, Garrett A., *Shakespeare and British World War Two Film* (Cambridge: Cambridge University Press, 2022).

Sussex, Elizabeth, *The Rise and Fall of British Documentary: The Story of the Film Movement Founded by John Grierson* (Berkeley, CA: University of California Press, 1975).

Sussex, Elizabeth, 'Cavalcanti in England', in Ian Aitken (ed.), *The Documentary Film Movement: An Anthology* (Edinburgh: Edinburgh University Press, 2008), 181–202.

## SELECT BIBLIOGRAPHY 221

Swallow, Betty M. and Helen Bradley, *Dear Helen: Wartime Letters from a Londoner to her American Pen Pal*, ed. Russell M. Jones and John H. Swanson (Columbia, MO: University of Missouri Press, 2009).

'Table D'Hôte', *BBC Radio Times*, 23 June 1939, 16.

'Talking Film Triumph', *The Daily Mail*, 10 November 1928, 13.

Tange, Hanne, 'Grassic Gibbon's Art of Community: *A Scots Quair* and the Condition of Scotland', *Studies in Scottish Literature*, 33.1 (2004), 247–262.

Tange, Hanne, 'Language, Class and Social Power in *A Scots Quair*', in Scott Lyall (ed.), *The International Companion to Lewis Grassic Gibbon* (Glasgow: Association for Scottish Literary Studies, 2015), 22–32.

Taylor, D. J., *Bright Young People: The Rise and Fall of a Generation, 1918–1940* (London: Vintage, 2008).

Taylor, Richard (ed.), *The Eisenstein Reader* (London: BFI, 1998).

Teekell, Anna, 'Elizabeth Bowen and Language at War', *New Hibernia Review*, 15.3 (2011), 61–79.

Thomas, Sue, *Jean Rhys's Modernist Bearings and Experimental Aesthetics* (London: Bloomsbury, 2022).

Thompson, Emily, *The Soundscape of Modernity: Architectural Acoustics and the Culture of Listening in America, 1900–1933* (Cambridge, MA: MIT, 2004).

Thompson, Kristin, 'The Concept of Cinematic Excess', *Ciné-Tracts*, 1.2 (Summer 1977), 54–63.

Thompson, Kristin, 'Early Sound Counterpoint', *Yale French Studies*, 60 (1980), 115–140.

Todd, Ian Scott, 'Editing Corpses in Evelyn Waugh's Hollywood', *Twentieth Century Literature*, 59.3 (2013), 414–440.

Trotter, David, *Cinema and Modernism* (Oxford: Blackwell, 2007).

Trotter, David, *Literature in the First Media Age: Britain Between the Wars* (Cambridge, MA: Harvard University Press, 2013).

Trotter, David, 'Mobility, Network, Message: Spy Fiction and Film in the Long 1930s', *Critical Quarterly*, 57.3 (2015), 10–21.

Trotter, David, 'Literature between Media', in Vincent Sherry (ed.), *The Cambridge History of Modernism* (Cambridge: Cambridge University Press, 2017), 386–403.

Trotter, David, *The Literature of Connection. Signal, Medium, Interface, 1850–1950* (Oxford: Oxford University Press, 2020).

Uricchio, William, 'Historicizing Media in Transition', in David Thorburn and Henry Jenkins (eds), *Rethinking Media Change: The Aesthetics of Transition* (Cambridge, MA: MIT, 2004), 23–38.

'*Vile Bodies*: Difficulties of Stage Presentation', *Daily Telegraph*, 9 October 1931, 8.

von Ankum, Katharina, 'Material Girls: Consumer Culture and the "New Woman" in Anita Loos' *Gentlemen prefer Blondes* and Irmgard Keun's *Das kunstseidene Mädchen*', *Colloquia Germanica*, 27.2 (1994), 159–172.

Waddell, Nathan, 'Introduction', in George Orwell, *A Clergyman's Daughter* (Oxford: Oxford University Press, 2021), ix–xxxvi.

Wark, Wesley K. (ed.), *Spy Fiction, Spy Films and Real Intelligence* (Abingdon: Routledge, 2006).

Watson, Roderick, 'Alien Voices from the Street: Demotic Modernism in Modern Scots Writing', *Yearbook of English Studies*, 25 (1995), 141–155.

Watt, Harry, *Don't Look at the Camera* (London: Paul Elek, 1974).

Waugh, Evelyn, *The Diaries of Evelyn Waugh*, ed. Michael Davie (Harmondsworth: Penguin, 1979).

## 222 SELECT BIBLIOGRAPHY

Waugh, Evelyn, 'My Favourite Film Star', in Donat Gallagher (ed.), *The Essays, Articles and Reviews of Evelyn Waugh* (London: Methuen, 1983), 68–70.

Waugh, Evelyn, '*Felix Culpa?* Review of the *Heart of the Matter* by Graham Greene', in Donat Gallagher (ed.), *The Essays, Articles and Reviews of Evelyn Waugh* (London: Methuen, 1983), 360–365.

Waugh, Evelyn, 'Ronald Firbank', in Donat Gallagher (ed.), *The Essays, Articles and Reviews of Evelyn Waugh* (London: Methuen, 1983), 56–59.

Waugh, Evelyn, 'Why Hollywood is a Term of Disparagement', in Donat Gallagher (ed.), *The Essays, Articles and Reviews of Evelyn Waugh* (London: Methuen, 1983), 325–331.

Waugh, Evelyn, 'The Balance', in Ann Pasternak Slater (ed.), *The Complete Short Stories and Selected Drawings* (London: Everyman's Library, 1998), 3–38.

Waugh, Evelyn, *The Loved One: An Anglo-American Tragedy* (London: Penguin, 2000).

Waugh, Evelyn, *Vile Bodies* (London: Penguin, 2000).

Waugh, Patricia, 'Precarious Voices: Moderns, Moods, and Moving Epochs', in David Bradshaw, Laura Marcus, and Rebecca Roach (eds), *Moving Modernisms: Motion, Technology, and Modernity* (Oxford: Oxford University Press, 2016), 191–216.

Wilkins, Heidi, *Talkies, Road Movies and Chick Flicks: Gender, Genre and Film Sound in American Cinema* (Edinburgh: Edinburgh University Press, 2016).

Williams, F, 'Truth about the Talkies', *The Picturegoer*, 21.121 (January 1931), 52.

Williams, Keith, *British Writers and the Media, 1930–1945* (Basingstoke: Macmillan, 1996).

Williams, Keith, '"The Unpaid Agitator": Joyce's Influence on George Orwell and James Agee', *James Joyce Quarterly*, 36.4 (1999), 729–763.

Winston, Brian, *Claiming the Real: The Documentary Film Revisited* (London: BFI, 1995).

Wood, James, 'A Plausible Magic: The Novels of Henry Green', in Marina MacKay and Lyndsey Stonebridge (eds), *British Fiction after Modernism: The Novel at Mid-Century* (Basingstoke: Palgrave Macmillan, 2007), 50–58.

Woollacott, Angela, 'Colonial Origins and Audience Collusion: The Merle Oberon Story in 1930s Australia', in Desley Deacon, Penny Russell, and Angela Woollacott (eds), *Transnational Lives: Biographies of Global Modernity, 1700–Present* (London: Palgrave Macmillan, 2010), 96–108.

# Index

Since the index has been created to work across multiple formats, indexed terms for which a page range is given (e.g., 52–53, 66–70, etc.) may occasionally appear only on some, but not all of the pages within the range.

*6.30 Collection* 110–11
*39 Steps, The* 137, 141–4
*49th Parallel* 183–4

Addinsell, Richard 144–5
Afra, Kia 9–10
Alexandrov, Gregori 29–30
Altman, Rick 3–4, 11–14
    on theories of montage 47–8
Ambler, Eric 20–1, 147–9, 155
    on the film industry 42–3
    *Mask of Dimitrios, The* 148–9
    *Uncommon Danger* 147
Anstey, Edgar 115
Arliss, Leslie 192–3
Army Film and Photographic Unit 43, 183–4
Asynchronicity 182–3, 197–8
Auden, W. H. 69–70, 117
    work on *Night Mail* 117–19
Audio-vision
    definition of 1, 11–14
    history of 8–10
    in Phenomenology 12

Balázs, Béla
    *The Spirit of Film* 9–10, 31
    on silence 143, 148–9
Barrett, Gerard 173–4
Barry, Iris 6–8
Barry, Joan 25
BBC
    radio feature documentary 108–9, 116
    'opping 'oliday 108–9
Belton, John 11–12, 24–5
Betts, Ernest 29–30
*Blackmail* 1, 19, 22–8
    silent version 22–4
    sound version 24–8

Bluemel, Kristin 120–1
Bowen, Elizabeth 17, 20–1, 87–94, 167–8
    'A Matter of Inspiration' 36
    BBC radio 87–9
    'Careless Talk' 92, 94
    'Dead Mabelle' 34–6
    'Notes on Writing a Novel' 88–9
    on dialogue 87–90
    'Oh, Madam…' 90–2, 94
    'Songs My Father Sang Me' 92–4
    'The Demon Lover' 176–7
    'The Happy Autumn Fields' 177–80
    *The Heat of the Day* 180–3
    'Why I Go to the Cinema' 35–6, 40 n.68
Britten, Benjamin 117–19
Brooks, Peter 167 n.2, 181
Bryant, Marsha 116–17
Buhler, James 8–9, 29–31

Cabaret 19–20, 47–52, 67–74
*Cabaret* 67–8
Cameron, Ken 115–16
Calvert, Phyllis 184–5, 187–91
*Captain Blood* 139–40
Cavalcanti, Alberto 111–17
Chaplin, Charlie 1–2, 29–30
Chion, Michel
    on 'added value' 106–7
    on audio-vision 1, 11–12
    on silence 143–4, 149
    on sound as punctuation 80–1
    on text and speech 24
Clarke, Ben 133–5
*Close Quarters* 183–4
*Coal Face* 115, 117
*Coastal Command* 183–4
Cochran, C. B. 50–1, 54–5
Colman, Ronald 81–2

## 224 INDEX

Compton-Burnett, Ivy 99–105
  *A House and its Head* 100–4
  *Manservant and Maidservant* 103–4
  On dialogue 99–100, 104
Connor, Steven 5–27
Cook, Pam 184 n.81, 187
Coultass, Clive 183–4
Coward, Noël 50–1, 71–2
Crooning 153–4
Crown Film Unit 183–6

Davis, Cynthia 158
Deer, Patrick 171 n.20, 173–4
*Desert Victory* 183–4
*Desert Song, The* 48–9
Donnelly, K. J. 11–12, 59
  on audiovisual combination 13
  on music in melodrama 191–2
  on sound as punctuation 80–1
  on synchronized speech 76, 79–81

Eisenstein, Sergei 8–10
  *The Film Sense* 9–10
  Statement on Sound 29–31
*Elstree Calling* 49–50
Empire Marketing Board 107
*Enough to Eat?* 115–16
Everson, William K. 187 n.97, 190–1

Fairbanks, Douglas 7–8
*Fanny by Gaslight* 183–4, 187
Feigel, Lara 172–3
Ferguson, Rex 171
Flaherty, Robert 106–7, 109–10
  *Man of Aran* 42 n.77, 109
  *Nanook of the North* 106–7, 109
Fields, Gracie 81–2
Fogerty, Elsie 82–3
Foltz, Jonathan 16–17
Frost, Laura 7–8

Gainsborough Pictures 167–8, 183–98
*Gaslight* 144–7
Gaumont-British 141, 183–4
Gellen, Kata 3–5, 8, 16
General Post Office 107, 119–20
Gitelman, Lisa 5–6
Goldberg, Jonathan 196–7
Granger, Stewart 184–5, 187–8, 190–1
Grassic Gibbon, Lewis 20, 37
  'A Novelist Looks at the Cinema' 37–8

*Memoirs of a Materialist* 37
*Sunset Song* 120–6, 135–6
Green, Henry 38–9, 94–9, 167–8
  *Caught* 168–73
  *Living* 38–9, 96–7
  on 'non-representational' dialogue 94–6,
    98–9, 104–5
  *Party Going* 97–8
Greene, Graham 18, 40–2, 137, 149–50
  'A Film Principle' 40–1
  *Brighton Rock* 40–1, 150–5
  *Ministry of Fear, The* 149–50
  on *Dood Wasser* 40–1
  on *Jazz Comedy* 41–2
  on *Song of Ceylon* 41–2, 112–13
  work as film reviewer 40–2
  work as script writer 40–1
Grierson, John 109–12, 115–16
  *Drifters* 109–10
Groth, Helen 15–16

Haffenden, Elizabeth 193–5
Hamilton, Patrick 16–17, 20–1, 44, 137,
  144–5, 155–6
  *Hangover Square* 161–6
  *Rope* 44
Hanley, James 21, 167–8, 197–8
  *Grey Children* 107
  *No Directions* 173–6
Harcourt-Smith, Simon 192–3
Harper, Sue 184–5, 189–93
Harris, Laurel 2 n.5, 16, 154 n.49
Hepburn, Allan 2–3, 87–8, 91–2, 138 n.5
Hitchcock, Alfred 1, 19, 22, 44, 49
  'Direction' 25 n.7
  *Elstree Calling* 49
  on reaction shots 25
  on 'screen language' 27–8
  *Rebecca* 140–2
  *Rope* 44
  *Suspicion* 140–2
  *The 39 Steps* 141–3
  *Blackmail* 22–5
*Housing Problems* 115–17
Humble, Nicola 184–5

Intertitles 1, 6–8, 24
Isherwood, Christopher 42–4, 46–7,
  67–74, 102–3
  *Christopher and His Kind* 68–9
  *Goodbye to Berlin* 67–9

*Mr Norris Changes Trains* 67–9
on film's impact on his writing 43–4, 71–2
on theatre 69–71
*Prater Violet* 71–4

Jacobs, Lea 11–12, 15, 80–1
Jung, Carl Gustav
on synchronicity 11, 11 n.51

Kalinak, Kathryn 139 n.7, 139–40
Korda, Alexander
mentorship of Merle Oberon 82–3
*The Divorce of Lady X* 20, 76, 83–7
Korngold, Erich Wolfgang 139–40
Kozloff, Sarah 79, 104

*Lady Vanishes, The* 137–8
Lastra, James 11–12, 76–9, 89
on 'perceptual fidelity' 76–7
on intelligibility 77–8
Legg, Stuart 110–11, 118
Leigh, Walter 110–15
Lejeune, C. A. 187
*Lion has Wings, The* 183–4
Lockwood, Margaret 184–8, 192, 196
Lodge, David
'Dialogue in the Modern Novel'
75, 99–100
Loos, Anita 7–8, 58 n.50

MacKay, Marina 2–3, 174, 197 n.119
*Madonna of the Seven Moons* 70–191
*Magic Bow, The* 196–7
Malamet, Elliott 154–5
*Man in Grey, The* 183–90
Mansell, James 110–11, 115 n.42
Marcus, Laura 1–3, 6–7, 25 n.8, 26–7, 29–30,
75, 107, 109–10
Mason, James 184–6, 196
Matthews, Jessie 81–2
May, Hans 190–1
McCracken, Allison 153–4
McDonald, Matthew 24–5
'Media representation' 46–7, 62, 65–6, 71–2
'Mediatized textuality' 16–17, 37, 46–7, 66, 74,
94, 125–6, 200–1
definition of 4–5
Melodrama 167–8, 183–98
in *The Heat of the Day* 180–1
Mellor, Leo 106–7, 175
'documentary impulse' 106–7, 106 n.1

Mengham, Rod 179–80
Mepham, John 75, 103–4
Merleau-Ponty, Maurice 12–13
*The Phenomenology of Perception* 12
Minney, R. J. 184–6
Mirrlees, Hope 125
Musical theatre 47–9

Network 137, 150
in the thriller 137–9, 155
'network society' 141
*Night Mail* 115, 117–19

Oberon, Merle 82–7
Speech training 83 n.41
Olivier, Laurence 82–7
Ondra, Anny 25
Operetta 47–9, 71–4
Orwell, George 20, 45, 107–8, 126–36
*A Clergyman's Daughter* 107–8, 127–31
*Down and Out in Paris and London*
126–7, 132–3
film reviews 45
*Homage to Catalonia* 126–7
*Keep the Aspidistra Flying* 107–8,
127, 131–5
*The Road to Wigan Pier* 126–7
Ostrer, Maurice 185–6

*Pett and Pott* 113–15
Piette, Adam 167–8, 167 n.3, 174
Potter, Simon 108–9, 111 n.27,
113 n.36, 116
Puckett, Kent 168
Pudovkin, Vsvolod 29–31
*Film Acting* 30–1
*Film Technique* 30–1
Purdon, James 1–2, 137–8

Rae, Patricia 130 n.93, 131
Rawlinson, Mark 168–9
*Rebecca* 140–2
Revue 19–20, 47–8, 50–2
Revue film 49–52
Rhys, Jean 18, 137, 155–61
*After Leaving Mr Mackenzie* 156
*Good Morning, Midnight* 158–61
*Quartet* 156
*Smile Please* 39–40
*Voyage in the Dark* 156–8
Robinson, Gregory 6–8

## 226  INDEX

Roc, Patricia 184–5
Rotha, Paul 29–30, 114–15
  *Documentary Diary* 108 n.12
  *The Film till Now* 29–30

Schaller, Karen 33–4
Scoring 138–42, 145–6
Seiler, Claire 2 n.7, 182–3
Singer, Ben
  on melodrama 186–7
*Singing Fool, The* 28–9
Snaith, Anna 16 n.75, 156–7
*Song of Ceylon, The* 20, 41–2, 111–15
Sound-on-disc 28–9, 76–7
Sound-on-film 28–9
Spence, Ralph 7–8
Stead, Lisa 40 n.68, 161 n.74, 184–5
Stonebridge, Lyndsey 2–3, 3 n.8, 172–3,
  172 n.25
Strauss, Johann 73, 140–1
Strauss, Richard 139–40
*Suspicion* 140–1
Synch point 42, 59
  definition of 13–15
  dialogue as synch point 76,
    79–80
Synchronicity 8–18
  applied by Carl Gustav Jung 11
  definition of 1
  mid-century discussion of 9–11
  in relation to literature 15–17
  in relation to synchronization
    10–11
Synchronization 9–11, 76, 80–1

*Target for Tonight* 183–4
Teekell, Anna 181–2
Thompson, Kristin
  on cinematic excess 167–8
  on counterpoint 81 n.34
Thriller 20–1, 137–47
Transmediation 46–7, 58, 71, 74
Trotter, David 1–6, 141
*True Glory, The* 183–4

Uricchio, William 6

Viertel, Berthold
  *Little Friend* 43–4, 71–2

Watt, Harry 117–18, 119 n.56
Waugh, Evelyn
  *The Balance* 55–6
  cinema's impact on writing 36–7, 55–6
  criticism of cinema 65–6
  *The Loved One* 21, 199–204
  *Vile Bodies* 16–17, 19–20, 52–66
  on revue shows 50–1, 54–5
  on Ronald Firbank 54–5
Waugh, Patricia 165–6
Waxman, Franz 139–40
*Went the Day Well?* 183–4
*Western Approaches* 183–4
*Wicked Lady, The* 183–5, 192–6
Williams, Keith 127
Wright, Basil 40–2, 111, 113

Ziegfeld, Florenz 50–2
'Ziegfeld Girls' 56–8